Handbook of Mortgage Processing

by Cheryl J. Diehl

Susan R. Bray, Editor

Mortgage Lending Handbook Series

MORTGAGE BANKERS ASSOCIATION OF AMERICA
Washington, DC

Mortgage Bankers Association of America
1125 15th Street, NW
Washington, DC 20005

ISBN 0-945359-16-0

Disclaimer

This publication is designed to present, as simply and as accurately as possible, general information on the loan origination process. It should be noted that the information presented is not all inclusive. Forms, regulations, and overall processes may change because of changes within the industry. This publication should not be used as a substitute for referring to the applicable rules and regulations and is sold with the understanding that the publisher is not engaged in rendering legal, accounting, or other personalized professional service. If legal or other expert assistance is required, the services of a competent professional should be sought.

Table of Contents

Acknowledgments xiii

Preface xv

Chapter 1
Introduction to Mortgage Loan Processing 1

- Development of Mortgage Banking 1
- Function and Organization of the Loan Production Department 2
- The Role Of Processors in Mortgage Lending 5
- Preventing Fraud and Unethical Practices 11
- Residential Mortgage Lending Products 12
  - Fixed Rate Mortgage (FRM)
  - Adjustable Rate Mortgage (ARM)
  - Alternate Doc Programs
  - Biweekly Mortgage
  - Balloon Mortgage
  - Buydown Mortgage
  - Convertible Mortgage
  - Graduated Payment Mortgage (GPM)
  - Low Doc Programs
  - Reverse Annuity Mortgage (RAM)
  - Shared Appreciation Mortgage (SAM)
  - 10- to 15-Year Mortgage

Investors/Insurers of Residential Loan Production 15
- Department of Veterans Affairs
- Federal Home Loan Mortgage Corporation
- Federal Housing Administration
- Federal National Mortgage Association
- Government National Mortgage Association
- Private Mortgage Insurance Companies

Processing Terminology 16
- Appraisal
- Closing Costs
- Conforming Mortgage Loans
- Conventional Mortgage
- Credit Report
- Direct Endorsement (HUD-FHA) and Automatic/Lender Appraisal Processing Program (VA) Underwriting
- Disclosure Statements
- Discount Points
- Interest
- Lock-in Agreement
- Loan-to-Value Ratio (LTV)
- Maximum Mortgage Amount
- Mortgage
- Mortgage Insurance Premium (MIP)
- Mortgagees and Mortgagors
- Nonconforming Mortgage Loan
- Note
- PITI
- Principal
- Qualification Ratios
- Verification of Deposit (VOD)
- Verification of Employment (VOE)

Chapter 2
Selling Mortgage Services 25

The Role of Loan Officers 25
How Rates and Service Affect Referrals 26
Sales Tools and Advertising 27
Dealing with Applicants 30
The Role of Automated Systems 30

Chapter 3
Preparing to Take the Application 33

Responsibility for Taking the Application 33
The Sales Agreement 34
Case Examples 37
Before the Interview Begins 39
Disclosures and Restrictions 40
The Real Estate Settlement Procedures Act
Federal Truth in Lending Statement
Equal Credit Opportunity Act of 1975 (ECOA)
The Privacy Act
The Processor's Role in Taking the Application 46
VA Documentation
HUD-FHA Documentation
Verifying Information Directly 47
Fees and Charges 48

Chapter 4
Completing the Application 51

The Uniform Residential Loan Application 51
Statement on Joint Obligation or Reliance on Spouse's Income

Interest Rate
Names on Title
Manner in Which Title Will be Held
Social Security Number
Marital Status
Information for Government Monitoring Purposes
Discrepancies and Inconsistencies in the Loan Application 60
Warning Signals
Verification
Case Example

Chapter 5
The Appraisal 65

Loan-to-Value (LTV) and Loan Amount 66
Appraiser Licensing and Certification 66
Uniform Standards
HUD-FHA and VA Fee Panels
Ordering a HUD-FHA Appraisal 69
Appraisal by Fee Panel
The HUD-FHA File Folder
Ordering a VA Appraisal 79
LAPP Procedures
Ordering a Conventional Appraisal 81
Monitoring the Appraisal 83
Evaluating the Appraisal 83
Reconsideration
Repair Requirements
Lender Responsibility for Appraisals 93
Warning Signals
Case Examples

Chapter 6 Verifying Application Data 97

Ordering Verifications 99

Verification of Cash for Down Payment and Closing 100

- Earnest Money Deposits
- Bank Deposits
- Retirement Funds
- Equity in Other Real Estate
- U.S. Savings Bonds
- Cash Value of Life Insurance Policies
- Gifts
- Stocks and Bonds
- Cash Settlements and Inheritances

Verification of Employment 119

Self Employed Persons 121

- Sole Proprietorship
- Partnership
- Corporation
- S Corporation

Interest, Dividends, and Trust Funds 124

Retirement Benefits and Social Security 124

Real Estate 126

Alimony, Child Support, and Separate Maintenance 126

Credit History 128

Direct Verification 133

- Alternative, "Low Doc" Programs

Fraud Prevention 140

- Warning Signals
- Verification of Employment (VOE)
- Payroll Check Stub
- W-2 Form
- Tax Return Form 1040
- Schedule A, Itemized Deductions

Schedule C, Profit/Loss from Business Owned
Schedule E, Rents and Royalties
Case Examples
Down Payments/Assets to Close 147
Warning Signals
Verification of Deposit (VOD)
Case Examples
Credit Report 151
Case Examples

Chapter 7
The Final Application and Submission to Underwriting 155

Addendum to the URLA 156
The Worksheet 162
HUD-FHA and VA Worksheets
Agency Case Number
Section of the Act
Loan Amount
Percent
Signatures
Submission of the HUD-FHA Cases to Underwriting 171
Underwriting 173
Experience
Review and Control

Chapter 8
Closing the Loan 177

Two Related Transactions 178
Preparation of Documents 179

Instruction to Closing Agent
The Note
The Mortgage or Deed of Trust
Truth in Lending Disclosure
Disbursement 224
Recording 225
Conclusion 226

Glossary 229

EXHIBIT LIST FOR HANDBOOK OF MORTGAGE PROCESSING

I-1: Overview of the Loan Production Process
I-2: Organization Chart for a Loan Production Department
I-3: Sample Job Descriptions for Senior and Junior Level Processors
I-4: Acceptable Conventional Mortgage Insurers or Alternative Forms of Coverage (Fannie Mae)

II-1: Rate Sheet

III-1: Sales Agreement
III-2: Good Faith Estimate of Borrower's Settlement Costs
III-3: Good Faith Estimate of Borrower's Settlement Costs
III-4: Truth in Lending Disclosure

IV-1: Uniform Residential Loan Application
IV-2: Interest Rate Disclosure Statement

V-1: Request for HUD-FHA Case Number and Appraiser
V-2: HUD Application for Property Appraisal and Commitment
V-3: Uniform Residential Appraisal Report
V-4: VA Request for Determination of Reasonable Value
V-5: Loans in Process Record
V-6: HUD-FHA Conditional Commitment
V-7: VA Certificate of Reasonable Value

VI-1: Sample Verification that Earnest Money Deposit Has Been Paid in Cash
VI-2: Verification of Deposit
VI-3: Sample Letter Requesting Verification of Vested Interest in Retirement Fund and Right to Withdraw
VI-4: HUD-1 Settlement Statement

VI-5: Sample Analysis of Expected Proceeds from Sale of Real Estate (under contract)
VI-6: Sample Analysis of Expected Proceeds from Sale of Real Estate (not yet under contract)
VI-7: Sample List of Savings Bonds Owned
VI-8: Sample Gift Letter
VI-9: Sample Verification of Pending Cash Settlement, Inheritance, etc.
VI-10: Request for Verification of Employment
VI-11: Sample Request for Verification of Retirement or Other Income
VI-12: Sample Schedule of Real Estate Owned
VI-13: Credit Report
VI-14: Sample Request for Verification of Mortgage Indebtedness
VI-15: Sample Request for Verification of Payment of Rent
VI-16: Sample Request for Credit Union Verification
VI-17: Sample Request for Verification of Child Care Expenses

VII-1: HUD-FHA Addendum Form 92900-A
VII-2: Mortgage Credit Analysis Worksheet (HUD) Form 92900-WS
VII-3: Loan Analysis (VA) Form 26-6393
VII-4: Transmittal Summary Fannie Mae Form 1008
VII-5: List of HUD-FHA Case Number Suffixes
VII-6: FHA's Three Insurance Funds

VIII-1: Conventional Loan Closing/Title Instructions
VIII-2: HUD-FHA Multistate Note, Mortgage and Deed of Trust
VIII-3: Conventional Multistate Note, Mortgage and Deed of Trust
VIII-4: VA Note and Mortgage
VIII-5: Addendum to HUD-1 Settlement Statement
VIII-5: HUD-FHA Firm Commitment

Acknowledgements

Cheryl J. Diehl, the author, is a mortgage banking consultant who travels nationwide conducting seminars. She has taught for the Institute of Financial Education, the University of Texas at Arlington-Continuing Education, Oklahoma City University-School of Law-Continuing Education Department, many state Mortgage Bankers Associations and various other organizations. She has written several training guides used in her seminars. She has conducted quality control reviews for HUD and acted as fee personnel. She currently does quality control for various lenders.

ACKNOWLEDGEMENTS:

Nina Bennett
Nina Bennett Mortgage Consulting
Dallas, Texas

Delia Brannon
Foster Mortgage Corporation
Ft. Worth, Texas

Carolyn Gresham
Associates Mortgage Corporation
Las Colinas, Texas

Diana Messmer
AmeriTrust Mortgage
Indianapolis, Indiana

CLOSING INSTRUCTIONS SUPPLIED BY:

Eldon Youngblood
Youngblood, Claycombe & King
Dallas, Texas

We thank the following for helping with the preparation of this text: Joyce Kappeler, MBA education department; Don Cupit, CMB, Norwest Mortgage, Greensboro, NC; Brian Hershkowitz, MBA government and agency relations department; Bill Brewster, formerly of MBA government and agency relations department; Anne Dow, MBA procurement officer; Katherine George, CAE, Catalina Communications, Alexandria, VA; Nancy Washe, VMP Mortgage Forms, Fraser, MI; Karen Jones, CREDCO, Silver Spring, MD; and Chuck Ebert of the Washington, DC Association of Realtors.

A special thanks goes to the Ethics in Real Estate Transactions Task Force for providing us with case examples of fraud prevention that were used throughout the text.

We also extend appreciation to Warren Lasko, EVP, whose thoughtful foresight provided the impetus for this first of the Mortgage Lending Handbook series.

Susan R. Bray
Editor

Preface

The origination of mortgages is the foundation of the mortgage lending industry. Each closed loan means another American has been successful in the purchase of a home or the refinancing of an existing loan on more favorable terms—things of which we all can be proud. But closed mortgages play another part in the American economy as well. A closed mortgage becomes an integral part of a multi-trillion dollar circle of capital that channels money from borrowers to investors and back to new borrowers.

Thus the role of mortgage loan processing, the basis of this *Handbook,* is crucial to our industry. Processors work with borrowers, fellow real estate professionals, and others to keep mortgage applications moving toward closing. They take information from the applicant; record and verify it; arrange for valuation of the collateral through a property appraisal; and assemble the application package for an underwriter's evaluation.

We have designed this *Handbook of Mortgage Processing* to help processors understand and thrive in a profession that is essential to loan production and mortgage banking. The information herein will help processors increase their professionalism and mortgage lending skills. The better informed processors are about mortgage lending, the more likely it is that loans will pass smoothly to closing and on to the secondary market.

This *Handbook* covers conventional as well as government-insured processing and includes information about loan types, fraud prevention, and new technology. There is also practical instruction on how to cope with the everyday lending situations beginning or experienced processors face: 'low doc' loans, self-employed applicants, verification problems, and so on. The *Handbook* addresses the concerns of all mortgage processors—whether they work for mortgage bankers, savings or commercial banks, mortgage brokers, credit unions, or other lenders.

We in the mortgage lending community depend on the commitment and professionalism of these loan processors. We hope that these dedicated individuals will find *The Handbook of Mortgage Processing* a worthy reference for an important and exacting job.

Warren Lasko
Executive Vice President
Mortgage Bankers Association of America

1

Introduction to Mortgage Loan Processing

Development of Mortgage Banking

Mortgage banking is the origination, sale, and servicing of mortgages, secured by either residential or income producing real estate. In the United States, early suppliers of mortgage lending were primarily friends, relatives, and wealthy individuals. As individual specialists began arranging loans, preparing the basic legal forms and developing appraisal techniques, the loan would be matched up with a private individual who retained the security until the loan was paid. Around the turn of the century, some of these specialists began to represent institutions such as life insurance companies.

The early mortgage banker served as a conduit for bringing investment funds from capital-surplus regions to areas that lacked financial institutions. Differing strategies were employed to perform this function—some mortgage bankers making loans and selling them while retaining the servicing, other mortgage bankers holding the loans as an investment trust, and still others acting as mortgage brokers to bring borrowers and individual lenders together.

Today the mortgage banker is more of a facilitator than a balancer, shopping national money markets for capital and providing it to all areas of the country. The primary role of the mortgage banker remains the same, however, to serve as a middleman, arranging loans and then selling them to other lenders and investors both within the United States and abroad.

With residential real estate, the process begins with the mortgage banker using short-term borrowings to make mortgage loans to home buyers. These loans are then grouped together for sale in packages to outside investors, usually large institutions. The proceeds of the sale are used to replenish the lending capital, and start the cycle over again.

Even after the loans are sold, however, the mortgage banker remains in the picture as the servicer of the loans. Servicing consists of collecting the monthly payments, forwarding the proceeds to investors who have purchased the loans, maintaining escrow accounts for payment of taxes and insurance, and acting as the investors' representative if any problems arise with the loans.

Function and Organization of the Loan Production Department

The loan production department includes those functions needed to originate and close a mortgage. (See Exhibit I-1.) Loan production includes the management of origination staff (at local, regional, and national levels); the tasks of origination (taking the application, processing, closing, and in some cases underwriting); and the wholesale (purchase of correspondent or brokered loans) and retail operations (direct consumer contact, telephone origination). A sample organizational chart for a loan production department is shown in Exhibit I-2.

A mortgage production division includes the functions of origination, processing, underwriting, closing, and delivery. The loan production process involves a series of interrelated activities performed by individuals who make up the loan production team.

A key role is played by the **loan officer,** also called a **loan originator, loan representative,** or **loan consultant**. This per-

EXHIBIT I-1: OVERVIEW OF THE LOAN PRODUCTION PROCESS

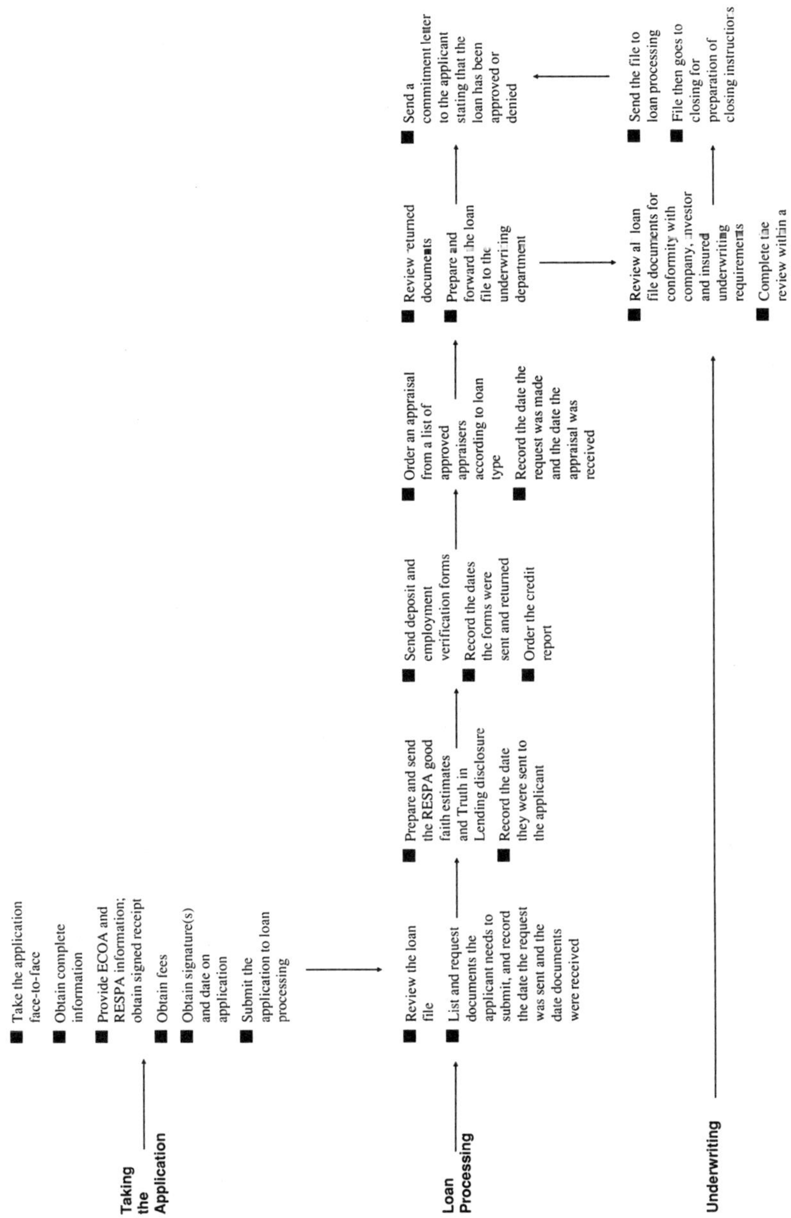

EXHIBIT I-2: ORGANIZATIONAL CHART FOR A LOAN PRODUCTION DEPARTMENT

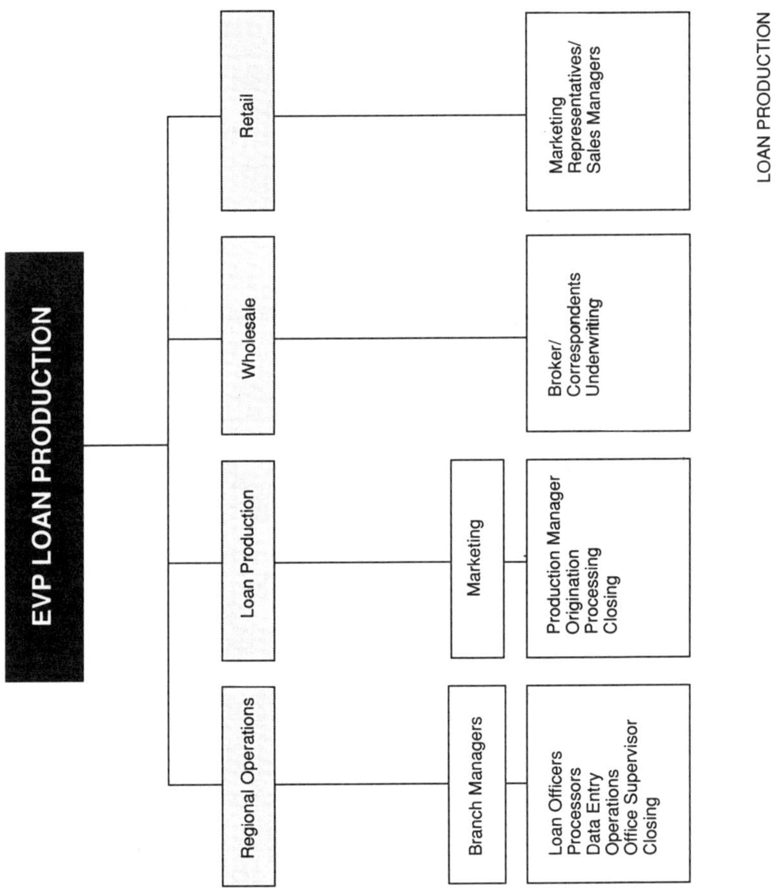

son generates mortgage loan activity by selling the company's loan services and taking the initial application. Loan officers talk with the borrower to be sure that he or she meets the specific loan guidelines.

Another important person is the **underwriter.** This person examines the work of the loan processor and analyzes the data. The underwriter makes a judgment decision based on the confirmed information in the file and is responsible for verifying that the loan has been processed under specific loan guidelines—and in fact meets those guidelines.

The **loan closer** receives the loan after it has been approved by the underwriter. The closer prepares and assembles the closing documents, funds the mortgage loan, and records the mortgage documents.

The **escrow** or **closing officer** acts as an independent third party for the loan transaction and ensures that financial adjustments, the signing of documents, and the disbursement of funds are properly done. In some places this is done by an attorney or title officer.

The person who receives the loan after it has been funded is the **loan shipper.** This person will usually ship the mortgage loan documents as collateral to the warehouse lender. Once the warehouse line is repaid, the loan shipper sends the entire package to the investor.

The Role of Processors in Mortgage Lending

What is a typical processor expected to accomplish? Loan processing functions include assembling loan files; ordering verifications, appraisals, credit reports, disclosure statements, and other documents; reviewing documents for signatures, completeness, accuracy, and legibility; and ensuring investor requirements are met.

The steps of setting up the loan file, reviewing the documents for accuracy, and submitting a complete credit and property package to the underwriter ensure that an investment quality loan is produced. Sample job descriptions for senior and junior level processors are included as Exhibit I-3.

Processors may work for any type of real estate lender: mortgage bankers, savings banks, credit unions, or commercial banks. With any of these lenders, the processor will work on loans that will be underwritten and closed (and perhaps sold and shipped to the investor) by other people in the same organization.

If a processor is employed by mortgage brokers or correspondents, loans are originated, processed, and perhaps underwritten by the broker or correspondent and then are sent to a wholesaler. The wholesaler, as a separate entity, usually underwrites (or re-underwrites) and closes the loans. This relationship of brokers or correspondents to wholesalers is sometimes called third-party origination or purchased production.

Whatever the type of lender, the relationship of the processor to others in the loan origination department is determined to a large extent by how the department is organized.

The processing function can be organized in a variety of ways. Although most processing is done in the office where the mortgage is originated with the loan officer and the borrower close at hand, there are some mortgage operations with regionalized processing centers that support smaller satellite origination offices or loan application centers. In some cases, the organization is structured so that loan applications are taken by processors.

Two examples of job function structuring are seen in a specialized approach and a "turnkey" or all-encompassing approach. A company may decide to have processors specialize in a particular function. For example, one company may have processors be responsible for a loan application from the time the application is taken until after it is closed.

Other processors take the "turnkey" approach, that is they perform all functions—setting up the loan file, reviewing mail, following up, submitting the loan, specifying loan conditions, and preparing settlement documents. This results in a smaller caseload, and there is a greater possibility that the processor will

EXHIBIT I-3: JOB DESCRIPTIONS FOR SENIOR AND JUNIOR LEVEL PROCESSORS

Company Name

Job Title:	**Senior Processor**
Department:	Loan Production
Section:	Loan Processing
Reports to:	Office or Branch Supervisor/Processing Supervisor

I. JOB SUMMARY:

Evaluate all information supplied on residential loan applications. Verify, through outside sources, the validity of the information, calculate debt-to-income and loan-to-value ratios, and assemble a completely documented file for submission to underwriting where a decision on whether the loan application should be approved is made.

II. DUTIES & RESPONSIBILITIES:

Maintain updated manual of all new policies or modifications to the guidelines and standards of the company, federal housing programs, investors, and private mortgage insurers.

Train processor trainees in company policy as regards the correct method of processing a loan application from start to finish.

Assist junior processors when necessary.

Open files: order credit reports and appraisals and send out verification forms and conduct regular follow-up with outside sources for outstanding documents.

Update Realtors and loan officer on file status.

Maintain an open line of communication with the applicant throughout the processing period, assisting them with any questions and notifying them of any additional information required.

Monitor incoming mail and documents for information verifying the data collected by loan officers, and log into file and computer system and track development of information to ensure compliance with underwriting guidelines.

Process requests for extensions to the applicants' commitments in accordance with company policy.

Complete a final evaluation and analysis of the completed application package and prepare the file for approval, specifying any applicable conditions to the approval. Review the commitment and any additional required disclosures.

EXHIBIT I-3—*continued*

Assemble and print submission documents, assemble submission file and prepare file for closing department review.

Notify borrowers and realtors of underwriting decision.

Prepare, if applicable, the "Decline Letter," and ensure accurate disclosure of the reason(s) for the adverse action at whatever time during the processing period it is determined that applicants do not qualify.

Maintain record of all loans in process.

III. JOB DIMENSIONS:

Supervises Directly:	
Internal Relations:	Works regularly with loan officers and company staff involved in pricing, underwriting, and closing.
External Relations:	Realtors, appraisers, credit, and title companies and borrowers.
Other:	

IV. POSITION SPECIFICATIONS/REQUIREMENTS:

College degree preferred but may substitute equivalent experience in mortgage banking origination.

Minimum of 3 years overall mortgage lending experience with at least 12-18 months as a processor.

Working knowledge of FHLMC and/or FNMA and FHA/VA guidelines and private mortgage insurance requirements.

Good oral and written communication skills.
Ability to interact effectively with customers and other company staff to resolve problems.

Analytical ability, with an aptitude for figures.

Typing and computer skills.

EXHIBIT I-3—*continued*

Company Name

Job Title: **Junior Processor**
Department: Loan Production
Section: Loan Processing
Reports to: Office or Branch Supervisor

I. JOB SUMMARY:

Evaluate all information supplied on residential loan applications. Verify, through outside sources, the validity of the information, calculates debt-to-income and loan-to-value ratios and assemble a completely documented file for submission to underwriting, where a decision on whether the loan application should be approved is made.

II. DUTIES & RESPONSIBILITIES:

Open files: order credit reports and appraisals, and send out verification forms and conduct regular follow-up with outside sources of outstanding documents.

Update Realtors and loan officer on file status.

Maintain an open line of communication with the applicant throughout the processing period, assisting them with any questions and notifying them of any additional information required.

Monitor incoming mail and documents for information verifying the data collected by loan officers, and log into file and computer system and track development of information to ensure compliance with underwriting guidelines.

Process requests for extensions to the applicants' commitment in accordance with company policy.

Complete a final evaluation and analysis of the completed application package and prepare the file for approval, specifying any applicable conditions to the approval. Review the commitment and any additional required disclosures.

Assemble and print submission documents, assemble submission file and prepare file for closing department review.

Notify borrowers and realtors of underwriting decision.

Prepare, if applicable, the "Decline Letter," and ensure accurate disclosure of the reason(s) for the adverse action at whatever time during the processing period it is determined that applicants do not qualify.

Maintain record of all loans in process.

EXHIBIT I-3—*continued*

III. JOB DIMENSIONS:

Supervise Directly:	
Internal Relations:	Works regularly with loan officers and company staff involved in pricing, underwriting, and closing.
External Relations:	Realtors, appraisers, credit, and title companies and borrowers.
Other:	

IV. POSITION SPECIFICATIONS/REQUIREMENTS:

Minimum of a high school diploma and up to 3 years of mortgage banking experience, preferably in the loan processing division.

Good written and verbal communication skills.

Typing and computer skills.

be able to be paired one-on-one with an originator. A one-on-one pairing may not be the most efficient way of providing an even caseload throughout the branch; however, it is a major advantage for the originator to have a focal point for any particular case.

Another approach currently being tried with mortgage banking companies is one where the file is worked backwards. This process looks at the entire loan process and breaks it into small, step-by-step segments. One key element of the approach is to set the delivery date of the product and then work backwards, assigning to the production team the responsibility of meeting daily deadlines to ensure that a quality product is delivered when needed.

A consideration in any type of approach is the company's definition of a suitable caseload (number of cases processed) per processor. The caseload is based on what the organization finds to be cost-efficient. Ideally, a processor's workload should be designed for cost efficiencies taking into account flexibility for peak or slow workloads.

Each processing system has its own set of drawbacks and advantages. In the context of maximum quality production at the least possible cost, a company must decide which system will result in better communication, maximum flexibility, decreased turnover, and, ultimately, increased production.

Internally, processors interact with many other job functions in a lender's office, including loan officers, underwriters, and the closing staff. Externally, the processor may have contact with Realtors, appraisers, credit bureaus, banks, employers, title companies, and borrowers.

Preventing Fraud and Unethical Practices

Preventing fraud and unethical practices is one of the processor's basic responsibilities. It is essential that the loan processor be able to recognize potential problem loans while processing the application.

A great deal can be accomplished by simply developing an awareness of or sensitivity to potential problem areas in mortgage loans. Processors fail when they see their function or responsibility as merely checking to see if the required loan information and documentation is present for the underwriter's review.

The application process is much more than simply ensuring the presence of certain documents. The processor must use good judgment and common sense to determine if information is consistent and reasonable. If it is not, it is the processor's responsibility to advise the underwriter of any inconsistencies.

Possible fraudulent activity may center around similarities or patterns among applications received from clients of certain brokers or loan officers. For example, does a particular broker consistently send applicants who use gift letters, sweat equity, monies from tax refunds, or undeposited cash on hand to qualify? Or does a builder forward a high number of self-employed applicants?

Residential Mortgage Lending Products

For the half-century before 1980, practically all residential real estate loans were financed with the fixed-rate mortgage. Since 1980, we have experienced an explosion in the many types of residential mortgage lending products. Some of the more common types of loan financing alternatives are listed below.

Fixed Rate Mortgage (FRM)

Fixed-rate mortgages have an interest rate and monthly payments that remain constant over the life of the loan. This sets a maximum on the total amount of principal and interest you pay during the loan. The FRM is a monthly amortized, direct reduction instrument. Equal monthly payments for the term of the loan are used to directly reduce the amount owed, by first paying interest on the loan due since the last payment and then using the remainder to reduce principal.

Adjustable Rate Mortgage (ARM)

Adjustable or flexible rate mortgages have an interest rate that increases or decreases over the life of the loan, based upon market conditions. The starting rate will generally be lower than the rate offered on a standard fixed-rate mortgage. Changes in the interest rate are usually governed by a financial index.

Alternate Doc Programs

The alternate doc (short for "documentation") program is a quick qualifying loan program that substitutes readily available documents for conventional verification forms. This would involve, for example, substituting bank statements for a verification of deposit, or substituting the borrower's pay stub and W-2 form for the verification of employment.

Biweekly Mortgage

The biweekly mortgage features payments due every two weeks, totaling 26 payments annually. The key benefit to the borrower is that the mortgage is usually paid in full in about 19 years, several years earlier than the conventional fixed-rate, 30-year mortgage.

Balloon Mortgage

A balloon mortgage is characterized by periodic installments of principal and interest that do not fully amortize the loan. The balance of the mortgage is due in a lump sum at a specified date, usually at the end of the term.

Buydown Mortgage

Typically, the buydown mortgage is one made at a below-market interest rate. Lenders can make these mortgages because a builder, seller, or buyer has paid additional discount points applied to reduce the interest rate for a specified period.

Convertible Mortgage

The convertible mortgage is an adjustable-rate mortgage that allows the borrower to convert the mortgage to a fixed-rate mortgage during a predetermined time period. This product offers the borrower the flexibility of lower initial payments based upon an index, with the security of converting to a fixed-rate mortgage at a later date.

Graduated Payment Mortgage (GPM)

The graduated payment mortgage is a type of flexible payment mortgage wherein the payments begin at a lower amount then increase for a specified period of time before leveling off. Even though the payments change, the interest rate is usually fixed. So during the early years, payments are lower than the amount dictated by the interest rate. During the later years, the difference is made up by higher payments. At the end of the mortgage term, the entire debt will be paid off.

Low Doc Programs

The low doc (or documentation) program is a quick qualifying loan program that typically requires a large down payment. This program eliminates many verification documents that normally slow down the approval process.

Reverse Annuity Mortgage (RAM)

With the reverse annuity mortgage (or RAM), the lender makes periodic payments to the borrower using the borrower's equity in the home as security.

Shared Appreciation Mortgage (SAM)

In the shared appreciation mortgage (SAM), monthly payments are made at a relatively low interest rate. The borrower must agree to share with the lender a sizable percent (usually 30 percent to 50 percent) of the appreciation in the home's value when the home is sold or transferred, or after a specified number of years.

10- to 15-Year Mortgage

As one might guess, the 10- to 15-year mortgage is a loan amortized over a 10- to 15-year period.

Investors/Insurers of Residential Loan Production

Department of Veterans Affairs (VA)

The VA Home Loan Guaranty Program operates within the purview of the Department of Veterans Affairs. The VA Home Loan Guaranty Program encourages mortgage lenders to offer long-term, little or no down payment financing to eligible veterans by partially guaranteeing the lender against loss.

Federal Home Loan Mortgage Corporation

The Federal Home Loan Mortgage Corporation (Freddie Mac or FHLMC) is a congressionally chartered corporation that serves as one of the biggest secondary market investors. Freddie Mac primarily buys and securitizes conventional single-family fixed-rate and adjustable-rate loans.

Federal Housing Administration

The Federal Housing Administration (FHA) is a component of the Department of Housing and Urban Development (HUD). Its main activity is insuring residential mortgage loans made by private lenders. It monitors standards for construction and underwriting. FHA does not lend money, nor does it plan or construct housing.

Federal National Mortgage Association

The Federal National Mortgage Association (Fannie Mae or FNMA) is a corporation created by Congress to support the secondary mortgage market. Fannie Mae buys and securitizes residential mortgages insured by HUD-FHA or guaranteed by VA, as well as conventional home mortgages.

Government National Mortgage Association

The Government National Mortgage Association (Ginnie Mae or GNMA) is a department of HUD responsible for the administration of a mortgage-backed securities program. It channels new sources of funds into residential financing through the sale of privately issued securities guaranteed by GNMA.

Private Mortgage Insurance Companies

Private mortgage insurance (PMI) companies issue an insurance policy to the lender that insures against loss if the loan goes into default. PMI carriers insure a portion of the loan, which, when combined with the down payment, gives the lender the comfort level needed to approve a high risk or high loan-to-value loan.

Although borrowers pay the premium, there is no benefit to them from this insurance policy; only the lender can receive a payment from the carrier. Exhibit I-4 is a list of Fannie Mae's acceptable conventional mortgage insurers or alternative forms or coverage.

Processing Terminology

This section will acquaint processors with some of the basic terminology needed to process loans.

Appraisal

The appraisal is a report made by a professionally designated appraiser, establishing the current market value of the property subject to the sales contract. The appraisal justifies the loan amount being requested.

Closing Costs

Closing costs represent money paid by the borrower and seller to effect the closing of a mortgage loan. This normally

EXHIBIT I-4: ACCEPTABLE CONVENTIONAL MORTGAGE INSURERS (FANNIE MAE)

Exhibit 1 Acceptable Conventional Mortgage Insurers (or Alternative Forms of Coverage)

	MI Code	Mortgage Insurer's Name (or Code Definition)	
•	31	California Housing Insurance Fund (California first mortgages only)	
•	17	Commonwealth Mortgage Assurance Company	
•	09	Foremost Mortgage Insurance Company (Applicable only for renewals of existing policies; therefore, only seasoned mortgage deliveries may have this coverage.)	* * *
•	01	General Electric Mortgage Insurance Companies	
•	16	Home Guaranty Insurance Corporation (Applicable only for renewals of existing policies; therefore, only seasoned mortgage deliveries may have this coverage.)	* *
•	20	Integon Mortgage Guaranty Corporation (Applicable only for renewals of existing policies; therefore, only seasoned mortgage deliveries may have this coverage.)	* *
•	14	Maryland Housing Fund (Maryland first mortgages only)	*
•	06	Mortgage Guaranty Insurance Corporation	
•	11	PMI Mortgage Insurance Company	
•	30	New York City Rehabilitation Mortgage Insurance Corporation (first mortgages in designated New York City neighborhood preservation areas only)	
•	13	Republic Mortgage Insurance Company	
•	24	Triad Guaranty Insurance Company	
•	12	United Guaranty Residential Insurance Corporation	*
•	19	U.S. Mortgage Insurance Company	
•	02	Verex Assurance, Incorporated (Applicable only for renewals of existing policies; therefore, only seasoned mortgage deliveries may have this coverage.)	* *
•	22	Vermont Home Mortgage Guaranty Board (Vermont fixed-rate first mortgages with loan-to-value ratios of 90% and less only)	* *
•	07	Wisconsin Mortgage Assurance Corporation (Applicable only for renewals of existing policies; therefore, only seasoned mortgage deliveries may have this coverage.)	

Exhibit 1 Acceptable Conventional Mortgage Insurers (or Alternative Forms of Coverage) (cont. . .)

	MI Code	Mortgage Insurer's Name (or Code Definition)	
•	93	*No MI-Repurchase/Indemnification.* (No mortgage insurance is required for a negotiated transaction because the lender has agreed to repurchase the mortgage or to indemnify Fannie Mae for loss, under the terms of a recourse agreement or some other form of credit enhancement.)	*
•	94	*No MI-Pool Coverage.* (No individual mortgage insurance is required for a negotiated transaction because the lender has agreed to obtain mortgage pool insurance coverage.)	*
•	95	*No MI-Original LTV.* (No mortgage insurance is required because the original loan-to-value ratio for a first mortgage was 80% or less or the original combined loan-to-value ratio for a second mortgage was 70% or less.)	*
•	97	*No MI-Current LTV.* (No mortgage insurance is required because the current loan-to-value ratio for a first mortgage is 80% or less, or the current combined loan-to-value ratio for a second mortgage is 70% or less, as the result of loan amortization or property appreciation, as evidenced by a new appraisal.)	*
•	98	*No MI-Property Disposition/Loss Mitigation.* (No mortgage insurance is required because we waived it for a purchase money mortgage that we agreed to fund as a cash purchase as part of our property disposition or loss mitigation efforts.)	*

includes an origination fee, title insurance fees, survey fees, and attorneys' fees.

Conforming Mortgage Loan

A conforming mortgage loan is one that meets all requirements to be eligible for purchase and securitization by Fannie Mae and Freddie Mac.

Conventional Mortgage

"Conventional mortgage" is a term generally used to describe any mortgage not insured by the Federal Housing Administration (HUD-FHA), or Farmers Home Administration (FmHA), or one not guaranteed by the Department of Veterans Affairs (VA).

Credit Report

A credit report, issued by a consumer credit reporting agency, discloses the applicant's credit accounts and payment history, outstanding debts, and liens and judgments of public record. It is used to assist in the determination of a applicant's creditworthiness.

Direct Endorsement (HUD-FHA) and Automatic/Lender Appraisal Processing Program (VA) Underwriting

VA and HUD-FHA have programs that permit the mortgage lender to do all or part of the underwriting of a mortgage loan. These programs allow lenders to apply agency guidelines without obtaining prior approval by the agencies. This saves time for transmission of the loan file back and forth between the insuring or guaranteeing agency and the mortgage lender.

Both programs require that the mortgage lender and the individual who does the underwriting be approved by the appropriate government agency.

Disclosure Statements

Disclosure statements provide information relevant to specific transactions that is required by law. They must be signed by the applicant and include a good-faith estimate of settlement costs, Truth in Lending disclosure of the annual percentage rate, an adjustable-rate disclosure rider (if applicable), and other forms required by federal and state regulations.

Discount Points

Discount points or, simply, "points" are amounts collected by the lender at closing to increase the yield on the investment to an amount higher than what would be presented by the contract interest rate alone. One point is 1 percent of the loan amount.

Interest

Interest is consideration in the form of money paid for the use of money, usually expressed as an annual percentage.

Lock-in Agreement

A lock-in agreement is a guarantee offered for a specified period by the mortgage lender to the applicant for a particular interest rate and discount points. Lock-in periods generally last seven, 30, 60, or 90 days. If applicants do not sign lock-in agreements, their interest rate will "float" with the market, and their loan will carry the interest rate available at the time of settlement.

Loan-to-Value Ratio (LTV)

One of the most important considerations in evaluating the risk associated with a real estate loan is the loan-to-value ratio. This is the relationship of the amount of the loan to the value of the property that serves as security for the loan. Lenders usually express the maximum amount they are willing to lend in terms of loan-to-value ratios.

Maximum Mortgage Amount

Government and conventional lending programs have limits on the amount an applicant may borrow for a mortgage: the "maximum mortgage amount." In some cases closing costs and upfront mortgage insurance premiums may be added to the loan amount and exceed the limit. With HUD-FHA, Fannie Mae, and Freddie Mac loans, the maximum mortgage amount is set by law.

With VA loans, the maximum mortgage amount is based on the veteran's entitlement. Conventional loans made for private investors are usually the largest, sometimes up to $1 million or more.

Mortgage

The mortgage is a pledge of the property as security for the loan. It includes a complete and accurate legal description of the property, along with the same basic information about the debt that appears on the note.

In some states, a deed of trust is used in place of a mortgage. A deed of trust is a type of security instrument conveying title in trust for a particular piece of property to a third party. It is used to secure the payment of the note.

Mortgage Insurance Premium (MIP) or Funding Fee

When mortgages are insured, either privately or by HUD-FHA, the insurer collects a mortgage insurance premium. The amount of the premium and the manner in which it is collected vary with the insurer and the insurance program. In most HUD-FHA transactions, the mortgagee must collect risk-based premiums, which have two components: the upfront mortgage insurance premium and the annual periodic premium. On VA guaranteed loans a risk based funding fee is collected upfront.

Mortgagees and Mortgagors

From the generic term, mortgage, we get the words used to describe borrower and lender—mortgagor and mortgagee. The mortgagor is the borrower and the mortgagee is the lender.

Nonconforming Mortgage Loan

A nonconforming mortgage loan is one in which the loan amount, or some other aspect of the loan, exceeds limits set by law or guidelines for the purchasing investor.

Note

The note creates the borrower's legal obligation to repay the debt secured by the mortgage. This note, once properly executed by the borrower, may also be recorded. The note includes the date of closing, the loan amount and the interest rate, the place where payments are made, the due date of the first and subsequent payments, the frequency of payments, and the date by which the borrower must pay the loan in full.

PITI

PITI is an acronym for the items included in a monthly mortgage payment: principal, interest, taxes, and insurance.

Principal

Principal is the original balance of money lent, excluding interest. It also is the remaining balance of the loan, excluding interest.

Qualification Ratios

Lenders commonly use qualification ratios to help make a decision whether to approve a borrower's loan. The two ratios used most often are the housing cost ratio and the debt ratio. These ratios compare the borrower's anticipated monthly housing expense and total monthly obligations to his or her stable monthly gross income. Investors and insurers may find different ratios acceptable, depending on the loan type and the loan-to-value.

Verification of Deposit (VOD)

A verification of deposit form requests and secures verifications of amounts on deposit at financial institutions. The

VOD establishes that sufficient cash is available to meet closing requirements.

Verification of Employment (VOE)

A verification of employment form requests and secures documentation of a mortgage applicant's work history and occupation. The VOE establishes stable employment and income sufficient to meet loan payments. Self-employment is verified by personal financial statements, tax returns, and a corporate profit and loss statement.

This chapter has introduced you to the role of processing in mortgage lending as well as some of the tasks and terminology involved with processing. The next chapters of this book will explore in greater detail how mortgage applications are processed and provide some checkpoints for fraud prevention.

2

Selling Mortgage Services

The customer is anyone bringing business to the mortgage banker. Traditionally, mortgage bankers have viewed real estate brokers and builders as their principal customers. More recently, however, it has become apparent that borrowers, bypassing traditional conduits, have become an important source of new and repeat business.

The Role of Loan Officers

The loan officer remains the principal contact between the mortgage banking firm and its customers, no matter who they are. It is usually the loan officer who makes the first contact with "the outside world" and in many cases represents the only contact.

The loan officer finds customers, whether directly or through referrals, and takes borrower applications. He or she also follows up on the application and serves as the link between the customer and the mortgage banker's "back room" employees—processors, underwriters, closers, and others. Quite often, to the outside world, the loan officer is the mortgage banker.

The competition for the mortgage business is intense. There may be dozens of mortgage banking firms and other lending institutions actively seeking mortgage applications in a lively market area. Yet, a real estate broker rarely recommends more than four lenders to a purchaser, and more commonly three. Because most customers end up with just one lender, the rest are left out of the competition. The loan officer's primary objective is to assure that his or her company is one of the three or four the real estate broker recommends.

One sales approach some companies have found effective is telemarketing. While the average loan officer making calls in person can make only an average of three to four quality contacts a day, an outbound telemarketer can make four to five quality contacts an hour. (An outbound telemarketer is a loan officer dialing outbound calls; an inbound telemarketer is one who receives calls.)

Outbound telemarketing can be used to contact previous clients, call targeted lists of potential refinance candidates, and stay in touch with targeted real estate and builder agents. Inbound telemarketers who are located at the company's office can be more accessible than loan officers carrying beepers or using a carphone. In addition, they can handle inquiries for rates, qualification questions, applications, or loan status.

Another approach is to rely on mortgage brokers to bring business through the doors, with processing being done by the broker or the purchasing lender (wholesaler).

Although lenders have experimented with a variety of alternatives to the traditional staff loan officer, it does not appear that ongoing, direct contact with brokers and builders, which has been the mainstay of new customer generation in the past, will disappear. The knowledgeable loan officer, maintaining regular contacts with traditional customers and building the confidence of those customers with his or her expertise and reliability, will continue to be the most significant source of new business to the mortgage banker.

How Rates and Service Affect Referrals

From the point of view of the real estate broker or builder, the appeal of available financing terms can be a powerful tool when selling a house. If the prospective homebuyer can get a financing plan tailored to his or her individual situation, and knows there should be no problem qualifying for financing, the real estate broker can close substantial part of the sale.

If the loan officer provides the broker or builder with up-to-date information, then the real estate broker or builder can provide the homebuyers with the tailored financing programs that will help sell the properties.

Brokers and builders want to be able to separate their prospects into categories that permit them to direct their energies into the sales most likely to close. Loan officers who regularly call on their broker and builder customers, armed with current information about market conditions and trends, have taken the first step toward cementing customer loyalty. If they reinforce their calls with regular meetings to inform clients about new developments, they will have gone still another step. These meetings can help provide brokers and builders with prospect pre-qualification information.

The nature of the loan officer's efforts in developing customers is subject to a certain extent to the types of products offered by the firm. For example, surveys indicate that real estate brokers who refer clients to mortgage banking firms for their financing deal heavily with younger, first-time homebuyers. Those brokers might suggest HUD-FHA or VA financing to their clients.

Before soliciting referrals from these brokers, it pays to make certain the firm offers government-supported loan products. If the company specializes in conventional loans, it might be a better use of a loan officer's time to seek out and cultivate other sources of referrals.

Sales Tools and Advertising

The rate sheet (Exhibit II-1) does not replace but reinforces the loan officer's direct personal contact. It is simply a tool to keep the broker or builder customer aware of current market conditions and of the lender's competitive position. It does not substi-

EXHIBIT II-1: SAMPLE RATE SHEET

See How We Rate.

YOUR LOAN OFFICER HAS PROCESSED, CLOSED LOANS
AND HAS UNDERWRITING AND OPERATIONAL MANAGEMENT EXPERIENCE.
PLEASE GIVE ME A CALL SO I MAY MAKE YOUR TRANSACTIONS SMOOTH.

NOTICE: Quotes set forth are not for disclosure to consumers. If there is no firm contract, agents should reconfirm terms when contract is ratified. This sheet is to be used for the benefit of real estate brokers and agents only. This is not an advertisement or a solicitation of loans and is not to be used to inform potential applicants of loan offerings. Our company will provide quotations in the legally required manner for each applicant.

All rates quoted are subject to change without notice.

Fixed Rate

30 YEAR FIXED TO $153,100

10.625	2+1
10.75	1+1
10.875	0+1

15 YEAR FIXED TO $153,000

10.375	2+1
10.5	1+1
10.625	0+1

JUMBO 30 YEAR FIXED TO $1,000,000

10.625	2+1
10.75	1+1
10.875	0+1

****
****

JUMBO 15 YEAR FIXED TO $1,000,000

10.625	2+1
10.75	1+1
10.875	0+1

QUOTES GOOD FOR 2 MONTHS: 38/38 RATIOS ON JUMBO LOANS WITH 20% DOWN

Variable Rate

ONE YEAR ADJUSTABLE TO $153,100

7.375	3½+1

ONE YEAR ADJUSTABLE JUMBO

7.75	2+1 (95%)
7½	2+1 (90%)

3 TO 1 ADJUSTABLE

9.125	2+1
9.375	1+1

3 TO 1 ADJUSTABLE CAN BE CONVERTED TO A FIXED RATE ANY TIME FROM YEARS 3 THROUGH 5
OR
AUTOMATICALLY CONVERTS TO A ONE YEAR ADJUSTABLE IN YEAR 4.

Government Loans

30 YEAR FHA/VA

10.5	.75+1
10.0	3+1
9.5	5.75+1

15 YEAR FHA/VA

10½	
10	.75+1
9.5	3+1

FHA ARM

8½	3+1

IN HOUSE FHA & CONVENTIONAL APPRAISER

WE NOW HAVE IN HOUSE CREDIT REPORTS: REPORTS IN FOUR WORKING DAYS.

Miscellaneous

****ONLY 20% DOWN REQUIRED ON NO INCOME DOCUMENTATION PROGRAM; AVAILABLE ON ALL LOAN
**** PROGRAMS. NO INCOME DOCUMENTATION PRICED THE SAME AS OUR JUMBO MONEY.
*******FHA/VA PRICING AVAILABLE FOR 30 & 75 DAYS. SECOND HOMES AND NON OWNER OCCUPIED AVAILABLE ON ALL LOAN PROGRAMS.

tute for the loan officer's personal commitment to providing service.

Because rates and fees are not always competitive, many firms are reinforcing the loan officer's personal contact with major marketing and public relations programs. Some of these programs are aimed at the traditional broker and builder customers, but recently the target has moved to the individual consumer. This bypasses the traditional referral route. Where such campaigns are used, the loan officer's job becomes even more demanding.

It is one thing to be able to explain a technical product in technical terms to someone with at least a basic understanding of the industry. It is an entirely different aspect to explain that same technical product in non-technical terms to someone who not only has never had a mortgage, but also is confused, rushed, and anxious.

Mortgage advertising campaigns for consumers reinforce name recognition rather than product detail. With limited time or space, this advertising identifies the company and builds an attractive image. Details must be filled in by loan officers. This relationship only reinforces the need for the loan officer to be a true expert in the business of marketing loans.

The branch manager and his or her staff can be a positive force in using public relations to develop potential customers, both within the industry and among the home-buying public. Branch personnel in companies of all sizes are usually familiar with local conditions. They are best equipped to respond to local media inquiries about market conditions or the technicalities of mortgage lending.

The loan officer who cultivates media contacts—as well as contacts with traditional customers—is likely to stay ahead of the competition. Positive contacts in good times can also serve to avoid being identified with the "bad guys" in down times.

Dealing With Applicants

In initial contacts with loan applicants, the loan officer must be careful not to promise too much. If processing and underwriting take 90 days, it is bad business to promise closing in 60 days. If the rates quoted will be locked in for 60 days and there is even a remote possibility that the lender will be unable to close in that time, it is essential that the possibility of a rate change, and the reasons for it, be explained to the customer up front.

It is also important not to give the borrower written assurance of a locked-in rate without a caveat pointing out that there is no guarantee the loan can be closed within the lock period. An explanation by the loan officer of how investor commitments influence rates can go a long way toward instilling borrower confidence.

Consumer information brochures available from the Mortgage Bankers Association (MBA), among other sources, can reinforce loan officer efforts. If the prospective customer knows what to expect at the time the mortgage application is taken, considerable time can be saved in face-to-face meetings with lender staff.

The Role of Automated Systems

Automated systems permit the loan officer or other employees to enter application data directly into laptop computers or into the company's mainframe computer by modem. Depending on the type, these automated systems can prequalify borrowers, permit full application data entry, print documents, and interface with other systems, such as credit bureaus.

Whether or not such a system is used is a management decision based on whether the increase in closed loans justifies the cost. Today, however, the trend in mortgage origination is to cut the cost of origination wherever possible. Use of technology can dramatically increase the number of good loan applications taken and also the number of loans closed. Some of these systems not only organize data but use it to make underwriting decisions. These systems used for automated loan evaluation involve either rules-based systems, expert systems, or both.

A rules-based system is one that follows guidelines and uses logic to examine specific data elements based on the computer's reaction to other data elements. Compensating factors can be built into the process by assigning a mathematical value for their worth, and determining whether compensating factors are allowable under the circumstances.

The rules-based system is particularly adept at quality control and compliance. This type of system offers mortgage bankers a machine that allows fact-based decisionmaking.

It is difficult to work with rules-based systems for tasks such as underwriting, where decisions are seldom straightforward, even for good loans. To deal with more complicated loans, some lenders are implementing the expert system. An expert system operates by following instructions derived from the intuitive process of an expert. By following underwriters around, and asking them about all aspects of their decisionmaking, programmers can translate this into computer programs that designate acceptable levels of risk.

However, since underwriters traditionally bring subjectivity and experience to their work, these systems work only by generalizing the case being examined to fit general principles. The level of a system's built-in generalization requirements can affect the number of cases that the expert system can handle and increase human review.

Why do loan production shops need these technological systems? Automation can enable lenders to make quicker decisions, take higher levels of acceptable risk, and pattern pipelines and portfolios for market dominance. Their value lies not only in competitive advantage but in streamlining operations, to better handle the increased loan production for the coming decade.

Taking application data through the system directly to the underwriter's screen not only results in more efficiency but should reduce fraud and inconvenience to borrowers. Today's personal computers can track performance standards and market penetration; give exception reports for possible problem areas; reduce paperwork; and automatically order appraisals, credit, and other reports. The possibilities are endless with continuing improvements in the technology.

Fresh ideas continue to emerge in the origination process, for originators constantly become more efficient in delivering what their customers demand. Now, what happens after the customer has been brought to the company?

3

Preparing to Take the Application

How the application is taken profoundly affects everything that comes later, not only in the origination process, but also for the life of the loan. The borrower's confidence in the lender and understanding of the mortgage process are built at the time of application, and the impact of what happens here is long lasting. It is essential that this initial contact with the lender establish a positive relationship.

In the interview, the person taking the application assumes three responsibilities: first, to impress on the applicants the need for a careful study of their financial situation and the fact that the company is genuinely interested in helping them; second, to obtain information to judge the soundness of the loan, so that missing bits and pieces won't necessitate more meetings and slow the process; and third, to ensure that no law is violated in taking the application.

Responsibility for Taking the Application

In most situations, a loan officer takes the initial application; then a processor takes over and, using the information from the rough application, puts together a finished loan application package. In some companies, a processor takes the application, and in others, the responsibilities are divided: Loan officers take applications from borrowers who are referred by real estate brokers or builders, while processors or branch managers may take them from those walk-in applicants. Industry-wide, most applications are probably taken by loan officers.

A complete, accurate application is essential if the company is to provide superior service to its customers. If the loan application is taken by a knowledgeable professional, the person taking the application can identify disqualifying factors immediately and avert wasted time.

Those taking the loan application can also be the first to spot fraud. At this point, one of the most important documents is the sales contract for the purchase of the property.

The Sales Agreement

The sales agreement (Exhibit III-1) is one of the first pieces of documentation that can be quickly reviewed for possible inconsistencies in mortgage loan transactions. While 95 percent of most contracts contain what is called "boilerplate" or "canned" terms and conditions, the remaining 5 percent is what is unique about a particular loan and should always be reviewed carefully for conflicts.

Warning Signals

Here are some typical warning signals for bad sales agreements:

- The seller is a real estate broker, relative, or employer.
- No real estate broker is involved.
- There is a lease-option clause.
- The price is substantially below market value.
- A second mortgage is indicated.
- Deposit checks have inconsistent dates.
- The name and address on the deposit check are different from the buyer's.

EXHIBIT III-1: SALES AGREEMENT

WASHINGTON, DC ASSOCIATION OF REALTORS® INC.
Second Floor
777 Fourteenth Street, N.W.
Washington, D.C. 20005

Single Family Home Sales Contract — District of Columbia

1. (DATE OF CONTRACT) ______________ , 19 _____ , RECEIVED from the undersigned Purchaser a deposit in the amount set forth in Paragraph 2a.(i) hereof in the form of (CASH/CHECK/NOTE) ____________ , which if in the form of cash or check shall be deposited expeditiously by the undersigned agent in an (INTEREST/NON-INTEREST) ______________ bearing escrow account in a District of Columbia financial institution after final ratification of this contract. Any interest shall be paid to Purchaser at settlement, or to Seller in the event of a forfeiture of deposit pursuant to Paragraph 12.c. The deposit shall be applied as part payment of the Purchase Price, in the amount set forth in Paragraph 2c. hereof, of the premises known as ______________________________________ , Washington, D.C., Zip Code ______ Lot ________, Square ________, with improvements thereon (collectively, the "Property"), including built-in heating plant and air-conditioning system, all plumbing and lighting fixtures, kitchen equipment, including range, refrigerator, built-in dishwasher, trash-compactor and disposal, all wall-to-wall carpeting, cornices, curtain and drapery rods, awnings, T.V. antennas, screens, storm doors and storm windows, venetian blinds, shades, indoor shutters, trees, shrubs and plants, alarm system (with a transfer fee of $ ________ and a monthly service fee of $ ________) and ______________________________ , if the foregoing are installed on the Property and owned by Seller as of the above date, upon the terms of sale set forth herein.

2. **PAYMENT OF PURCHASE PRICE.** The Purchase Price of the Property shall be paid as follows:

a. **Cash Downpayment**	(i)	Deposit with Contract	$ __________	
	(ii)	Balance of Downpayment at Settlement	$ __________	
		TOTAL DOWNPAYMENT		$ __________
b. **Financing**	(i)	First Trust	$ __________	
	(ii)	Second Trust	$ __________	
	(iii)	Trust (Seller to Take Back)	$ __________	
		TOTAL FINANCING		$ __________
c. TOTAL PURCHASE PRICE OF PROPERTY				$ __________

3. **FINANCING**

a. **First Trust: (If FHA or VA financing is used, see Addendum attached.)** The Purchaser is to (PLACE/TAKE TITLE SUBJECT TO/ASSUME) ______________ a (CONVENTIONAL FIXED RATE/ARM/FHA/VA) ______________ first deed of trust in lender's usual form secured by said Property in the amount set forth in Paragraph 2b.(i) hereof due in _____ years and bearing interest at the rate of _____ percent per annum or, in cases other than assumptions, the prevailing rate at time of settlement, payable approximately $ ______________ monthly, plus one-twelfth of annual taxes, fire insurance, and private mortgage insurance, if required by lender.

b. **Second Trust:** The Purchaser is to (PLACE/TAKE TITLE SUBJECT TO/ASSUME) ______________ a second deed of trust in lender's usual form secured by said Property in the amount set forth in Paragraph 2b.(ii) hereof due in ____ years and bearing interest at the rate of _____ percent per annum, payable approximately $ ______________ monthly.

c. **Trust (Seller to Take Back):** The deferred purchase money note in the am[illegible] [illegible]h in Paragraph 2b.(iii) hereof as part of the purchase price is to be secured by a _____ deed of trust in usual form on said Property, to be paid in mon[illegible] [illegible]s of $ ______________ or more, without penalty, at maker's option, including interest at the rate of _____ percent per annum. The entire [illegible] [illegible]hall be due and payable in full within ______________. If this Paragraph 3c. is applicable, this contract shall not be assigned without the prior [illegible] of the Seller. (See additional terms on the reverse side hereof)

4. **CONVENTIONAL FIXED RATE/ARM FINANCING CONTINGENC**[illegible] is contingent on the ability of Purchaser to secure or receive a written commitment for the herein described financing, to take title subject to any e[illegible] trust, or to obtain lender's approval of any assumption, if required, within _____ calendar days from the date of final ratification of this contract, wh[illegible] or approval Purchaser agrees to pursue diligently. Purchaser reserves the right to increase the cash downpayment and/or to accept a modified com[illegible]ancing. If Purchaser has diligently pursued obtaining financing and has provided all information requested in a timely manner, as required by Paragra[illegible], and the lender needs additional time to finish processing the loan, prior to the expiration of the ____________ day period Purchaser or Seller [illegible] contingency period for an additional 15 days by notifying all parties of the intention to do so, and by providing them with evidence from the lender [illegible]ion received by it to date shows that the loan should be approved. If, after making every reasonable effort, Purchaser is unable to obtain the herein s[illegible]g and notifies Seller of this fact in writing within the term of this contingency, this contract shall become null and void and Purchaser's deposit sha[illegible] full. IF PURCHASER FAILS TO GIVE ANY OF THE ABOVE NOTICES, THIS CONTINGENCY SHALL AUTOMATICALLY EXPIRE AND THIS CONTRACT S[illegible] IN FULL FORCE AND EFFECT, UNLESS OTHERWISE STATED HEREIN.

5. **SETTLEMENT.**

a. **Date of Settlement.** With[illegible] from the date of final ratification of this contract, or as soon thereafter as a report on the title can be secured if promptly ordered, and survey obtaine[illegible] and loan processed, all if promptly applied for, Seller and Purchaser agree to make full settlement in accordance with the terms hereof.

b. **Place of Settlement.** THE [illegible]CHASER HAS THE RIGHT TO SELECT THE SETTLEMENT OFFICE. Purchaser hereby authorizes the undersigned Agent to order the examination of title, a survey, and the preparation of necessary conveyancing papers through ______________________ (to be named within 10 days of final ratification).

c. **Payment of Downpayment.** Purchaser agrees to pay by certified check at settlement a downpayment in the amount set forth in Paragraph 2a. hereof, of which sum the above deposit shall be a part. If the deposit exceeds the downpayment, any excess shall apply first to settlement costs and the balance shall be refunded to Purchaser at settlement.

d. **Payment of Conventional Loan Fees.** If a new loan is to be placed under this contract, the Purchaser agrees to pay by certified check at settlement a loan fee (i.e., points) of ________ % of the principal sum of the loan. The Seller agrees to pay a loan fee of _____ % of the principal sum of the loan. The above fees are based on the present mortgage money market, and the Purchaser will comply with any reasonable increase or decrease in such fees. All other lender's fees shall be paid by Purchaser by certified check at settlement based on lender's good faith estimate of closing costs (including Private Mortgage Insurance Premium) as required by lender.

e. **Payment of Settlement Costs.** Purchaser agrees to pay by certified check at settlement the settlement charges in connection with the examination of title, the survey, the preparation of all necessary conveyancing papers, tax certificate, conveyancing, settlement fee, notary fees and recording charges, except those incident to clearing existing encumbrances. The D.C. Recordation Tax will be paid by the Purchaser and the D.C. Transfer Tax will be paid by the Seller. Seller hereby agrees to pay a reasonable closing fee for services rendered to Seller, and to pay any above-mentioned costs incurred if upon examination the title should be found defective and it is not remedied as stated herein.

f. **Taking Title.** Property is to be conveyed in the names of ______________________________ .

6. **TENANCY.** The Property is sold and shall be conveyed free of any existing tenancy, except as follows: ______________________________ (hereinafter the "Tenant(s)"). Without the prior written consent of Purchaser (which shall not be unreasonably withheld) Seller shall not (a) modify the terms of or terminate such tenancy, except for non-payment of rent; or (b) enter into any new leases or tenancies with respect to the Property. Seller represents to Purchaser and Agent that on ______________, 19 _____ Seller has provided to the Tenant(s) a written notice of the intended sale of the Property and a bona fide offer of sale. If the Property is tenant occupied, Purchaser hereby represents that Purchaser (WILL/WILL NOT) ______________ occupy the Property. (See additional terms on the reverse side hereof.)

7. **D.C. SOIL DISCLOSURE REQUIREMENTS.** The characteristic of the soil on the subject Property as described by the Soil Conservation Service of the United States Department of Agriculture in the Soil Survey of the District of Columbia published in 1976 and as shown on the Soil Maps of the District of Columbia at the back of that publication is ______________________________ . For further information, the Purchaser can contact a soil testing laboratory, the District of Columbia Department of Environmental Services, or the Soil Conservation Service of the Department of Agriculture.

8. **AGENCY.** Seller recognizes ______________________________ (referred to herein as "Agent") as Agent negotiating this contract and agrees to pay a brokerage fee(s) for services rendered as specified in a separate listing agreement, and the party making settlement is hereby irrevocably directed and authorized to deduct and pay such brokerage fee(s) from the proceeds of the sale.

9. **AGREEMENT.** "Without limiting the means of ratifying this contract, the parties agree that ratification of this contract may be accomplished by signing same or by transmitting assent through a wired or electronic medium which produces a tangible record of the transmission (such as a telegram, mailgram or datagram), and that such ratification shall be binding on the parties." We, the undersigned, hereby ratify, accept and agree to this contract and acknowledge receipt of a copy thereof. ADDITIONAL PARAGRAPHS NUMBERED 10 THROUGH 16 SET FORTH ON THE REVERSE SIDE HEREOF ARE INCORPORATED HEREIN AND MADE A PART HEREOF AND ALL PARTIES ACKNOWLEDGE THAT THEY HAVE READ SAID PARAGRAPHS.

THIS IS A LEGALLY BINDING CONTRACT. IF YOU DO NOT UNDERSTAND ALL OF THE TERMS OF THIS DOCUMENT, SEEK COMPETENT LEGAL ADVICE BEFORE SIGNING IT.

ADDENDUM ATTACHED. ____Yes ____ No.

______________________	______________________
SELLER (Print name also)	PURCHASER (Print name also)
______________________	______________________
SELLER (Print name also)	PURCHASER (Print name also)
______________________	______________________
ADDRES[illegible] [illegible]f other than premises)	ADDRESS OF PURCHASER
______________________	______________________
BROKER	SALES ASSOCIATE

THE SELLER OR PURCHASER, WHICHEVER ONE PROVIDES FINAL RATIFICATION, SHALL COMPLETE THE FOLLOWING:

DATE OF FINAL RATIFICATION ______________ TIME OF FINAL RATIFICATION ______________ BY ________ (INITIALS ONLY) 9/89

EXHIBIT III-1—*continued*

10. ADDITIONAL FINANCING CONDITIONS.

a. **Additional Seller Take Back Financing Provisions.** Each monthly installment on the note described in Paragraph 3c. when so paid shall be applied first to the payment of late charges, then to interest on the amount of principal remaining and the balance thereof credited to principal. In case of default on any payment, the entire amount then remaining unpaid shall become due and payable fifteen (15) days after written notice is sent to maker by certified mail, return receipt requested, unless maker cures said default prior to the expiration of said fifteen (15) day period. Said trust and note may not be assumed or title taken subject to said trust and note without the prior written consent of the noteholder. The note shall provide that (i) maker shall pay a late charge of five percent (5%) of any monthly installment not received by the noteholder within fifteen (15) days of the due date; and (ii) default in the payment of any prior encumbrance or charge against the Property shall be construed to be a default on the payment of this note. The deed of trust shall provide that unless waived by the noteholder, maker will submit to noteholder, on a yearly basis, evidence of payment by the due date of all real property taxes and assessments and all insurance premiums for policies on the Property.

b. **General Financial Provisions.**

(i) In the event that mortgages are used rather than deeds of trust, the word "mortgage" shall be substituted automatically.

(ii) If this contract provides for the assumption of existing trust(s) or for purchase subject to existing trust(s), it is understood that the balance of such trust(s) and the cash downpayment are approximate amounts. A COPY OF THE EXISTING TRUST(S) AND NOTE(S) ARE ATTACHED HERETO. Any change(s) required by the lender in order that the trust may be assumed will be subject to the Purchaser's consent, if assumption is promptly applied for.

(iii) Trustees in all deeds of trust are to be named by the parties secured thereby.

(iv) Seller shall allow inspections of all the Property and furnish any pertinent information required by Purchaser or Purchaser's financing agency in reference to obtaining a loan commitment.

(v) If this contract provides for financing, Purchaser placing financing agrees to make application immediately and file all necessary papers that are required to complete processing and agrees that failure to do so within seven (7) days after final ratification of this contract, or to promptly comply with all further requests from lender for additional information, shall give Seller the right to declare the deposit forfeited or avail himself of any legal or equitable rights as provided in the paragraph labeled "FORFEITURE OF DEPOSIT/LIQUIDATED DAMAGES."

(vi) Seller agrees to comply with reasonable lender requirements for repairs.

11. CONSUMER REPORT AUTHORIZATION. A financial or credit information statement signed by Purchaser is to be submitted together with this contract. Purchaser hereby authorizes the Agent to disclose (and to provide a signed copy) to Seller or any lender the financial or credit information statement provided to the Agent by Purchaser. In the event the terms of this contract require Seller to take back financing from Purchaser, this contract shall be contingent upon approval of a satisfactory Consumer Report (Credit Report) by Seller within 5 days after receipt of said report by Seller, provided, however, that Seller orders or notifies Agent to order said report immediately after the final ratification of this contract. If Seller does not approve the credit standing of Purchaser, and Purchaser is so notified in writing by Seller within 5 days after receipt of the Consumer Report, this contract shall be null and void and the deposit returned to Purchaser. Purchaser hereby authorizes the Agent to order and obtain a Consumer Report from a Consumer Reporting Agency to be used only in connection with this transaction. Further, in the event the Agent is acting on behalf of a creditor, Seller or other party directly affected by said transaction, Purchaser hereby authorizes the Agent to forward all or any portion of the information contained in the Consumer Report to the creditor, Seller or other party directly involved. Cost of said Consumer Report is to be borne by Purchaser. Except as stated herein, the Consumer Report is confidential and the information contained therein shall not be knowingly released to others without the written consent of Purchaser. Purchaser hereby certifies that all income and credit information furnished in connection with this purchase is true and accurate to the best of Purchaser's knowledge.

12. ADDITIONAL SETTLEMENT PROVISIONS.

a. **Performance.** Settlement is to be made at the settlement office designated in Paragr[illegible] Delivery to the settlement office of the cash payment and settlement costs as herein stated, the executed deed of conveyance and such other papers as are r[illegible] either party by the terms of this contract shall be considered good and sufficient tender of performance in accordance with the terms hereof. It is agree[illegible]sing out of this transaction at settlement may be used to pay off any existing encumbrances, including interest, as required by lender.

b. **Adjustments.** Rents, taxes, water, sewer, oil, escrow for taxes and insu[illegible]e (except FHA Mortgage Insurance Premium), and interest on existing encumbrances, if any, and other operating charges are to be adjusted to the [illegible]ment. Rent security deposits, if any, plus interest, shall be transferred to Purchaser at time of settlement. Taxes, general and special, are to be adjuste[illegible] the certificate of taxes issued by the D.C. Department of Finance and Revenue, except that assessments for improvements completed prior to the date [illegible] hereof, whether assessment therefor has been levied or not, shall be paid by Seller or allowance made therefor at the time of settlement.

c. **Forfeiture of Deposit/Liquidated Damages.** If Purchaser fail[illegible] settlement as hereby required, the deposit herein provided for shall be forfeited as liquidated damages (in which event Purchaser shall be relieved [illegible]bility hereunder), unless Seller notifies Purchaser and Agent in writing within thirty (30) days after the date provided for settlement herein of his elect[illegible]self of any legal or equitable rights, other than the said liquidated damages, which he may have under this contract. In the event Seller so elects to av[illegible]gal or equitable rights as aforesaid, Seller shall execute and deliver to Agent with such notice an Agreement of Release (as defined below) for execut[illegible]er, and upon such execution by Purchaser and delivery of the Agreement of Release to Agent, the deposit shall be returned to Purchaser by Agent [illegible]me and Agent shall not be liable to Seller for return of said deposit. In the event of the forfeiture of the deposit as liquidated damages or in the eve[illegible] of damages by a court or a compromise agreement between Seller and Purchaser, Seller shall allow or pay Agent one-half thereof as compensation [illegible]ndered, said amount not to exceed the amount of the full brokerage fee. Nothing herein shall prevent Agent from holding Seller liable for the full a[illegible] commissions to which Agent may be entitled. Seller and Purchaser agree that Agent who holds the deposit given by Purchaser shall have the right to [illegible]eposit and accrued interest thereon upon settlement of this contract, and that in the event settlement does not occur for any reason the deposit and [illegible]st thereon shall only be given or returned by Agent to any of the parties to this contract (i) when an "Agreement of Release", in which all parties auth[illegible] the disposition of the deposit as therein specified, has been signed by all such parties and delivered to Agent, or (ii) as directed by a court order. If ei[illegible] or Purchaser refuses to execute an Agreement of Release when requested to do so in writing and a court finds that such party should have executed same, t[illegible]y who so refused to execute an Agreement of Release shall pay the reasonable expenses, including, without limitation, reasonable attorney's fees, incurred by the other party in the litigation. The parties hereto hereby agree that Agent shall have no liability to any party on account of Agent's disbursement of the deposit or on account of Agent's failure to disburse the deposit, except only in the event of Agent's gross negligence or willful misconduct. The parties further agree that Agent shall not be liable for the failure of any depository in which the deposit is placed, and that Seller and Purchaser each will indemnify, defend and save harmless Agent from and against every claim, liability, cost, damage, loss or expense arising out of the disbursement of the deposit or failure to disburse the deposit by Agent, except in the case of Agent's gross negligence or willful misconduct.

d. **Conveyance.** Seller agrees to execute and deliver a good and sufficient special warranty deed. Purchaser agrees to have the deed of conveyance recorded promptly.

13. PROPERTY.

a. **Property Condition.** Seller, at the time of settlement or occupancy (whichever occurs first), will leave the Property free and clear of trash and debris and broom clean, will leave the electrical, plumbing, heating, air-conditioning and any other mechanical systems and equipment included in this contract in operating condition, and will deliver the Property in substantially the same physical condition as of the date of this contract. Purchaser has the privilege of a pre-settlement inspection of the Property. All notices of violations of municipal orders or requirements noted or issued by any department or agency of the District of Columbia, or prosecutions in any courts on account thereof, against or affecting the Property at the date of this contract shall be complied with by Seller and the Property conveyed free thereof, with the exception of the means of egress regulations.

b. **Termite Inspection.** Prior to the time of settlement, Seller shall order a termite inspection, and no later than the time of settlement Seller shall pay the costs of termite inspection and provide to Purchaser a written certification from a licensed exterminator that, based upon a careful visual inspection of accessible areas of the house, any garage, and any accessory buildings, there is no evidence of infestation of termites or wood-boring insects. If such infestation exists, Seller is to exterminate, using a licensed exterminator. Seller at his own expense and prior to settlement shall repair any prior or current visible damage caused by termites or wood-boring insects.

c. **Risk of Loss.** The risk of loss or damage to said Property by fire or other casualty is assumed by Seller until the executed deed of conveyance is delivered to the Purchaser or is recorded by the settlement office conducting the conveyance, whichever shall occur first.

d. **Title.** The Property, including the personal property described in Paragraph One above, is sold free of encumbrances, except as stated herein. Title is to be good of record and marketable subject, however, to covenants, rights of way, easements, conditions and restrictions of record,if any, on the date of execution of this contract by Purchaser; otherwise the deposit is to be returned and sale declared off at the option of the Purchaser, unless the defects are of such character that they may readily be remedied by legal action, but the Seller and Agent are hereby expressly released from all liability for damages by reason of any defect in the title. In case legal steps are necessary to perfect the title, such action must be taken promptly by and at the Seller's expense, whereupon the time herein specified for full settlement by the Purchaser will thereby be extended for the period necessary for such action.

14. ADDITIONAL TENANCY PROVISIONS. Seller and Purchaser further acknowledge that, in addition to the rights under the bona fide offer of sale, the Tenant(s) has an additional fifteen (15) day right of first refusal to purchase the Property during the period specified by District of Columbia law and regulations. Seller further represents and agrees that within two (2) days after final ratification of this contract Seller will hand-deliver to the Tenant(s) and send by first-class mail the notice of right of first refusal required by District of Columbia law and regulations and a copy of this contract. In the event that prior to the date of this contract Seller has not provided to the Tenant(s) a written notice of the intended sale of the Property and a bona fide offer of sale, Seller represents and agrees that within two (2) days after final ratification of this contract Seller will hand-deliver and send by first class mail to the Tenant(s) a written notice of the intended sale of the Property, a bona fide offer of sale, the required notice of right of first refusal and a copy of this contract. Upon or after execution of a contract of sale of the Property between Seller and the Tenant(s), at the option of Purchaser (exercisable by written notice to Seller) this contract shall be void and the deposit hereunder shall be returned to Purchaser. If, however, the Tenant(s) shall fail to exercise the foregoing rights to purchase the Property or shall execute and deliver a valid rejection of said rights, then this contract shall remain in full force and effect. The Seller shall keep Purchaser and Agent apprised of all negotiations, correspondence, contracts and other developments with respect to negotiations with the Tenant(s). All actions required hereunder to be taken by Seller shall be taken in accordance with District of Columbia law and regulations. If there is no existing tenancy, Seller agrees to give possession of the Property at the time of settlement, and if Seller fails to do so and occupies the Property, Seller shall become and thereafter be a tenant at sufferance of Purchaser, and hereby expressly waives all notice to quit provided by law.

15. NOTICES. All notices required or permitted herein shall be in writing and effective as of the date on which such notice is mailed in any United States Post Office by certified or registered mail, postage prepaid, or hand-delivered to Seller at the Property address, to the Agent or Purchaser at the addresses designated herein, or to such other addresses as the parties may designate in writing from time to time.

16. CONTRACTING PARTIES. The principals to this contract mutually agree that it shall be binding upon them, their heirs, executors, administrators, personal representatives, successors and assigns; that the provisions hereof shall survive the execution and delivery of the deed herein stated and shall not be merged therein; that this contract contains the final and entire agreement between the parties hereto, and neither they nor their agents shall be bound by any terms, conditions, statements, warranties or representations, oral or written, not herein contained. The Agent and the cooperating agent assume no responsibility for the condition of the Property nor for the performance of this contract by any or all parties hereto.

- The earnest deposit check has not been cashed.
- The borrower is not shown as the purchaser.
- The seller is noted as a contract buyer.
- There is an excessive real estate commission.
- There is a contract addendum.
- The contract is dated after the credit documents.
- Multiple contracts exist.

Case Examples

Following are five case examples of mortgage fraud.

1. Recently, a lender discovered an unusual commissions pattern for one of its brokers. Each case submitted by that broker showed a 25 to 30 percent real estate commission. After calling the involved sellers, the lender discovered that the excessive commissions were being used by the broker to pay the mortgagors' down payments.
2. In Virginia, an owner-occupant transaction referenced the mortgagor as purchasing the property subject to an existing three-year lease agreement with a certain tenant. This inconsistency was not questioned by the lender, and the mortgagor obtained a high ratio owner-occupant mortgage. When the mortgage insurer became aware of the problem, the lender was required to buy down the mortgage by $12,000.
3. Beware of double contracting. A case in Alaska illustrates how a contract was drawn up to fit the lender's loan-to-value requirements. The first contract was for $100,000; however, the mortgagor had insufficient assets for the down payment of $20,000 (20 percent of value/selling price). The second contract was drawn showing a sales price of $125,000, which allowed the mortgagor to obtain a $100,000 loan. Thus, the mortgagor was able to obtain 100 percent of financing. Question any multiple-contract loan package to ascertain the true sales price.

4. Southern Florida provided two examples of the same problem—a relative selling to a relative. Specifically, a husband and wife team were selling properties to each other so they could pull out their equity and still retain ownership. The two contracts, dated the same date, clearly showed that Mr. XYZ was buying from Ms. XYZ and vice versa. Both loans were high ratio owner-occupant loans, and the fraud could have been detected by simply reviewing last names on the contracts.
5. One Texas lender failed to read the contract addendum on five loans. The basic contract in each case made no mention of any seller credit to the mortgagor for the down payment. However, the addendum, dated two to three days after the original contract, clearly indicated that the seller was to pay most or all the mortgagor's down payments.

While this last example is related to lender negligence and not necessarily fraud, the lender was required to pay over $250,000 to the insurer of these loans since they all subsequently went into foreclosure. Read any addendum to the contract. It is typically less than one full page and often addresses changes in sales price, down payment requirements, and responsibility for the payment of points and settlement charges.

The person taking the application should set an appointment time whenever possible, planning on about an hour for each appointment. It is helpful, however, to remain flexible enough to take an occasional application on little or no notice.

When arranging for a time and place to meet, the interviewer should ask the borrower for basic information that will have to be confirmed later in both the application and verification phases, such as sales price, deposit, down payment, mortgage amount and terms, interest rate, discounts, and type of loan the applicant has in mind.

Every applicant on the loan should be present at the first application appointment. The applicants will be asked to disclose their entire past and present financial position, so absolute privacy is a must. Some loan officers go to the applicant's home for this reason. Sometimes a partitioned booth in the office will suffice, but a private office is preferable. A systematic and professional approach gives borrowers confidence and speeds the application taking process.

Before the Interview Begins

It is important that the interviewer know as much about the transaction as possible before meeting with the applicants to take the application. It is here that the loan officer's advance work with the real estate broker or builder pays dividends. If the broker has done much of the preliminary work, the applicant already will have been primed with much of the information needed in preparation for the application session.

The interviewer may also need to talk to a real estate broker or builder in advance, to get more information or confirm details. If the applicant has responded to an advertisement or if the broker has not properly prepared the applicants, the person taking the application will have to do most of this work.

First, it must be established that there is a valid sales contract to finance the purchase of a property. The contract may, by its terms, require the borrower to use HUD-FHA, VA, or conventional financing. If it does not, there must be agreement on the type of loan for which the borrower will apply.

Wherever possible, the applicant's wishes relating to the type of financing should be honored, but borrowers sometimes do not know one loan program from another. The interviewer also may find that what the applicant has in mind does not fit with the company's lending policies, so the interviewer must be prepared to suggest alternatives. This may require him or her to have detailed knowledge of the loan differences so that they can be explained to the applicant.

Before the appointment, the processor should let the applicant know what preliminary documentation to bring: names and address of employers, banks, and creditors, including account numbers; canceled checks for mortgages for the most recent 12-month period; information on VA or Social Security benefits; and information on the details of military service, if relevant to the application.

The applicant should be asked to bring adequate funds to cover all services that will be provided before closing. In addition, he or she should be informed of any funds that will not be returned even if the loan is rejected, such as the appraisal and credit report fees.

Some items will almost always create documentation problems later in the process, and those problems can often be avoided with proper preparation of and by the applicant.

Disclosures and Restrictions

There are restrictions on how information is gathered as well as disclosures that have to be provided to the applicant at or shortly after the time of application, and the interviewer may want to have them prepared in advance.

The Real Estate Settlement Procedures Act

The Real Estate Settlement Procedures Act of 1974 (RESPA) was originally designed to regulate lending practices, closings, and settlement procedures by minimizing unnecessary costs and difficulties commonly encountered in purchasing a house.

RESPA requires lenders to provide, in advance, general information about settlement costs and, within three days after receiving the application, a statement of the estimated cost of settlement and monthly payments.

The general information requirement is met by providing a copy of a booklet written by HUD titled *A Home Buyer's Guide To Settlement Costs,* either at or before the application appointment. RESPA also requires a more detailed disclosure before settlement. (See Exhibit III-2 and III-3.)

In addition to the disclosures about settlement costs and monthly payments discussed above, RESPA also requires that the lender provide a good faith estimate of the cost of the loan over its term, including a statement of the cost as an annual percentage rate.

Federal Truth in Lending Statement

A key provision of the Consumer Protection Act of 1968 was the disclosure of the annual percentage rate (APR). The APR does not necessarily bear any relationship to the stated interest rate on the loan. This estimate is often referred to as the "Reg Z" estimate, because the details are provided in Regulation Z of the Federal Reserve regulations.

As with the estimate of closing costs referred to above, the Reg Z estimate must be provided within three days after the application is taken. Another statement providing the actual long-term cost data, known as a "Truth in Lending Statement," must be provided no later than the time of settlement if there have been other than very minor changes. If the APR has not changed but other costs have, no new statement is required. Hence, an accurate good-faith estimate can be prepared to prove these requirements have been met.

There is no prescribed form for these disclosures, and lenders are free to develop their own. Exhibit III-2 and III-3 both meet the current requirements, as does the sample Truth in Lending Disclosure Statement in Exhibit III-4.

Equal Credit Opportunity Act of 1975 (ECOA)

ECOA is another federal law affecting loan origination. It was amended in 1975 and became effective in 1977. ECOA prohibits discrimination in any aspect of a credit transaction on the basis of sex, marital status, race, color, religion, handicap, national origin, age (provided the applicant has the legal capacity to contract), receipt of income from a public assistance program, or the good-faith exercise of rights under the Consumer Credit Protection Act.

EXHIBIT III-2: GOOD FAITH ESTIMATE OF BORROWER'S SETTLEMENT COSTS—RESPA (VERSION 1)

LENDER:
ADDRESS:

DATE:

APPLICANT(S) ______ AMOUNT OF SALE

PROPERTY ADDRESS ______

☐ FHA ☐ V.A. ☐ CONVENTIONAL

LOAN AMOUNT INTEREST RATE

This list gives an estimate of most of the charges you will have to pay at the settlement of your loan. The figures shown as estimates, are subject to change. The figures shown are computed based on sales price and proposed mortgage amount as stated on your loan application.

ESTIMATED SETTLEMENT CHARGES

NUMBERS FROM HUD-1 FORM	DESCRIPTION OF CHARGES	ESTIMATED AMOUNT OR RANGE From	To
801.	LOAN ORIGINATION FEE	$	to
802.	LOAN DISCOUNT	$	to
803.	APPRAISAL FEE	$	to
804.	CREDIT REPORT	$	to
805.	INSPECTION FEE	$	to
806.	MORTGAGE INSURANCE APPLICATION FEE	$	to
807.	ASSUMPTION FEE	$	to
808.	UNDERWRITING FEE	$	to
		$	to
		$	
(SEE BELOW)* 901.	INTEREST ADJUSTMENT	$	to
902.	MORTGAGE INSURANCE PREMIUM	$	to
		$	to
1101.	SETTLEMENT OR CLOSING FEE	$	to
1105.	DOCUMENT PREPARATION FEE	$	to
1107.	ATTORNEYS' FEES	$	to
1108.	TITLE INSURANCE	$	to
1201.	RECORDING FEES	$	to
1202.	CITY/COUNTY TAX/STAMPS	$	to
1203.	STATE TAX/STAMPS	$	to
1301.	SURVEY	$	to
1302.	PEST INSPECTIONS	$	to
OTHERS: ______	______	$	to
______	______	$	to
______	______	$	to
1400 & 103	ESTIMATED SETTLEMENT CHARGES		
		TOTAL EST. CHARGES	

(FROM ABOVE) * This interest calculation represents the greatest amount of interest you could be required to pay at settlement. The actual amount will be determined by which day of the month your settlement is conducted. To determine the amount you will have to pay, multiply the number of days remaining in the month in which you settle times $ ______ , which is the daily interest charge for your loan.

"THIS FORM DOES NOT COVER ALL ITEMS YOU WILL BE REQUIRED TO PAY IN CASH AT SETTLEMENT, FOR EXAMPLE, DEPOSIT IN ESCROW FOR REAL ESTATE TAXES AND INSURANCE. YOU MAY WISH TO INQUIRE AS TO THE AMOUNTS OF SUCH OTHER ITEMS." YOU MAY BE REQUIRED TO PAY OTHER ADDITIONAL AMOUNTS AT SETTLEMENT.

The Undersigned Acknowledges Receipt of:

1. This Good Faith Estimate of Charges.
2. The HUD Guide for Home Buyers, "Settlement Costs," and if applicable the "Consumer Handbook on ARM Mortgages."

APPLICANT ______ BY ______

APPLICANT ______ PER ______ DATE ______

"S" designates those costs to be paid by Seller.

REV. (4/78)
VMP-17 (9206)

VMP MORTGAGE FORMS • (313)293-8100 • (800)521-7291

EXHIBIT III-3: GOOD FAITH ESTIMATE OF BORROWER'S SETTLEMENT COSTS—RESPA (VERSION 2)

GOOD FAITH ESTIMATE
OF BORROWER'S SETTLEMENT COSTS

Lender:
Address:
Applicant(s):

Property Address:

Sales Price:
Loan Amount:
Type of Loan:
Date Prepared:

This form does not cover all items you will be required to pay in cash at settlement, for example, deposit in escrow for real estate taxes and insurance. You may wish to inquire as to the amounts of such other items. You may be required to pay other additional amounts at settlement.

Listed below is the GOOD FAITH ESTIMATE OF SETTLEMENT CHARGES MADE pursuant to the requirements of the REAL ESTATE SETTLEMENT PROCEDURES ACT (RESPA). These figures are only estimates and the actual charges due at settlement may be different.

800. ITEMS PAYABLE IN CONNECTION WITH LOAN:
801. Loan Origination Fee % $
802. Loan Discount % $
803. Appraisal Fee $
804. Credit Report $
805. Lender's Inspection Fee $
806. Mortgage Insurance Application Fee $
807. Assumption Fee $
808. $
809. $
810. $
811. $
812. $
813. $

900. ITEMS REQUIRED BY LENDER TO BE PAID IN ADVANCE:
901. Interest From to @ /Day $
902. Mortgage Insurance Premium $
904. $

1100. TITLE CHARGES:
1101. Closing or Escrow Fee $
1102. Abstract or Title Search $
1103. Title Examination $
1104. Title Insurance Binder $
1107. Attorney Fees $
1108. Title Insurance $
1111. $
1112. $

1200. GOVERNMENT RECORDING & TRANSFER CHARGES:
1201. Recording Fees: Deed: $; Mortgage: $; Release: $ $
1202. City/County Tax/Stamps: Deed: $; Mortgage: $; Release: $ $
1203. State Tax/Stamps: Deed: $; Mortgage: $ $
1204. $
1205. Recording Notice of Commencement $

1300. ADDITIONAL SETTLEMENT CHARGES:
1301. Survey $
1302. Pest Inspection $
1303. $
1305. Construction Disbursing or Inspection Agent Fee $
1306. $

TOTAL ESTIMATED SETTLEMENT CHARGES $
"S" designates those costs to be paid by Seller.

Monthly Payment Estimate:
Interest Rate:
Term:

Principal and Interest $
Taxes/Insurance
PMI
TOTAL $

THIS SECTION TO BE COMPLETED BY LENDER ONLY IF A PARTICULAR PROVIDER OF SERVICE IS REQUIRED. Listed below are providers of service which we require you use. The charges or ranges indicated in the Good Faith Estimate above are based upon the corresponding charge of the below designated providers.

ITEM NO.	NAME & ADDRESS OF PROVIDER	TELEPHONE NO.	BUSINESS RELATIONSHIP EXISTS?
			☐ Yes ☐ No
			☐ Yes ☐ No
			☐ Yes ☐ No

AGREEMENT:
I/We acknowledge I/we have received a copy of the booklet "Settlement Costs," and if applicable the Consumer Handbook on ARM Mortgages, and I/we fully understand the amounts indicated above are **estimates only** and may vary from the actual settlement charges I/we will be required to pay at closing. Further, I/we fully understand that the loan origination fee, interest rate, loan term, and monthly payment indicated above are subject to change at any time and without notice **prior to** the issuance of a formal written loan commitment by the lender.

Applicant ______________________ Applicant ______________________

Date ______________________ Date ______________________

VMP-770 (9206) 6/92
VMP MORTGAGE FORMS • (313)293-8100 • (800)521-7291

EXHIBIT III-4: TRUTH IN LENDING DISCLOSURE—REG Z

NOTICE TO BORROWER(S) REQUIRED BY FEDERAL LAW AND FEDERAL RESERVE REGULATION Z
REAL PROPERTY TRANSACTION SECURED BY A FIRST LIEN ON DWELLING

LENDER:

DATE
LOAN NO.
TYPE

BORROWERS
ADDRESS
CITY/STATE/ZIP
PROPERTY

ANNUAL PERCENTAGE RATE The cost of your credit as a yearly rate.	**FINANCE CHARGE** The dollar amount the credit will cost you.	Amount Financed The amount of credit provided to you or on your behalf.	Total of Payments The amount you will have paid after you have made all payments as scheduled.
%	$	$	$

ITEMIZATION: You have a right at this time to an ITEMIZATION of AMOUNT FINANCED.
☐ I do not want an itemization__________(Initials) ☐ I want an itemization__________(Initials)

PAYMENT SCHEDULE:

NUMBER OF PAYMENTS	AMOUNT OF PAYMENTS	WHEN PAYMENTS ARE DUE	NUMBER OF PAYMENTS	AMOUNT OF PAYMENTS	WHEN PAYMENTS ARE DUE

DEMAND FEATURE: ☐ This loan does not have a Demand Feature. ☐ This loan has a Demand Feature as follows:

VARIABLE RATE FEATURE: ☐ This loan has a Variable Rate Feature. Variable Rate Disclosures have been provided to you earlier.

SECURITY: ☐ You are giving a security interest in the property located at:

ASSUMPTION: ☐ Someone buying this property ☐ cannot assume the remaining balance due under original mortgage terms.
☐ may assume subject to lenders conditions the remaining balance due under original mortgage terms.

FILING/RECORDING FEES: $

PROPERTY INSURANCE: ☐ Property hazard insurance in the amount of $ with a loss payable clause to the lender is a required condition of this loan. Borrower can purchase this insurance from any insurance company acceptable to the lender, but may be purchased through the lender at an estimated cost of for a year term.

LATE CHARGES: If your payment is not received when due, a late charge of % of the overdue payment amount will be added.

PREPAYMENT PENALTY: ☐ You may be charged a penalty to prepay this loan in full or in part.
See your contract documents for any additional information regarding non-payment, default, required repayment in full before scheduled date, and prepayment refunds and penalties.

E = ESTIMATED

I/We hereby acknowledge reading and receiving a complete copy of this disclosure along with copies of documents referred to in this disclosure.

BORROWER/DATE BORROWER/DATE

BORROWER/DATE BORROWER/DATE

VMP-781 (8807).01 VMP MORTGAGE FORMS • (313)293-8100 • (800)521-7291 7/88

ECOA also imposes some very specific restrictions on lenders. There are questions that must not be asked of an applicant. Other types of information may be collected only to monitor compliance. There are still other questions that may be asked, but only if the interviewer has made it clear that the applicant is under no obligation to answer. For example, under ECOA, it is unlawful for a lender to:

- Make any oral or written statement, in advertising or otherwise, to borrowers or prospective borrowers, that would discourage, on a prohibited basis, a reasonable person from making or pursuing an application.
- Inquire whether income stated in an application is derived from alimony, child support, or separate maintenance payments—unless the creditor discloses to the borrower that such income need not be revealed if the borrower does not want the lender to consider it in determining the borrower's creditworthiness.
- Inquire about the sex, race, color, religion, or national origin of an application, except where allowed by law for monitoring purposes.
- Inquire about birth control practices, or intentions concerning the bearing and rearing of children, or capability to bear them.

Loan interviewers must be familiar with the detailed requirements and restrictions of ECOA, and they also need to recognize that the rules change. There must be a method for keeping track of those changes, on behalf of all employees taking applications are kept abreast of changes.

The Privacy Act

The Privacy Act states, in its simplest form, that the applicant is entitled to privacy. A lender, for example, may not require an applicant to provide any information that does not have a direct bearing on eligibility for the loan in question.

While it is acceptable to ask for almost any kind of documentation, it is improper to insist that the applicant provide it. For example, all information contained in income tax returns has bearing on eligibility, because the applicant's entire financial picture is relevant. Therefore, it is proper to insist on copies of tax returns.

On the other hand, a divorce decree includes information on irrelevant subjects, such as the reason for the divorce. One can insist on evidence of the financial rights and obligations established by the divorce decree, but not on a copy of the actual decree. Alternative forms of evidence (court verification, tax returns, deposit slips, attorney verification) might be necessary if the applicant declines to provide a copy of the divorce decree.

The Processor's Role in Taking the Application

The processor prepares for taking an application by assembling a set of blank documents, including the application and verification forms. These will allow the interviewer to complete them efficiently when the time comes. The processor may wish to have information handy about various types of loans available, including FHA, VA, and adjustable rate mortgages.

VA Documentation

If the applicant is a veteran and plans to apply for a VA loan, the processor needs to make sure he or she already has a Certificate of Eligibility or is prepared to provide a Certificate of Release or Discharge from Active Duty/DD Form 214. Note that earlier versions, referred to as "Reports of Separation," with the same and different form numbers, are obsolete. If the veteran has no DD Form 214, one will need to be requested.

Often, VA offices are available to reconstruct the veteran's service from his or her records without having to request a new DD Form 214. The processor may advise the veteran to try this alternative, by visiting the Veterans' Assistance Division in the nearest VA office. The VA also requires a recent "original or certified true copy" pay stub, which the processor must obtain prior to submitting the case for underwriting.

HUD-FHA Documentation

If the application is for a HUD-FHA mortgage, some additional documentation is necessary. The HUD-FHA application must include copies of the applicant's driver's license (or other photo identification) and Social Security number verification. The person taking the application may have to certify that the applicant was actually the person whose picture accompanies the application.

Verifying Information Directly

Conventional and government financing with alternative documentation allows borrowers to provide information directly, to secure faster loan approval. If company policy permits alternative documentation, at a minimum the processor should request W-2 forms for the last two years; a full month of the applicant's most recent pay stubs; three months of current bank statements (if this is the source of funds for down payment and closing costs); and 12 months of the most recent canceled checks (front and back sides) for the present or previous mortgage.

If the borrower is self-employed and owns over 25 percent of the business, he or she must furnish signed and dated personal and business income tax returns from the past two years. If more than three months have passed since the end of the tax year, an interim profit and loss statement is required prior to submission for underwriting. Sole proprietorships should provide a balance sheet from the last two years.

If the source of funds for down payment and closing costs will be a savings account, borrowers should be ready to provide documentation to establish a two month average balance for the account. The processor can ask the applicant's bank to provide the same information, but that may take time. To avoid delays, applicants should have their passbooks or recent original statements available (depending on the type of account) to establish average balances.

Directly verifying retirement income can be difficult. Those relying on retirement income must furnish copies of their current annuity statements and copies of IRS form 1099 or their bank statement reflecting direct deposit.

Some creditors, especially those dealing with so-called "travel and entertainment" card accounts, may refuse to report to credit reporting agencies. They also decline to respond to direct requests from lenders for verification. Applicants must furnish copies of recent statements covering a three- or four-month period from these creditors. This establishes not only the amount of debt but also the manner of recent payment.

Applicants who have recently been transferred by their employers may need to furnish copies of pay stubs covering the period immediately before the transfer, as well as W-2 forms for the preceding two years. In many cases, employers maintain particular payroll records at various locations. The records of an employee transferred from one state to another might not be available at the company's office in the new location. Independent verification of that income will save time. The exact date of transfer is also needed.

In addition, applicants need to be aware that providing statements, pay stubs, canceled checks, and so on helps simplify asset and debt verification and may speed the application process. Also, if backup verification is available at the point of application, the process can go more quickly.

Fees and Charges

Fees and charges vary widely from lender to lender and from one loan type to another, even with the same lender. Therefore, the person taking the application needs to be thoroughly familiar with the company policy on fees and charges. One lender might charge an additional fee for processing the application of a self-employed person, for example, because of the added work involved in analyzing self-employed income history.

Fees also may vary for processing different kinds of mortgages because of added disclosure requirements. On the other hand, some lenders absorb all fees under certain conditions as a means of competing for business. Whatever the fees charged, though, they must be disclosed under RESPA.

The next step in the process is actually taking the initial application.

4

Completing the Application

The loan application form is a key document. It includes the details that identify the potential borrower, the property, and the terms of the loan. It also includes information that supports the decision whether the borrower is able to close the loan and maintain the payments and whether the property is adequate security for the loan. Clearly, it is important that the loan application be complete and accurate.

The Uniform Residential Loan Application

The Uniform Residential Loan Application (URLA), FNMA Form 1003/FHLMC Form 65 (Exhibit IV-1), is the industry's standard application form. It is used on loans that will be sold to Freddie Mac and Fannie Mae as well as those made under HUD-FHA and VA loan programs. It is a good application, is readily available, and can be used regardless of who takes the initial application, or where. On HUD-FHA and VA loans there is a government addendum, which is signed by the applicants along with the URLA.

In some companies the initial application is normally taken by a real estate agent or builder. When an application is handled this way, someone should always check the data carefully and

EXHIBIT IV-1: UNIFORM RESIDENTIAL LOAN APPLICATION

Uniform Residential Loan Application

This application is designed to be completed by the applicant(s) with the lender's assistance. Applicants should complete this form as "Borrower" or "Co-Borrower", as applicable. Co-Borrower information must also be provided (and the appropriate box checked) when ☐ the income or assets of a person other than the "Borrower" (including the Borrower's spouse) will be used as a basis for loan qualification or ☐ the income or assets of the Borrower's spouse will not be used as a basis for loan qualification, but his or her liabilities must be considered because the Borrower resides in a community property state, the security property is located in a community property state, or the Borrower is relying on other property located in a community property state as a basis for repayment of the loan.

I. TYPE OF MORTGAGE AND TERMS OF LOAN

Mortgage Applied for: ☐ VA ☐ FHA ☐ Conventional ☐ FmHA ☐ Other:

Agency Case Number

Lender Case No.

Amount $ | Interest Rate % | No. of Months | **Amortization Type:** ☐ Fixed Rate ☐ GPM ☐ Other (explain): ☐ ARM (type):

II. PROPERTY INFORMATION AND PURPOSE OF LOAN

Subject Property Address (street, city, state, & ZIP) | No. of Units

Legal Description of Subject Property (attach description if necessary) | Year Built

Purpose of Loan ☐ Purchase ☐ Refinance ☐ Construction ☐ Construction-Permanent ☐ Other (explain):

Property will be: ☐ Primary Residence ☐ Secondary Residence ☐ Investment

Complete this line if construction or construction-permanent loan.

Year Lot Acquired | Original Cost $ | Amount Existing Liens $ | (a) Present Value of Lot $ | (b) Cost of Improvements $ | Total (a + b) $

Complete this line if this is a refinance loan.

Year Acquired | Original Cost $ | Amount Existing Liens $ | Purpose of Refinance | Describe Improvements ☐ made ☐ to be made Cost: $

Title will be held in what Name(s) | Manner in which Title will be held | Estate will be held in: ☐ Fee Simple ☐ Leasehold (show expiration date)

Source of Down Payment, Settlement Charges and/or Subordinate Financing (explain)

III. BORROWER INFORMATION

Borrower

Borrower's Name (include Jr. or Sr. if applicable)

Social Security Number | Home Phone (incl. area code) | Age | Yrs. School

☐ Married ☐ Unmarried (include single, divorced, widowed) ☐ Separated | Dependents (not listed by Co-Borrower) no. ages

Present Address (street, city, state, ZIP) ☐ Own ☐ Rent ______ No. Yrs.

Co-Borrower

Co-Borrower's Name (include Jr. or Sr. if applicable)

Social Security Number | Home Phone (incl. area code) | Age | Yrs. School

☐ Married ☐ Unmarried (include single, divorced, widowed) ☐ Separated | Dependents (not listed by Borrower) no. ages

Present Address (street, city, state, ZIP) ☐ Own ☐ Rent ______ No. Yrs.

If residing at present address for less than two years, complete the following:

Former Address (street, city, state, ZIP) ☐ Own ☐ Rent ______ No. Yrs. | Former Address (street, city, state, ZIP) ☐ Own ☐ Rent ______ No. Yrs.

Former Address (street, city, state, ZIP) ☐ Own ☐ Rent ______ No. Yrs. | Former Address (street, city, state, ZIP) ☐ Own ☐ Rent ______ No. Yrs.

IV. EMPLOYMENT INFORMATION

Borrower

Name & Address of Employer ☐ Self Employed | Yrs. on this job | Yrs. employed in this line of work/profession

Position/Title/Type of Business | Business Phone (incl. area code)

Co-Borrower

Name & Address of Employer ☐ Self Employed | Yrs. on this job | Yrs. employed in this line of work/profession

Position/Title/Type of Business | Business Phone (incl. area code)

If employed in current position for less than two years or if currently employed in more than one position, complete the following:

Name & Address of Employer ☐ Self Employed | Dates (from - to) | Monthly Income $ | Name & Address of Employer ☐ Self Employed | Dates (from - to) | Monthly Income $

Position/Title/Type of Business | Business Phone (incl. area code) | Position/Title/Type of Business | Business Phone (incl. area code)

Name & Address of Employer ☐ Self Employed | Dates (from - to) | Monthly Income $ | Name & Address of Employer ☐ Self Employed | Dates (from - to) | Monthly Income $

Position/Title/Type of Business | Business Phone (incl. area code) | Position/Title/Type of Business | Business Phone (incl. area code)

Freddie Mac Form 65 10/92 | Page 1 of 4 | Fannie Mae Form 1003 10/92

EXHIBIT IV-1—*continued*

V. MONTHLY INCOME AND COMBINED HOUSING EXPENSE INFORMATION

Gross Monthly Income	Borrower	Co-Borrower	Total	Combined Monthly Housing Expense	Present	Proposed
Base Empl. Income*	$	$	$	Rent	$	
Overtime				First Mortgage (P&I)		$
Bonuses				Other Financing (P&I)		
Commissions				Hazard Insurance		
Dividends/Interest				Real Estate Taxes		
Net Rental Income				Mortgage Insurance		
Other (before completing, see the notice in "describe other income," below)				Homeowner Assn. Dues		
				Other:		
Total	$	$	$	**Total**	$	$

* **Self Employed Borrower(s) may be required to provide additional documentation such as tax returns and financial statements.**

B/C	**Describe Other Income** *Notice:* **Alimony, child support, or separate maintenance income need not be revealed if the Borrower (B) or Co-Borrower (C) does not choose to have it considered for repaying this loan.**	Monthly Amount
		$

VI. ASSETS AND LIABILITIES

This Statement and any applicable supporting schedules may be completed jointly by both married and unmarried Co-Borrowers if their assets and liabilities are sufficiently joined so that the Statement can be meaningfully and fairly presented on a combined basis; otherwise separate Statements and Schedules are required. If the Co-Borrower section was completed about a spouse, this Statement and supporting schedules must be completed about that spouse also.

Completed ☐ Jointly ☐ Not Jointly

ASSETS Description	Cash or Market Value
Cash deposit toward purchase held by:	$
List checking and savings accounts below	
Name and address of Bank, S&L, or Credit Union	
Acct. no.	$
Name and address of Bank, S&L, or Credit Union	
Acct. no.	$
Name and address of Bank, S&L, or Credit Union	
Acct. no.	$
Name and address of Bank, S&L, or Credit Union	
Acct. no.	$
Stocks & Bonds (Company name/number & description)	$
Life insurance net cash value Face amount: $	$
Subtotal Liquid Assets	$
Real estate owned (enter market value from schedule of real estate owned)	$
Vested interest in retirement fund	$
Net worth of business(es) owned (attach financial statement)	$
Automobiles owned (make and year)	$
Other Assets (itemize)	$
Total Assets a.	$

Liabilities and Pledged Assets. List the creditor's name, address and account number for all outstanding debts, including automobile loans, revolving charge accounts, real estate loans, alimony, child support, stock pledges, etc. Use continuation sheet, if necessary. Indicate by (*) those liabilities which will be satisfied upon sale of real estate owned or upon refinancing of the subject property.

LIABILITIES	Monthly Payt. & Mos. Left to Pay	Unpaid Balance
Name and address of Company Acct. no.	$ Payt./Mos.	$
Name and address of Company Acct. no.	$ Payt./Mos.	$
Name and address of Company Acct. no.	$ Payt./Mos.	$
Name and address of Company Acct. no.	$ Payt./Mos.	$
Name and address of Company Acct. no.	$ Payt./Mos.	$
Name and address of Company Acct. no.	$ Payt./Mos.	$
Name and address of Company Acct. no.	$ Payt./Mos.	$
Alimony/Child Support/Separate Maintenance Payments Owed to:	$	
Job Related Expense (child care, union dues, etc.)	$	
Total Monthly Payments	$	
Net Worth (a minus b) $	**Total Liabilities b.**	$

EXHIBIT IV-1—*continued*

VI. ASSETS AND LIABILITIES (cont.)

Schedule of Real Estate Owned (If additional properties are owned, use continuation sheet.)

Property Address (enter S if sold, PS if pending sale or R if rental being held for income)		Type of Property	Present Market Value	Amount of Mortgages & Liens	Gross Rental Income	Mortgage Payments	Insurance, Maintenance, Taxes & Misc.	Net Rental Income
			$	$	$	$	$	$
		Totals	$	$	$	$	$	$

List any additional names under which credit has previously been received and indicate appropriate creditor name(s) and account number(s):

Alternate Name	Creditor Name	Account Number

VII. DETAILS OF TRANSACTION

a. Purchase price	$
b. Alterations, improvements, repairs	
c. Land (if acquired separately)	
d. Refinance (incl. debts to be paid off)	
e. Estimated prepaid items	
f. Estimated closing costs	
g. PMI, MIP, Funding Fee	
h. Discount (if Borrower will pay)	
i. Total costs (add items a through h)	
j. Subordinate financing	
k. Borrower's closing costs paid by Seller	
l. Other Credits (explain)	
m. Loan amount (exclude PMI, MIP, Funding Fee financed)	
n. PMI, MIP, Funding Fee financed	
o. Loan amount (add m & n)	
p. Cash from/to Borrower (subtract j, k, l & o from i)	

VIII. DECLARATIONS

If you answer "yes" to any questions a through i, please use continuation sheet for explanation.	Borrower Yes	Borrower No	Co-Borrower Yes	Co-Borrower No
a. Are there any outstanding judgments against you?	☐	☐	☐	☐
b. Have you been declared bankrupt within the past 7 years?	☐	☐	☐	☐
c. Have you had property foreclosed upon or given title or deed in lieu thereof in the last 7 years?	☐	☐	☐	☐
d. Are you a party to a lawsuit?	☐	☐	☐	☐
e. Have you directly or indirectly been obligated on any loan which resulted in foreclosure, transfer of title in lieu of foreclosure, or judgment? (This would include such loans as home mortgage loans, SBA loans, home improvement loans, educational loans, manufactured (mobile) home loans, any mortgage, financial obligation, bond, or loan guarantee. If "Yes," provide details, including date, name and address of Lender, FHA or VA case number, if any, and reasons for the action.)	☐	☐	☐	☐
f. Are you presently delinquent or in default on any Federal debt or any other loan, mortgage, financial obligation, bond, or loan guarantee? If "Yes," give details as described in the preceding question.	☐	☐	☐	☐
g. Are you obligated to pay alimony, child support, or separate maintenance?	☐	☐	☐	☐
h. Is any part of the down payment borrowed?	☐	☐	☐	☐
i. Are you a co-maker or endorser on a note?	☐	☐	☐	☐
j. Are you a U.S. citizen?	☐	☐	☐	☐
k. Are you a permanent resident alien?	☐	☐	☐	☐
l. **Do you intend to occupy the property as your primary residence?** If "Yes," complete question m below.	☐	☐	☐	☐
m. Have you had an ownership interest in a property in the last three years?	☐	☐	☐	☐
(1) What type of property did you own–principal residence (PR), second home (SH), or investment property (IP)?				
(2) How did you hold title to the home–solely by yourself (S), jointly with your spouse (SP), or jointly with another person (O)?				

IX. ACKNOWLEDGMENT AND AGREEMENT

The undersigned specifically acknowledge(s) and agree(s) that: (1) the loan requested by this application will be secured by a first mortgage or deed of trust on the property described herein; (2) the property will not be used for any illegal or prohibited purpose or use; (3) all statements made in this application are made for the purpose of obtaining the loan indicated herein; (4) occupation of the property will be as indicated above; (5) verification or reverification of any information contained in the application may be made at any time by the Lender, its agents, successors and assigns, either directly or through a credit reporting agency, from any source named in this application, and the original copy of this application will be retained by the Lender, even if the loan is not approved; (6) the Lender, its agents, successors and assigns will rely on the information contained in the application and I/we have a continuing obligation to amend and/or supplement the information provided in this application if any of the material facts which I/we have represented herein should change prior to closing; (7) in the event my/our payments on the loan indicated in this application become delinquent, the Lender, its agents, successors and assigns, may, in addition to all their other rights and remedies, report my/our name(s) and account information to a credit reporting agency; (8) ownership of the loan may be transferred to successor or assign of the Lender without notice to me and/or the administration of the loan account may be transferred to an agent, successor or assign of the Lender with prior notice to me; (9) the Lender, its agents, successors and assigns make no representations or warranties, express or implied, to the Borrower(s) regarding the property, the condition of the property, or the value of the property.

Certification: I/We certify that the information provided in this application is true and correct as of the date set forth opposite my/our signature(s) on this application and acknowledge my/our understanding that any intentional or negligent misrepresentation(s) of the information contained in this application may result in civil liability and/or criminal penalties including, but not limited to, fine or imprisonment or both under the provisions of Title 18, United States Code, Section 1001, et seq. and liability for monetary damages to the Lender, its agents, successors and assigns, insurers and any other person who may suffer any loss due to reliance upon any misrepresentation which I/we have made on this application.

Borrower's Signature	Date	Co-Borrower's Signature	Date
X		X	

X. INFORMATION FOR GOVERNMENT MONITORING PURPOSES

The following information is requested by the Federal Government for certain types of loans related to a dwelling, in order to monitor the Lender's compliance with equal credit opportunity, fair housing and home mortgage disclosure laws. You are not required to furnish this information, but are encouraged to do so. The law provides that a Lender may neither discriminate on the basis of this information, nor on whether you choose to furnish it. However, if you choose not to furnish it, under Federal regulations this Lender is required to note race and sex on the basis of visual observation or surname. If you do not wish to furnish the above information, please check the box below. (Lender must review the above material to assure that the disclosures satisfy all requirements to which the Lender is subject under applicable state law for the particular type of loan applied for.)

BORROWER

☐ I do not wish to furnish this information

Race/National Origin: ☐ American Indian or Alaskan Native ☐ Asian or Pacific Islander ☐ White, not of Hispanic Origin ☐ Black, not of Hispanic origin ☐ Hispanic ☐ Other (specify) ____________

Sex: ☐ Female ☐ Male

CO-BORROWER

☐ I do not wish to furnish this information

Race/National Origin: ☐ American Indian or Alaskan Native ☐ Asian or Pacific Islander ☐ White, not of Hispanic Origin ☐ Black, not of Hispanic origin ☐ Hispanic ☐ Other (specify) ____________

Sex: ☐ Female ☐ Male

To be Completed by Interviewer	Interviewer's Name (print or type)	Name and Address of Interviewer's Employer
This application was taken by: ☐ face-to-face interview ☐ by mail ☐ by telephone	Interviewer's Signature / Date	
	Interviewer's Phone Number (incl. area code)	

Freddie Mac Form 65 10/92 Page 3 of 4 Fannie Mae Form 1003 10/92

EXHIBIT IV-1—*continued*

Continuation Sheet/Residential Loan Application

Use this continuation sheet if you need more space to complete the Residential Loan Application. Mark **B** for Borrower or **C** for Co-Borrower.	Borrower:	Agency Case Number:
	Co-Borrower:	Lender Case Number:

I/We fully understand that it is a Federal crime punishable by fine or imprisonment, or both, to knowingly make any false statements concerning any of the above facts as applicable under the provisions of Title 18, United States Code, Section 1001, et seq.

Borrower's Signature:	Date	Co-Borrower's Signature:	Date
X		X	

Freddie Mac Form 65 10/92 | Page 4 of 4 | Fannie Mae Form 1003 10/92 arrange a meeting in the office for the applicant to check and sign the final application. In HUD-FHA transactions, there must be a face-to-face meeting between the applicant and a lender employee sometime during the application process, unless the property is located more than 50 miles from the lender's nearest office.

In some cases, the application will have been taken by another lender, one who has decided not to make the loan. This decision may be made at any stage in the process, and there is generally no problem associated with transferring applications from lender to lender. The lender who ultimately makes the loan assumes responsibility for everything done in the application process, however.

The new lender is not obligated to repeat any of the work conducted by the original lender and thus may or may not reverify the application. Some companies accept other lenders' verification work without question. HUD-FHA and VA may require verbal reverification. Others reverify everything. The decision is an individual one based on the applicant's individual circumstances or company policy.

The initial application will be a draft, because some of the information may be changed as a result of the verification process, or because market conditions changed the terms of the loan before the final application was ready. The final updated application may be signed at the closing. The borrower may never sign a blank initial or final application.

If it can be avoided, do not ask an applicant to sign any blank verification forms. It takes a little longer to fill in verification forms while the applicant waits, but it avoids difficulties later. Verification forms do not have to be typed—they simply have to be legible.

We will now examine FNMA form 1003 and some of the areas that require special care when it is used.

Statement on Joint Obligation or Reliance on Spouse's Income

Make sure the applicant understands this statement on joint application. One, two, or all three blocks may be checked as appropriate, and the information in subsequent sections must be consistent with the block(s) checked.

Interest Rate

The processor should enter the interest rate (on line 2 of the form, under I. "Types of Mortgage and Terms of Loan" section), using decimals (9.25, not 9-1/4). The interest rate is completely negotiable. To be effective in the negotiations, a lender needs to know the attitudes and needs of its investors and must keep abreast of market conditions.

The lender also needs to know the comparative advantages to investors and borrowers of alternative combinations of interest rates, discounts, and loan types. In HUD-FHA and VA transactions, there is a requirement that the borrower acknowledge having been told that the agencies no longer regulate rates. This a good time to get the borrower's signature on these acknowledgments. The HUD-FHA text appears in Exhibit IV-2.

Names on Title

The processor should enter the names in which title will be held, exactly as they are to appear on the title, in the sixth line down under II, "Property Information and Purpose of Loan" section. Spelling is important here. This is likely the first document produced by the lender in which the names appear. The spelling as it appears here will probably be used throughout the origination process, so if it is wrong, the final documents will be wrong.

The processor should not rely on the broker or builder to have given the proper attention to spelling. Also, the order in which the names are listed is up to the borrowers in most cases, although the veteran whose eligibility is being used to qualify must be named first in a VA application, exactly as that name appears on the Certificate of Eligibility.

EXHIBIT IV-2: DISCLOSURE STATEMENT

Borrower's Notification and Interest Rate Disclosure Statement

U.S. Department of Housing and Urban Development
Office of Housing
Federal Housing Commissioner

Condition of Property

The property you are buying is not HUD/FHA approved and HUD/FHA does not warrant the condition or the value of the property. An appraisal will be performed to estimate the value of the property, but this appraisal does not guarantee that the house is free of defects. You should inspect the property yourself very carefully or hire a professional home inspection service to inspect the property for you. If you have a professional home inspection service perform an inspection of the property, you may include some of the cost of the inspection in your mortgage.

Interest Rate and Discount Points

- HUD does not regulate the interest rate or the discount points that may be paid by you or the seller or other third party. You should shop around to be sure you are satisfied with the loan terms offered and with the service reputation of the lender you have chosen.
- The interest rate, any discount points and the length of time the lender will honor the loan terms are all negotiated between you and the lender.
- The seller can pay the discount points, or a portion thereof, if you and the seller agree to such an arrangement.
- Lenders may agree to guarantee or "lock-in" the loan terms for a definite period of time (i.e., 30, 60, or 90 days) or may permit your loan to be determined by future market conditions, also known as "floating." Lenders may require a fee to lock in the interest rate or the terms of the loan. Your agreement with the lender will determine the degree, if any, that the interest rate and discount points may rise before closing.
- After your loan is approved at a given interest rate and discount points, any increase in the discount points which you are going to pay or an increase of more than one percent in the interest rate requires reunderwriting of the loan.
- If the lender determines you are eligible for the mortgage, your agreement with the seller may require you to complete the transaction or lose your deposit on the property.

Don't Commit Loan Fraud

It is important for you to understand that you are required to provide complete and accurate information when applying for a mortgage loan.

- Do not overstate your income or your assets.
- Disclose all loans and debts (including money that may have been borrowed to make the downpayment).
- Do not provide false letters-of-credit, cash-on-hand statements, gift letters or sweat equity letters.
- Do not accept funds to be used for your downpayment from any other party (seller, real estate salesperson, builder, etc.) involved in the transaction.
- Do not falsely certify that a property will be used for your primary residence when you are actually going to use it as a rental property.
- Do not act as a "strawbuyer" (somebody who purchases a property for another person and then transfers title of the property to that person), nor should you give that person personal or credit information for them to use in any such scheme.
- Do not apply for a loan by assuming the identity of another person.

Penalties for Loan Fraud: Federal laws provide severe penalties for fraud, misrepresentation, or conspiracy to influence wrongly the issuance of mortgage insurance by HUD. You can be subject to a possible prison term and fine of up to $10,000 for providing false information. Additionally, you could be prohibited from obtaining a HUD-insured loan for an indefinite period.

Report Loan Fraud: If you are aware of any fraud in HUD programs or if an individual tries to persuade you to make false statements on a loan application, you should report the matter by calling your nearest HUD office or the HUD Regional Inspector General, or call the HUD Hotline on 1(800)347-3735.

Lead Based Paint: If the property you are buying was built before 1978, there is a possibility that it may contain lead based paint. Be sure you receive a copy of the consumer pamphlet "Watch Out for Lead Paint Poisoning" and read it to learn about lead paint poisoning.

If you believe you have been subject to discrimination because of your race, color, religion, sex, handicap, familial status, or national origin, you should call the HUD Fair Housing and Equal Opportunity Complaint Hotline: 1(800)669-9777.

This statement must be delivered to you at the time of initial loan application. Return one copy to your lender as proof of notification and keep one copy for your records.

You, the borrower(s), must be certain that you understand the transaction. Sign here only after you have read this entire document. Seek professional advice if you are uncertain.

Borrower's Signature	Date:	Co-Borrower's Signature	Date:
X		X	

I, the lender, certify that this notification was delivered to the borrower(s) at the time of initial loan application.

Lender's Signature & Date:

X

VMP-605 (9201) form HUD-92900-B (12/91)
ref. Handbooks 4150.1 & 4155.1
VMP MORTGAGE FORMS (313)293-8100 (800)521-7291

Manner in Which Title Will be Held

The processor should enter in Section II the manner in which title will be held (joint tenancy, tenants in common, tenants by the entirety, and so on). It is important to be sufficiently familiar with the differences to explain them to an uninformed applicant.

If the applicant is unsure how to take title, offer referrals to an attorney, especially in the case of two unmarried applicants.

Social Security Number

A law requires lenders to report interest paid by their borrowers to the Internal Revenue Service (IRS) each year, and the Social Security number (SSN) (second line down under Section III "Borrower Information") or other taxpayer identification number (TIN) must be included as a part of the report.

While it has not been essential in the past, a lender must now insist on either the SSN or TIN at the time of every application. In addition, a copy of the Social Security card will have to accompany each HUD-FHA application.

Marital Status

The question of marital status (third line down under Section III "Borrower Information") is restricted by ECOA. A lender may ask the applicant, "Are you married, unmarried, or separated?"—but nothing more. Moreover, the information cannot be used in evaluating eligibility for the loan: It is collected only to monitor compliance with ECOA.

"Dependents" may be identified only by number and age, as this information is used in underwriting the loan. A dependent is someone who relies completely on the applicant for more than half of his or her support. Generally, a spouse or child working full time would not be considered a dependent.

Information for Government Monitoring Purposes

Each applicant should check the appropriate boxes (third page, bottom of form) relating to government monitoring. Providing this information is not mandatory, but if an applicant declines to provide the information, he or she must initial the appropriate box. When that happens, the person taking the application must complete the information on the basis of "observation or surname."

Institutions supervised by the Federal Reserve Board or the Federal Housing Finance Bank Board or insured by the Federal Deposit Insurance Corporation are required to collect this information for compliance with the Equal Credit Opportunity Act, Regulation B. The information is also required with respect to HUD-FHA and VA loans, even if the lender is a nonsupervised institution.

Lenders may want to consult legal counsel to implement procedures that will ensure compliance with ECOA.

Taking the initial application constitutes just that—a preliminary application. All of the information in it will be verified. When discrepancies occur, the processor will be required to reconcile the differences, and the applicant often will be asked to explain them.

The initial application contains the information needed to process the loan, but there is no certainty that it is accurate. It was noted earlier than an applicant should never be asked to sign application forms in blank, and there are several forms involved in the verification process that must be signed by the applicant. Common sense dictates that those forms be completed and signed as a part of the application process. Where that is simply impossible, however, a lender may mail the forms to the applicant or schedule another meeting to get signatures.

Discrepancies and Inconsistencies in the Loan Application

Any discrepancies and inconsistencies in the loan application and the loan file will need to be reconciled. When a loan application sounds too good to be true, it probably is. A good rule of thumb is compare, compare, compare to detect inconsistencies.

Mortgage finance fraud may be more—or less—than an obvious inconsistency or alteration to an applicant's credit package. It may be a subtle change, such a fourth digit and a comma added to the current balance of a verification of deposit (VOD) form. To be able to spot such potential fraud, the processor must know and understand the entire credit package. The original application is important because it sets the standard for the rest of the credit package. Comparing application information with the rest of the loan documents is critical.

Warning Signals

Here are some warning signals for mortgage finance fraud:

- There is a significant or unrealistic commute distance for the applicants.
- The new housing is too small to accommodate occupants.
- The buyer is downgrading from a larger to smaller home (except in the case of empty-nesters).
- The buyer currently resides in the property (purchasing it from the landlord).
- The borrower intends to rent or sell the current residence with no documentation.
- The down payment is other than cash.
- The deposit or down payment is a promissory note.
- The specific stocks and bonds (liquid assets) are not publicly traded (perhaps signaling a closely held corporation).
- The price and date of original purchase are not shown for refinances.
- The borrower is buying investment property but does not own the current residence.
- A post office box is the only indicated address for the employer.
- The same telephone number is used for home and business.

- The borrower holds stock in the employer (may be self-employed).
- Personal property value exceeds one year's salary.
- High-income borrower has little or no personal property.
- New housing expense exceeds 150 percent of current housing expense.
- The borrower's salary is inappropriate with respect to the amount of the loan.
- The source of deposit or down payment is repayment of a personal loan.
- The Social Security number is invalid.
- Significant or contradictory changes have occurred between the handwritten and typed loan application.
- The application is unsigned or undated.

Verification

These comparisons will aid verification:

- Compare date of verification forms to date of loan application.
- Compare source of funds for down payment to assets.
- Compare type and use of credit to type of employment and income.
- Compare current residence status (rent or own) to schedule of real estate owned.
- Compare value of property purchased to value of current residence (if owned).
- Compare stated owner occupancy of property purchased (and value) to schedule of real estate owned.
- Compare assets (amount and type) to overall credit quality of borrower.
- Compare borrower's age to number of years employed in his or her line of work.
- Compare borrower's income to type of employment.

Watch for any favorable information on the typed application that was not included on the original application. In one fraudulently originated loan, the applicant's second or part-time job was not listed on the original application. When interviewed by the mortgage insurer, the applicant freely admitted that the real estate broker advised him to lie about having the second job to ensure loan approval.

Common sense helps in spotting inconsistencies. For example, in one case the applicant was a high-income professional (a CPA earning $150,000 per year), who had no savings and was indebted to finance companies, furniture rental companies, and so on. Certainly this is plausible, but in this case the applicant was actually a maintenance man posing as a straw buyer. Always be suspicious if the facts don't add up. A simple call to the alleged employer would have exposed the fraud.

Case Example

A high-income professional, a doctor who was living in (and purchasing) a $295,000 home and owned other rental properties, was purchasing a $50,000 duplex in the inner city as an owner-occupant. After being confronted during an investigation, the mortgagor admitted that he was really trying to buy another rental property.

Always compare an applicant's income and value of the subject property to the value of the current residence to determine whether the applicant is moving into a less expensive home. Few people really do.

Often, the original application fails to address the source of funds to be used for the down payment. In one such case the lender did ask the applicant why the application lacked this important item. The applicant replied, "Don't worry. The seller is taking care of that."

Having completed the initial application, we will leave the borrower and go to the appraisal, another important component of the application package.

5

The Appraisal

Whether the application is for a conventional, HUD-FHA or VA loan, a property appraisal is often essential. The value of the property serves as the first benchmark for whether the lender should accept the property as security for the loan at all, and then, if the property is basically acceptable, how large a loan can be made based on that security.

Although borrowers usually pay for appraisals to be done, they are really done for the benefit of the lender. From the lender's point of view, the most important issue is whether the property is adequate security for the loan, not whether the buyer is paying a legitimate price for the property. In addition to the basic issues of location, condition, design, and so on, the lender's basic question is, "If there is a foreclosure or if I acquire this property by some other means, will I be able to sell it at a price that will satisfy the debt?"

Keep in mind that not every loan application requires an appraisal. In refinance cases HUD-FHA and VA may permit an application to be processed without an appraisal if the interest rate (and the monthly payment of principal and interest) is being reduced, and if the new mortgage amount does not exceed the original unpaid balance of the old mortgage. Check with investors or your local HUD-FHA or VA office to be sure.

This chapter will show how to select the appraiser, order the appraisal, monitor the appraiser to make certain the appraisal report is received promptly, and evaluate the appraisal report. The process varies with different loan types, so HUD-

FHA mortgages, VA mortgages, and conventional mortgages will be discussed separately.

Loan-to-Value (LTV) and Loan Amount

Loan-to-value ratio is one of the keys of loan origination. Lenders usually calculate the loan-to-value (LTV) ratio using the property's fair market value as the "V," or denominator, and the proposed loan amount as the "L," or numerator. If the resulting ratio fits within program guidelines and the application is otherwise acceptable, the loan can be approved.

The lender's decision as to the maximum loan amount on a specific property is based on the fair market value of that property and the LTV ratio guideiines. Guidelines for maximum loan amount vary. The maximum loan limit for Freddie Mac and Fannie Mae loans is set by law. VA allows lenders to make a loan based on 100 percent of the property's market value.

HUD-FHA has statutory loan-to-value ratios and limits, depending on the program under which the mortgage will be insured. Conventional lenders generally establish maximum loan-to-value ratios of 75 to 80 percent of value, although they may go higher for loans with private mortgage insurance. Private mortgage insurers charge increasing premiums as loan-to-value ratios increase.

Appraiser Licensing and Certification

The Real Estate Appraisal Reform Amendments are Title XI of the Financial Institutions Reform, Recovery and Enforcement Act of 1989 (FIRREA). These amendments led to a nationwide licensing and certification program for appraisers involved in federally related transactions. The purpose of Title XI is to protect federal financial and public policy interests in real estate related transactions involving lenders—or their affiliates or subsidiaries—that are regulated by the Federal Financial Institutions Regulatory Agencies.

Title XI requires that real estate appraisals used in connection with their federally related mortgage transactions be prepared in accordance with uniform standards, be presented in writing, and be developed by individuals who have a demonstrated competency and professional conduct that is subject to effective supervision.

All appraisers must be certified or licensed. Some states award certification based on minimum criteria issued by the Appraiser Qualification Board of the Appraisal Foundation. Other states may issue licenses based on requirements of Title XI of FIRREA if the Appraisal Subcommittee has not issued a finding that the state's policies, practices, or procedures are inconsistent with Title XI. (This requirement was effective on the date for compliance with FIRREA's licensing requirements.)

Uniform Standards

As part of the licensure and certification procedures, states and the federal financial regulatory agencies have adopted the Uniform Standards of Professional Appraisal Practice (USPAP), as promulgated by the Appraisal Standards Board of the Appraisal Foundation.

There are several national organizations of appraisers and if membership in an appraisal organization is a significant selective factor, the lender should probably approach several of the national organizations for referrals.

A designation should be no more than a starting point, however. An appraiser's true ability should be determined through interviewing carefully, checking references, and reviewing previous work as well as ongoing communications. The first time a lender uses an appraiser, the lender will probably be at some risk, not being able to establish in advance that an appraiser's work will be acceptable.

Work Review

Certainly the most important part of the selection process should be a review of previous and current work. Some certifying organizations require submission of sample reports as a prerequisite to the awarding of their designation. Those reports, however, are generally under the complete control of the applicant. He or she selects the property and can afford to devote considerably more time and attention to producing a model report than is generally possible in the day-to-day pressure of business.

One way around this problem is to assign a candidate an actual appraisal on a property where the lender has recently received what is considered to be an acceptable appraisal. While a comparison of the two appraisal reports on the same property should not find them identical, it should certainly result in finding them similar.

There are also appraisal firms that specialize in the review of appraisals. If one of these firms is available, an independent review of the candidate's work can be revealing.

If possible, lenders should avoid involving the candidate's competitors in the review process. The reasons should be obvious. Certainly, checking references is mandatory. The work done for other lenders in the past is a measure of the work that can be expected in the future. If an appraiser previously has worked for a competitor, the reason for having parted company should be explored with both the lender and the appraiser. Lenders should also respond frankly and willingly to inquiries from other lenders about their experiences with appraisers.

HUD-FHA and VA Fee Panels

HUD-FHA and VA have established basic qualifying standards that must be met before an appraiser is added to the "fee panel." The agencies assign appraisers from the fee panel to do appraisals. The appraisers assigned this way are not government employees but work on a fee basis, receiving payment based on the number and type of appraisals they complete.

The two government agencies also maintain a regular appraisal review system. Agency staff—or sometimes contractors—conduct regular desk and field reviews of the work done by fee panel members and investigate complaints from lenders about substandard work. The HUD-FHA and VA review appraisal system helps ensure sensible appraisals through specific qualification requirements for the fee appraisers themselves and ongoing review of their work.

Ordering a HUD-FHA Appraisal

Each HUD-FHA office maintains a panel of private appraisers who do work on HUD cases on an ad hoc basis. They are paid a fee for each appraisal they complete. All appraisals for HUD-FHA mortgages underwritten by HUD are done by members of these panels. Appraisals handled in the direct endorsement (DE) program may be done by members of the fee panel or by members of the mortgagee's appraisal staff.

When new construction in a subdivision is involved, HUD-FHA offices may issue "master conditional commitments" covering all models and variations in the subdivision. This procedure is optional with local HUD-FHA offices—not all of them use it.

Appraisal by Fee Panel

The following procedure applies when the appraisal of a new or existing single property is to be done by a member of the fee panel under the direct endorsement program. If a mortgagee staff appraiser will do the work, the steps involving the HUD-FHA office are omitted (except that a case number is still assigned before the appraisal is done). Detailed instructions and information are provided through HUD handbooks and local directives.

The beginning of the appraisal application process varies from office to office, depending largely on workload.

When only one or two case numbers are involved, or where the local HUD-FHA office does not have a heavy workload, usually the mortgagee first calls the assignment clerk at the local HUD-FHA office to ask for a case number and for the assignment of an appraiser. If the case is to be processed under the direct endorsement program, the assignment clerk should be told that at this time.

When several cases are involved, or when the office's workload is heavy, most offices have established procedures for requesting the assignment of case numbers and appraisers by mail or facsimile (fax) machine. The majority of the offices have a form similar to Exhibit V-1, Request for HUD-FHA Case Number and Appraiser. This office-specific form (which may not be available in all offices) is hand-delivered, mailed, or faxed to the assignment clerk at the HUD office. The clerk enters the case number and appraiser's name and then returns the form to the lender, usually on the following day.

Unless the DE staff appraiser is to be used, lenders may request the assignment of the case number and appraiser via computer on the CHUMS Lender Access System, or CLAS. CLAS allows lenders to enter data into a personal computer in their offices. That data then is transmitted to HUD via an electronic mailbox. Field office staff respond by sending the appraiser name and case number back to lenders through electronic mail within 24 hours.

Regardless of which system is used, the mortgagee then completes the application for property appraisal (HUD Form 92800 HUD Application for Property Appraisal and Commitment, Exhibit V-2) and forwards it to the appraiser.

The Uniform Residential Appraisal Report (URAR), also known as FNMA Form 1004 or FHLMC Form 70 (Exhibit V-3), is sent to the appraiser with the completed HUD-FHA application form (HUD Form 92800). Other exhibits may be required by the local HUD/FHA office. The appraiser will complete the report on the URAR.

On direct endorsement cases, the appraiser will send the pertinent exhibits to the DE lender, including: the original

EXHIBIT V-1: REQUEST FOR HUD-FHA CASE NUMBER AND APPRAISER

Request for HUD-FHA Case Number and Appraiser
(Using Locally-Prepared Form)

____

(Please Print or Type)

LENDER ______________________ FHA USE ONLY

DATE ______________________ CASE NUMBER ______________

TELEPHONE ______________________

PROCESSOR ______________________ APPRAISER ______________

LOAN OFFICER ______________________

1. BUILDING TYPE (Circle one and complete)
   a. TOWNHOUSE (Name and section #) ______________
   b. CONDOMINIUM (Name and section #) ______________
   c. OTHER (See #10 below)

2. CASE TYPE (Circle one)
   (DE lender must order DE except 234 and Existing CRV's)
   a. Regular HUD Processing
   b. VA-CRV Conversion
   c. Direct Endorsement VA-CRV (must be proposed)
   d. Direct Endorsement

3. ORIGINATING MORTGAGEE ID# ______________

4. SECTION OF THE ACT CODE ______________

5. PROPERTY ZIP CODE ______________

6. BUILDING STATUS

   a. Proposed (foundation not poured)
   b. Under construction
   c. Existing
   d. Substantial rehabilitation

7. NUMBER OF LIVING UNIT (No more than 4)

8. REFINANCE OF EXISTING LOAN? (Circle) YES NO
   IF YES, CIRCLE TYPE OF EXISTING LOAN: FHA VA CONV

9. MONTH (if less than 2 yrs old) AND YEAR COMPLETED) __________

10. STREET ADDRESS ______________
    CITY ______________ COUNTY ______________
    LOT/BLOCK/PLAT ______________

11. VA CRV CONVERSION: CRV EXPIRATION DATE ______________

    CRV NUMBER ______________
    IF COVERED BY 10-YEAR WARRANTY PLAN, NAME OF PLAN

EXHIBIT V-2: HUD APPLICATION FOR PROPERTY APPRAISAL AND COMMITMENT

VMP-425 (8706) 01 VMP MORTGAGE FORMS • (313)293-8100 • (800)521-7291

84.636-D

H.U.D.

OMB Approval Number 2502-0111

HUD APPLICATION FOR PROPERTY APPRAISAL AND COMMITMENT

HUD Section of Act | 1. CASE NUMBER

2. PROPERTY ADDRESS *(Include ZIP code and county)*

3. LEGAL DESCRIPTION

4. TITLE LIMITATIONS AND RESTRICTIVE COVENANTS:
1. ☐ CONDOMINIUM 2. ☐ PLANNED UNIT DEVELOPMENT

5. NAME AND ADDRESS OF FIRM OR PERSON MAKING REQUEST/APPLICATION *(Include ZIP code)*

6. LOT DIMENSIONS:
1. ☐ IRREGULAR: SQ/FT 2. ☐ ACRES:

7. UTILITIES (✓)	ELEC.	GAS	WATER	SAN. SEWER
1. PUBLIC				
2. COMMUNITY				
3. INDIVIDUAL				

8. EQUIP.: 1. ☐ RANGE/OVEN 2. ☐ REFRIG. 3. ☐ DISH-WASHER 4. ☐ CLOTHES WASHER 5. ☐ DRYER 6. ☐ GARBAGE DISP. 7. ☐ VENT FAN 8. ☐ W/W CARPET 9. ☐

9. BUILDING STATUS: 1. ☐ PROPOSED 2. ☐ SUBSTANTIAL REHABILITATION 3. ☐ UNDER CONSTRUCTION 4. ☐ EXISTING 5. ☐ ALTERATIONS, IMPROVEMENTS, OR REPAIRS

10. BUILDING TYPE: 1. ☐ DETACHED 2. ☐ SEMI-DETACHED 3. ☐ ROW 4. ☐ APT. UNIT

11. FACTORY FABRICATED? 1. ☐ YES 2. ☐ NO

12A. NO. OF BUILDINGS | 12B. NO. OF LIVING UNITS

13A. STREET ACCESS: 1. ☐ PRIVATE 2. ☐ PUBLIC

13B. STREET MAINT.: 1. ☐ PRIVATE 2. ☐ PUBLIC

14A. CONSTRUCTION WARRANTY INCLUDED? 1. ☐ YES 2. ☐ NO *(If "Yes," complete Items 14B and C also.)*

14B. NAME OF WARRANTY PROGRAM

14C. EXPIRATION DATE *(Month, day, year)*

15. CONSTR. COMPLETED *(Mo., yr.)*

16. NAME OF OWNER

17. PROPERTY: ☐ OCCUPIED BY OWNER ☐ NEVER OCCUPIED ☐ VACANT ☐ OCCUPIED BY TENANT *(Complete Item 18 also)*

18. RENT *(If applic.)* $ /MONTH

19. NAME OF OCCUPANT | 20. TELEPHONE NO. | 21. NAME OF BROKER | 22. TELEPHONE NO.

23. DATE AND TIME AVAILABLE FOR INSPECTION ☐ AM ☐ PM

24. KEYS AT *(Address)* | 25. ORIGINATOR'S IDENT. NO. | 26. SPONSOR'S IDENT. NO. | 27. INSTITUTION'S CASE NO.

28. PURCHASER'S NAME AND ADDRESS *(Complete mailing address. Include ZIP code.)*

EQUAL OPPORTUNITY IN HOUSING

NOTE—Federal laws and regulations prohibit discrimination because of race, color, religion, sex, or national origin in the sale or rental of residential property. Numerous State statutes and local ordinances also prohibit such discrimination. In addition, Section 805 of the Civil Rights Act of 1968 prohibits discriminatory practices in connection with the financing of housing.

If HUD/VA finds there is noncompliance with any antidiscrimination laws or regulations, it may discontinue business with the violator.

29. NEW OR PROPOSED CONSTRUCTION – *Complete Items 29A through 29G for new or proposed construction cases only.*

A. COMPLIANCE INSPECTIONS WILL BE OR WERE MADE BY: ☐ FHA ☐ VA ☐ NONE MADE

B. PLANS *(check one)* ☐ FIRST SUBMISSION ☐ REPEAT CASE *(If checked, complete Item 29C.)*

C. PLANS SUBMITTED PREVIOUSLY UNDER CASE NO.

D. NAME AND ADDRESS OF BUILDER | E. TELEPHONE NO. | F. NAME AND ADDRESS OF WARRANTOR | G. TELEPHONE NO.

30. COMMENTS ON SPECIAL ASSESSMENTS OR HOMEOWNERS ASSOCIATION CHARGES

31. ANNUAL REAL ESTATE TAXES $

32. MINERAL RIGHTS RESERVED? ☐ YES *(Explain)* ☐ NO

33. LEASEHOLD CASES *(Complete if applicable)*
LEASE IS: ☐ 99 YEARS ☐ RENEWABLE ☐ HUD/VA APPROVED
EXPIRES *(Date)*
ANNUAL GROUND RENT $

34. SALE PRICE OF PROPERTY $

34A. IS BUYER PURCHASING LOT SEPARATELY? ☐ YES ☐ NO *(If "Yes," see instruction page under "Sale Price")*

35. REFINANCING – AMOUNT OF PROPOSED LOAN $

36. PROPOSED SALE CONTRACT ATTACHED ☐ YES ☐ NO

37. CONTRACT NUMBER PREVIOUSLY APPROVED BY VA THAT WILL BE USED

CERTIFICATIONS FOR SUBMISSIONS TO HUD

In submitting this application for a conditional commitment for mortgage insurance, it is agreed and understood by the parties involved in the transaction that if at the time of application for a Firm Commitment the identity of the seller has changed, the application for a Firm Commitment will be rejected and the application for a Conditional Commitment will be reprocessed upon request by the mortgagee.

It is further agreed and understood that in submitting the request for a Firm Commitment for mortgage insurance, the seller, the purchaser and the broker involved in the transaction shall each certify that the terms of the contract for purchase are true to his or her best knowledge and belief, and that any other agreement entered into by any of these parties in connection with this transaction is attached to the sales agreement.

BUILDER/SELLER'S AGREEMENT: **All Houses:** The undersigned agrees to deliver to the purchaser a statement of appraised value on Form HUD-92800.5B. **Proposed Construction:** The undersigned agrees, upon sale or conveyance of title within one year from date of initial occupancy, to deliver to the purchaser Form HUD-92544, warranting that the house is constructed in substantial conformity with the plans and specifications on which HUD based its value and to furnish HUD a conformed copy with the purchaser's receipt thereon that the original warranty was delivered to him/her. **All Houses:** In consideration of the issuance of the commitment requested by this application, I (we) hereby agree that any deposit or down payment made in connection with the purchase of the property described above, whether received by the undersigned or an agent of the undersigned, shall upon receipt be deposited in escrow or in trust or in a special account which is not subject to the claims of my creditors and where it will be maintained until it has been disbursed for the benefit of the purchaser or otherwise disposed of in accordance with the terms of the contract of sale.

Signature of: ☐ Mortgagee ☐ Builder ☐ Seller ☐ Other X__________ Date __________ 19___

MORTGAGEE'S CERTIFICATE: The undersigned mortgagee certifies that to the best of his/her knowledge, all statements made in this application and the supporting documents are true, correct and complete.

Signature and Title of Mortgage Officer: X__________ Date __________ 19___

CERTIFICATIONS FOR SUBMISSIONS TO VA

1. On receipt of "Certificate of Reasonable Value" or advice from the Department of Veterans Affairs that a "Certificate of Reasonable Value" will not be issued, we agree to forward to the appraiser the approved fee which we are holding for this purpose.
2. CERTIFICATION REQUIRED ON CONSTRUCTION UNDER FHA SUPERVISION *(Strike out inappropriate phrases in parentheses)*

   I hereby certify that plans and specifications and related exhibits, including acceptable FHA Change Orders, if any, supplied to VA in this case, are identical to those (submitted to)(to be submitted to)(approved by) FHA, and that FHA inspections (have been)(will be) made pursuant to FHA approval for mortgage insurance on the basis of proposed construction under Sec.

38. SIGNATURE OF PERSON AUTHORIZING THIS REQUEST | 39. TITLE | 40. TELEPHONE NUMBER | 41. DATE

42. DATE OF ASSIGNMENT | 43. NAME OF APPRAISER

WARNING Section 1010 of title 18, U.S.C. provides: "Whoever for the purpose of ... influencing such Administration ... makes, passes, utters or publishes any statement knowing the same to be false ... shall be fined not more than $5,000 or imprisoned not more than two years or both."

HUD-92800 (3-87 Edition)

Supersedes HUD Form 92800-1, June 1984, which will not be used after June 30, 1987.

VMP-425 (8706) 01 VMP MORTGAGE FORMS • (313)293-8100 • (800)521-7291

HUD FILE COPY 1

EXHIBIT V-3: UNIFORM RESIDENTIAL APPRAISAL REPORT

Property Description & Analysis

UNIFORM RESIDENTIAL APPRAISAL REPORT

File No.

SUBJECT

Property Address ____ Census Tract ____
City ____ County ____ State ____ Zip Code ____
Legal Description ____
Owner/Occupant ____ Map Reference ____
Sale Price $ ____ Date of Sale ____
Loan charges/concessions to be paid by seller $ ____
R.E. Taxes $ ____ Tax Year ____ HOA $/Mo ____
Lender/Client ____

PROPERTY RIGHTS APPRAISED
Fee Simple
Leasehold
Condominium (HUD/VA)
De Minimis PUD

LENDER DISCRETIONARY USE
Sale Price $
Date
Mortgage Amount $
Mortgage Type
Discount Points and Other Concessions
Paid by Seller $
Source

NEIGHBORHOOD

LOCATION: Urban / Suburban / Rural
BUILT UP: Over 75% / 25-75% / Under 25%
GROWTH RATE: Rapid / Stable / Slow
PROPERTY VALUES: Increasing / Stable / Declining
DEMAND/SUPPLY: Shortage / In Balance / Over Supply
MARKETING TIME: Under 3 Mos. / 3-6 Mos. / Over 6 Mos.

PRESENT LAND USE %: Single Family ____ 2-4 Family ____ Multi-Family ____ Commercial ____ Industrial ____ Vacant ____

LAND USE CHANGE: Not Likely / Likely / In process / To: ____

PREDOMINANT OCCUPANCY: Owner / Tenant / Vacant (0-5%) / Vacant (over 5%)

SINGLE FAMILY HOUSING: PRICE $(000) / AGE (yrs): Low ____ High ____ Predominant ____

NEIGHBORHOOD ANALYSIS (Good / Avg. / Fair / Poor)
Employment Stability
Convenience to Employment
Convenience to Shopping
Convenience to Schools
Adequacy of Public Transportation
Recreation Facilities
Adequacy of Utilities
Property Compatibility
Protection from Detrimental Cond.
Police & Fire Protection
General Appearance of Properties
Appeal to Market

Note: Race or the racial composition of the neighborhood are not considered reliable appraisal factors.
COMMENTS: ____

SITE

Dimensions ____
Site Area ____ Corner Lot ____
Zoning Classification ____ Zoning Compliance ____
HIGHEST & BEST USE: Present Use ____ Other Use ____

UTILITIES (Public / Other): Electricity ____ Gas ____ Water ____ Sanitary Sewer ____ Storm Sewer ____

SITE IMPROVEMENTS (Type / Public / Private): Street ____ Curb/Gutter ____ Sidewalk ____ Street Lights ____ Alley ____

Topography ____
Size ____
Shape ____
Drainage ____
View ____
Landscaping ____
Driveway ____
Apparent Easements ____
FEMA Flood Hazard Yes* ____ No ____
FEMA* Map/Zone ____

COMMENTS (Apparent adverse easements, encroachments, special assessments, slide areas, etc.): ____

IMPROVEMENTS

GENERAL DESCRIPTION: Units ____ Stories ____ Type (Det./Att.) ____ Design (Style) ____ Existing ____ Proposed ____ Under Construction ____ Age (Yrs.) ____ Effective Age (Yrs.) ____

EXTERIOR DESCRIPTION: Foundation ____ Exterior Walls ____ Roof Surface ____ Gutters & Dwnspts. ____ Window Type ____ Storm Sash ____ Screens ____ Manufactured House ____

FOUNDATION: Slab ____ Crawl Space ____ Basement ____ Sump Pump ____ Dampness ____ Settlement ____ Infestation ____

BASEMENT: Area Sq. Ft. ____ % Finished ____ Ceiling ____ Walls ____ Floor ____ Outside Entry ____

INSULATION: Roof ____ Ceiling ____ Walls ____ Floor ____ None ____ Adequacy ____ Energy Efficient Items: ____

ROOM LIST

ROOMS	Foyer	Living	Dining	Kitchen	Den	Family Rm.	Rec. Rm.	Bedrooms	# Baths	Laundry	Other	Area Sq. Ft.
Basement												
Level 1												
Level 2												

Finished area **above** grade contains: ____ Rooms; ____ Bedroom(s); ____ Bath(s); ____ Square Feet of Gross Living Area

INTERIOR

SURFACES (Materials/Condition): Floors ____ Walls ____ Trim/Finish ____ Bath Floor ____ Bath Wainscot ____ Doors ____ Fireplace(s) # ____

HEATING: Type ____ Fuel ____ Condition ____ Adequacy ____
COOLING: Central ____ Other ____ Condition ____ Adequacy ____

KITCHEN EQUIP.: Refrigerator / Range/Oven / Disposal / Dishwasher / Fan/Hood / Compactor / Washer/Dryer / Microwave / Intercom

ATTIC: None / Stairs / Drop Stair / Scuttle / Floor / Heated / Finished

IMPROVEMENT ANALYSIS (Good / Avg. / Fair / Poor)
Quality of Construction
Condition of Improvements
Room Sizes/Layout
Closets and Storage
Energy Efficiency
Plumbing-Adequacy & Condition
Electrical-Adequacy & Condition
Kitchen Cabinets-Adequacy & Cond.
Compatibility to Neighborhood
Appeal & Marketability
Estimated Remaining Economic Life ____ Yrs.
Estimated Remaining Physical Life ____ Yrs.

AUTOS

CAR STORAGE: Garage / Carport / None; No. Cars ____; Condition ____
Attached / Detached / Built-In
Adequate / Inadequate / Electric Door
House Entry / Outside Entry / Basement Entry

COMMENTS

Additional Features ____

Depreciation (Physical, functional and external inadequacies, repairs needed, modernization, etc.): ____

General market conditions and prevalence and impact in subject market area regarding loan discounts, interest buydowns and concessions: ____

Freddie Mac Form 70 10/86 — Fannie Mae Form 1004 10/86

VMP -22F — VMP MORTGAGE FORMS • [illegible] • [illegible]

EXHIBIT V-3—*continued*

Valuation Section

UNIFORM RESIDENTIAL APPRAISAL REPORT

File No.

Purpose of Appraisal is to estimate Market Value as defined in the Certification & Statement of Limiting Conditions.

COST APPROACH

BUILDING SKETCH (SHOW GROSS LIVING AREA ABOVE GRADE)

ESTIMATED REPRODUCTION COST-NEW-OF IMPROVEMENTS:

Dwelling ______ Sq. Ft. @ $ ______ $ ______

______ Sq. Ft. @ $ ______ ______

Extras ______ ______

Special Energy Efficient Items ______ ______

Porches, Patios, etc. ______ ______

Garage/Carport ______ Sq. Ft. @ $ ______ ______

Total Estimated Cost New $ ______

	Physical	Functional	External	
Less Depreciation				$

Depreciated Value of Improvements $ ______

Site Imp. "as is" (driveway, landscaping, etc.) $ ______

ESTIMATED SITE VALUE $ ______

(If leasehold, show only leasehold value.)

INDICATED VALUE BY COST APPROACH $

(Not Required by Freddie Mac and Fannie Mae)

Does property conform to applicable HUD/VA property standards? Yes No

If No, explain: ______

Construction Warranty Yes No

Name of Warranty Program ______

Warranty Coverage Expires ______

SALES COMPARISON ANALYSIS

The undersigned has recited three recent sales of properties most similar and proximate to subject and has considered these in the market analysis. The description includes a dollar adjustment, reflecting market reaction to those items of significant variation between the subject and comparable properties. If a significant item in the comparable property is superior to, or more favorable than, the subject property, a minus (–) adjustment is made, thus reducing the indicated value of subject; if a significant item in the comparable is inferior to, or less favorable than, the subject property, a plus (+) adjustment is made, thus increasing the indicated value of the subject.

ITEM	SUBJECT	COMPARABLE NO. 1		COMPARABLE NO. 2		COMPARABLE NO. 3	
Address							
Proximity to Subject							
Sales Price	$		$		$		$
Price/Gross Liv. Area	$ ☐	$ ☐		$ ☐		$ ☐	
Data Source							
VALUE ADJUSTMENTS	DESCRIPTION	DESCRIPTION	+(–)$ Adjustment	DESCRIPTION	+(–)$ Adjustment	DESCRIPTION	+(–)$ Adjustment
Sales or Financing Concessions							
Date of Sale/Time							
Location							
Site/View							
Design and Appeal							
Quality of Construction							
Age							
Condition							
Above Grade Room Count	Total Bdrms Baths	Total Bdrms Baths		Total Bdrms Baths		Total Bdrms Baths	
Gross Living Area	Sq. Ft.	Sq. Ft.		Sq. Ft.		Sq. Ft.	
Basement & Finished Rooms Below Grade							
Functional Utility							
Heating/Cooling							
Garage/Carport							
Porches, Patio, Pools, etc.							
Special Energy Efficient Items							
Fireplace(s)							
Other (e.g. kitchen equip., remodeling)							
Net Adj. (total)		+ –	$	+ –	$	+ –	$
Indicated Value of Subject			$		$		$

Comments on Sales Comparison: ______

INDICATED VALUE BY SALES COMPARISON APPROACH $ ______

INDICATED VALUE BY INCOME APPROACH (If Applicable) Estimated Market Rent $ ______ /Mo. x Gross Rent Multiplier ______ $ ______

This appraisal is made ☐ "as is" ☐ subject to the repairs, alterations, inspections or conditions listed below ☐ completion per plans and specifications.

Comments and Conditions of Appraisal: ______

RECONCILIATION

Final Reconciliation: ______

This appraisal is based upon the above requirements, the certification, contingent and limiting conditions, and Market Value definition that are stated in

☐ FmHA, HUD & or VA instructions.

☐ Freddie Mac Form 439 (Rev. 7/86)/Fannie Mae Form 1004B (Rev. 7/86) filed with client ______ 19 ______ ☐ attached.

I (WE) ESTIMATE THE MARKET VALUE, AS DEFINED, OF THE SUBJECT PROPERTY AS OF ______ **19** ______ **to be $** ______

I (We) certify: that to the best of my (our) knowledge and belief the facts and data used herein are true and correct; that I (we) personally inspected the subject property, both inside and out, and have made an exterior inspection of all comparable sales cited in this report; and that I (we) have no undisclosed interest, present or prospective therein.

Appraiser(s) SIGNATURE ______ NAME

Review Appraiser (If applicable) SIGNATURE ______ NAME

☐ Did ☐ Did Not Inspect Property

Freddie Mac Form 70 10/86 Fannie Mae Form 1004 10/86

appraisal; front, back and street scene photograph of the subject property; front photograph of all comparables; location map; and diagram of the property. The appraiser sends a copy of the appraisal to the HUD/FHA office, thereby furnishing evidence to the assignment clerk at the local office that the appraiser has completed the assignment.

On agency approved cases, HUD-FHA will send a copy of the complete report to the lender with the conditional commitment, once one is issued. (If an application to HUD-FHA is to be based on a VA appraisal the process for ordering a VA appraisal, described later, is followed.)

The HUD-FHA File Folder

If HUD-FHA is to do the appraisal and issue a conditional commitment, an empty case binder that meets the specifications outlined in HUD Mortgagee Letter 87-18 is prepared and sent to the HUD-FHA office. This happens at the same time the application for property appraisal is sent to the appraiser. This file folder must meet detailed specifications as to size, weight of paper, built-in prongs, and several specific pieces of information that must be printed or stamped on the folder.

Later documents forwarded to the HUD-FHA office will be sent without any folder. If the case is to processed using a VA certificate of reasonable value, the folder is prepared at this time, but it is not sent to HUD-FHA until later.

In the direct endorsement program, it will not be sent to HUD-FHA until after closing, when the entire file is forwarded for the first time.

HUD Form 92800 is a four-page form with carbons already inserted. The application is completed without removing any of the carbons. When it is ready to go to the appraiser, the second copy is removed and retained by the mortgagee. VA Form 26-1805, Request for Determination of Reasonable Value (Exhibit V-4), may also be used to request a conditional commitment from HUD-FHA, but the HUD-FHA form may not be used in VA cases.

EXHIBIT V-4: VA REQUEST FOR DETERMINATION OF REASONABLE VALUE

VMP-427 (9205) VMP MORTGAGE FORMS • (313)293-8100 • (800)521-7291

86-273-8

VA

OMB Approved No. 2900-0045
Respondent Burden: 12 minutes

☐ **V.A. REQUEST FOR DETERMINATION OF REASONABLE VALUE (Real Estate)**
☐ **HUD APPLICATION FOR PROPERTY APPRAISAL AND COMMITMENT**

HUD Section of Act | 1. CASE NUMBER

2. PROPERTY ADDRESS *(Include ZIP code and county)*
3. LEGAL DESCRIPTION
4. TITLE LIMITATIONS AND RESTRICTIVE COVENANTS
1 ☐ CONDOMINIUM 2 ☐ PLANNED UNIT DEVELOPMENT

5. NAME AND ADDRESS OF FIRM OR PERSON MAKING REQUEST/APPLICATION *(Include ZIP Code)*

6. LOT DIMENSIONS:
1 ☐ IRREGULAR SQ/FT 2 ☐ ACRES

7. UTILITIES (✓)	ELEC	GAS	WATER	SAN SEWER
1. PUBLIC				
2. COMMUNITY				
3. INDIVIDUAL				

8. EQUIP: 1 ☐ RANGE/OVEN 2 ☐ REFRIG 3 ☐ DISH WASHER 4 ☐ CLOTHES WASHER 5 ☐ DRYER 6 ☐ GARBAGE DISP 7 ☐ VENT FAN 8 ☐ W/W CARPET 9 ☐

9. BUILDING STATUS: 1 ☐ PROPOSED 2 ☐ SUBSTANTIAL REHABILITATION 3 ☐ UNDER CONSTRUCTION 4 ☐ EXISTING 5 ☐ ALTERATIONS, IMPROVEMENTS, OR REPAIRS
10. BUILDING TYPE: 1 ☐ DETACHED 2 ☐ SEMI DETACHED 3 ☐ ROW 4 ☐ APT UNIT
11. FACTORY FABRICATED? 1 ☐ YES 2 ☐ NO
12A. NO. OF BUILDINGS
12B. NO. OF LIVING UNITS
13A. STREET ACCESS: 1 ☐ PRIVATE 2 ☐ PUBLIC
13B. STREET MAINT: 1 ☐ PRIVATE 2 ☐ PUBLIC

14A. CONSTRUCTION WARRANTY INCLUDED? 1 ☐ YES 2 ☐ NO *(If "Yes," complete Items 14B and C also.)*
14B. NAME OF WARRANTY PROGRAM
14C. EXPIRATION DATE *(Month, day, year)*
15. CONSTR. COMPLETED *(Mo., yr.)*

16. NAME OF OWNER
17. PROPERTY: ☐ OCCUPIED BY OWNER ☐ NEVER OCCUPIED ☐ VACANT ☐ OCCUPIED BY TENANT *(Complete Item 18 also)*
18. RENT *(If applic.)* $ /MONTH

19. NAME OF OCCUPANT
20. TELEPHONE NO.
21. NAME OF BROKER
22. TELEPHONE NO.
23. DATE AND TIME AVAILABLE FOR INSPECTION ☐ AM ☐ PM

24. KEYS AT *(Address)*
25. ORIGINATOR'S IDENT. NO.
26. SPONSOR'S IDENT. NO.
27. INSTITUTION'S CASE NO.

28. PURCHASER'S NAME AND ADDRESS *(Complete mailing address. Include ZIP code)*

EQUAL OPPORTUNITY IN HOUSING

NOTE — Federal laws and regulations prohibit discrimination because of race, color, religion, sex, or national origin in the sale or rental of residential property. Numerous State statutes and local ordinances also prohibit such discrimination. In addition, Section 805 of the Civil Rights Act of 1968 prohibits discriminatory practices in connection with the financing of housing.

If HUD/V.A. finds there is noncompliance with any antidiscrimination laws or regulations, it may discontinue business with the violator.

29. NEW OR PROPOSED CONSTRUCTION — *Complete Items 29A through 29G for new or proposed construction cases only.*

A. COMPLIANCE INSPECTIONS WILL BE OR WERE MADE BY: ☐ FHA ☐ V.A. ☐ NONE MADE
B. PLANS *(check one)*: ☐ FIRST SUBMISSION ☐ REPEAT CASE *(If checked, complete Item 29C.)*
C. PLANS SUBMITTED PREVIOUSLY UNDER CASE NO.
D. NAME AND ADDRESS OF BUILDER
E. TELEPHONE NO.
F. NAME AND ADDRESS OF WARRANTOR
G. TELEPHONE NO.

30. COMMENTS ON SPECIAL ASSESSMENTS OR HOMEOWNERS ASSOCIATION CHARGES
31. ANNUAL REAL ESTATE TAXES $
32. MINERAL RIGHTS RESERVED? ☐ YES *(Explain)* ☐ NO
33. LEASEHOLD CASES *(Complete if applicable)*: LEASE IS ☐ 99 YEARS ☐ RENEWABLE ☐ HUD/V.A. APPROVED; EXPIRES *(Date)*; ANNUAL GROUND RENT $

34. SALE PRICE OF PROPERTY $
34A. IS BUYER PURCHASING LOT SEPARATELY? ☐ YES ☐ NO *(If "Yes," see instruction page under "Sale Price")*
35. REFINANCING—AMOUNT OF PROPOSED LOAN $
36. PROPOSED SALE CONTRACT ATTACHED ☐ YES ☐ NO
37. CONTRACT NUMBER PREVIOUSLY APPROVED BY V.A. THAT WILL BE USED

CERTIFICATIONS FOR SUBMISSIONS TO HUD

In submitting this application for a conditional commitment for mortgage insurance, it is agreed and understood by the parties involved in the transaction that if at the time of application for a Firm Commitment the identity of the seller has changed, the application for a Firm Commitment will be rejected and the application for a Conditional Commitment will be reprocessed upon request by the mortgagee.

It is further agreed and understood that in submitting the request for a Firm Commitment for mortgage insurance, the seller, the purchaser and the broker involved in the transaction shall each certify that the terms of the contract for purchase are true to his or her best knowledge and belief, and that any other agreement entered into by any of these parties in connection with this transaction is attached to the sales agreement.

BUILDER/SELLER'S AGREEMENT: **All Houses:** The undersigned agrees to deliver to the purchaser a statement of appraised value on Form HUD-92800.5B. **Proposed Construction:** The undersigned agrees, upon sale or conveyance of title within one year from date of initial occupancy, to deliver to the purchaser Form HUD-92544, warranting that the house is constructed in substantial conformity with the plans and specifications on which HUD based its value and to furnish HUD a conformed copy with the purchaser's receipt thereon that the original warranty was delivered to him/her. **All Houses:** In consideration of the issuance of the commitment requested by this application, I (we) hereby agree that any deposit or down payment made in connection with the purchase of the property described above, whether received by the undersigned or an agent of the undersigned, shall upon receipt be deposited in escrow or in trust or in a special account which is not subject to the claims of my creditors and where it will be maintained until it has been disbursed for the benefit of the purchaser or otherwise disposed of in accordance with the terms of the contract of sale.

Signature of: ☐ Mortgagee ☐ Builder ☐ Seller ☐ Other X ____________ Date ________ 19__

MORTGAGEE'S CERTIFICATE: The undersigned mortgagee certifies that to the best of his/her knowledge, all statements made in this application and the supporting documents are true, correct and complete.

Signature and Title of Mortgage Officer: X ____________ Date ________ 19__

CERTIFICATIONS FOR SUBMISSIONS TO V.A.

1. On receipt of "Certificate of Reasonable Value" or advice from the Department of Veterans Affairs that a "Certificate of Reasonable Value" will not be issued, we agree to forward to the appraiser the approved fee which we are holding for this purpose.
2. CERTIFICATION REQUIRED ON CONSTRUCTION UNDER FHA SUPERVISION *(Strike out inappropriate phrases in parentheses)*
   I hereby certify that plans and specifications and related exhibits, including acceptable FHA Change Orders, if any, supplied to V.A. in this case, are identical to those (submitted to) (to be submitted to)(approved by) FHA, and that FHA inspections (have been)(will be) made pursuant to FHA approval for mortgage insurance on the basis of proposed construction under Sec.

38. SIGNATURE OF PERSON AUTHORIZING THIS REQUEST
39. TITLE
40. TELEPHONE NUMBER
41. DATE
42. DATE OF ASSIGNMENT
43. NAME OF APPRAISER

WARNING: Section 1010 of title 18, U.S.C. provides: "Whoever for the purpose of . . . influencing such Administration . . . makes, passes, utters or publishes any statement knowing the same to be false . . . shall be fined not more than $5,000 or imprisoned not more than two years or both."

V.A. FORM **26-1805** DEC 1991 — SUPERSEDES V.A. FORM 26-1805, SEP 1987, WHICH WILL NOT BE USED

VMP-427 (9205) VMP MORTGAGE FORMS • (313)293-8100 • (800)521-7291

VA/HUD FILE COPY 1

In preparing the application HUD Form 92800, it is important to complete certain items correctly.

Items 2 and 3: Property Address and Legal Description

If item 2 or 3 is inaccurate, there is the chance that the appraiser will go to the wrong property. If that happens, the error might not be discovered until well into the origination process, and considerable time will have been wasted.

Item 5: Lot Dimensions

Enter the actual measurements of the lot if that is practical. If the lot is too irregular, check "irregular" and enter the total area of the lot in square feet or acres. Do not cross-reference this item to the legal description.

Item 9: Building Status

"Proposed" means no construction has started. (Footings may have been dug, but not poured.) "Under construction" means some construction has been completed. (Footings have been poured, or something further.) "Existing" means construction is complete. The property is occupied or ready for occupancy.

Item 14A: Construction Warranty Included

Check the appropriate block. A "construction warranty" is an approved insured warranty plan such as HOW. It is not the standard builder warranty required in all new construction cases. If "yes" is checked, complete items 14B and C. If "no" is checked, go to item 15.

Item 15: Construction Completed

If "existing" was checked in item 9, enter the month and year construction was completed. If this was more than two years ago, only the year need be entered. If any other "building status" was checked in item 9, leave blank.

Item 19: Name of Occupant

This must be completed if either of the "occupied" blocks was checked in item 17. If "never occupied" or "vacant" was checked, leave this blank.

Item 20: Telephone Number

Enter the telephone number where the person named in item 19 can be reached during the day.

Item 23: Date and Time Available for Inspection

Enter the date the property will be available for inspection and check "a.m." or "p.m." or both to indicate when it can be inspected. If the appraiser cannot gain access to the property at the time checked, delays can be expected.

Item 24: Keys At

Enter the address where the keys to the property can be found when the property is available for inspection. If this is the property, enter "property." Otherwise enter a complete address.

Item 25: Originator's Identification Number

Enter the 10-digit identification number assigned to the mortgage by HUD-FHA. This is sometimes referred to as the mortgagee number.

Item 28: Purchaser's Name and Address

Enter the purchaser's name and current address and attach a copy of the contract of sale if the property has been sold. If the property has not yet been sold, enter "not yet sold." This is important. HUD-FHA assigns priority to appraisals being ordered to support sales of properties that are already under contract and for new construction cases. Appraisal of existing properties not under contract are done only after all those in the first two categories are complete.

Item 29: New or Proposed Construction

Complete these blocks only if "proposed" or "under construction" was checked in item 9. For item B (plans), mark the block to indicate whether the same plans and specifications have already been submitted in connection with an earlier application to HUD-FHA. For item C (plans submitted previously under case number), enter the HUD-FHA case number under which they were submitted, if the same plans and specifications have already been submitted with an earlier application and "Repeat Case" was checked in B.

Item 33: Leasehold Cases

This is used primarily in Maryland and Hawaii but may be found elsewhere, especially in resort areas. If title is in fee simple, leave blank.

Certification for Submission to HUD

The mortgagee's certificate must be signed by an authorized official of the mortgagee submitting the application. In the case of an existing house, any of the three parties identified may sign the "builder/seller's agreement." In proposed construction cases it must be signed by the builder or seller.

Ordering a VA Appraisal

VA, unlike HUD-FHA, will accept applications for appraisals from the veteran, lender, builder, owner, or sponsor. Typically, lenders act on behalf of others requesting appraisals, since their employees are most familiar with the process.

Ordering the VA appraisal is similar to ordering one from HUD-FHA, although there are a few minor differences. The VA Request for Determination of Reasonable Value (VA Form 26-1805) and the Uniform Residential Appraisal Report (URAR) are used. The requester telephones the VA regional office, provides the necessary data, and is given the case number and name of the designated appraiser.

In certain cases, the lender gets the case number and the name of the fee appraiser and mails certain copies of the VA Form 26-1805 and any exhibits directly to the fee appraiser. When the fee appraiser has finished the appraisal, he or she forwards copies 1, 3, 4, and 5 of the VA Form 26-1805, two copies of the completed appraisal report, and exhibits to VA.

When five or more similar properties are involved, a single application covers all of them, and VA issues a master certificate of reasonable value (MCRV). The MCRV assigns a separate value to each lot, to each basic house, and to each available alternate. These three values are combined to produce reasonable values for specific properties.

LAPP Procedures

Under the VA's Lender Appraisal Processing Program (LAPP), lenders are able to perform in-house review appraisals and ascertain property value based on the fee appraiser's report. Under LAPP, lenders follow the usual telephone or computer assisted assignment procedure to get the case number and the name of the fee appraiser. The VA assignment clerk, or automated system in use, will inform the lender of the case number and the name of the fee appraiser assigned to the case. When making the request the lender must identify the case as being processed under LAPP.

Cases processed under this program will receive case numbers from the common numbering system; however, a new designation for type of case is denoted by the prefix LAP. It is essential that lenders note on VA Form 26-1805 this LAP prefix before the case number and show in capital letters under the lender name and address on the appraisal request form the following: LENDER APPRAISAL PROCESSING PROGRAM (LAPP) CASE. The lender then immediately forwards VA Form 26-1805 to the fee appraiser.

In preparing the VA 26-1805, some blocks are completed in a different way than for HUD-FHA loans, and some are not used at all.

Form Heading

Check the block "VA Request for Determination of Reasonable Value (Real Estate)."

Item 25: Originator's Number

Leave blank.

Item 28: Purchaser's Name and Address

This must be completed for appraisal of an existing property.

Item 37: Contract Number Previously Approved by VA that Will be Used

VA reviews each sales contract entered into by a veteran. If a builder, developer, or real estate broker wishes, VA will review and approve standard contract forms in advance, thus saving time in processing individual cases.

When such contracts are reviewed and approved, they are assigned numbers. If a number has been assigned to the contract that will be used in this case, enter the number here. If no number is entered here, a copy of the contact must be submitted with the application.

Ordering a Conventional Appraisal

The procedures for ordering conventional appraisals vary widely from lender to lender and from investor to investor. However, many investors require lenders to follow Fannie Mae and Freddie Mac guidelines.

Working with appraisals of properties for a conventional loan puts more responsibility on the lender, because the lender may use appraisers of its own selection, either on staff or on a fee basis. It is the lender's responsibility to hire appraisers with ethical and professional standards, monitor their work in progress, and perform quality control checks on their completed appraisals. Most investors hold the lender responsible for the accuracy of the appraisal and insist that the appraisal be done in a way that will determine the true value of the property.

Thus it is important for conventional lenders to maintain a comprehensive list of approved appraisers. It is from this list that processors must choose an appraiser for a loan being processed. Failure to use an appraiser from the list may result in a second review appraisal being ordered, which causes delays and expense.

How do appraisers get on a lender's approved list? In general, they seek approval from lenders with whom they want to do business and submit evidence of their competency. In addition to a resume (with address, employment history, and so on), lenders generally require sample appraisals of one or more property types, such as single family homes, condominiums, or one- to four-units.

For almost all conventional mortgages, the appraisal report is prepared on FNMA Form 1004/FHLMC Form 70 (Exhibit V-3), the Uniform Residential Appraisal Report (URAR). The top section of the URAR, identified in the left margin as "To be completed by Lender," is usually filled in by the lender before sending the form to the appraiser. Some lenders order appraisals by telephone or fax, so the appraiser fills in this section from information provided by the lender.

The key to creating a successful system of approving appraisers lies in communication of standards and guidelines to the appraiser. Investor requirements will change from time to time, and the lender should systematically inform staff and fee appraisers of these changes. By effectively communicating requirements, the lender can do its job of originating quality loans more efficiently and at lower cost.

When ordering an appraisal for a property, lenders should give the appraiser a complete sales contact. The contract will tell the appraiser about financing data and sales concessions for the subject property that will be, or have been, granted by anyone associated with the transaction. If the lender has pertinent information that is not included in the sales contract, the appraiser should be told about it.

Monitoring the Appraisal

The lender's responsibility does not end when the appraisal has been ordered. Time is of the essence, especially if a borrower has already applied for a loan. It is frustrating for loan applicants to wait, and since files usually cannot be completed without an appraisal, it is a good habit for processors to stay aware of progress on an appraiser's report.

A suspense or "tickler" file should be established to remind processors and other of the status of outstanding appraisal reports. (Exhibit V-5 is a sample loan-in-process. Where reports have not been received by the deadline, processors should follow up with the appraiser immediately.

Occasionally an appraiser will be unable to get into the property, and the processor will have to contact the applicant or the real estate broker to allow admittance. When an appraiser consistently fails to return reports on time, it is important for the production manager to find out why. If there are no extenuating circumstances, the appraiser should be dropped from the approved list.

When the appraisal report has been received, it is best to pay the appraiser promptly. Appraisers otherwise may be a bit less conscientious for the slow-paying lender—this in turn could retard the lender's ability to move loan applications through the system.

Evaluating the Appraisal

Lenders have a strong, vested interest in securing a quality appraisal of properties involved in loan applications, so a thorough review of incoming appraisals is essential. The appraisal must be evaluated as soon as possible after it is returned by the appraiser and passed by the employee assigned this responsibility—often the processor.

The evaluation must not wait until the rest of the package is complete: problems discovered late in the process are bound

EXHIBIT V-5: SAMPLE GENERAL LOAN-IN-PROCESS RECORD

Sample Loan-In-Process Record

Applicant	Broker/Builder Requested	Received	Type of Loan Comments
Application	xxxxxxxx		
Certificate of Eligibility			
Appraisal (Fee $)			Fee Paid by:
Sales Contract			
Survey			
Credit Report (Fee $)			Fee Paid by:
Employment Verif #1			
Employment Verif #2			
Employment Verif #3			
Employment Verif #4			
Employment Verif #5			
Tax Returns			
Deposit Verif #1			
Deposit Verif #2			
Deposit Verif #3			
Deposit Verif #4			
Mortgage Verification			
Credit Verif #1			
Credit Verif #2			
Real Estate Equity			
Gift Letter			
Savings Bond List			
Other Documentation			
Firm Commitment (CRV, PMI)			
Final Inspection			
Health Auth Approval			
Builder Warranty			
Completion Escrow			
Other Documentation			
Submitted (FHA, VA, PMI)			
Closing			
Warehouse	xxxxxxxx		
Shipping	xxxxxxxx		

to cause delays, at best, and could well negate the value of the work done up to that time.

If there is ever a reason to reject or modify an application, the reason must be discovered as early as possible in the process to avoid unnecessary work and duplication of efforts. The lender's review also identifies conditions imposed by the appraiser, most of which must be met before the loan is closed.

In HUD-FHA cases processed outside the direct endorsement program, the lender receives a copy of the appraisal report along with a conditional commitment (HUD Form 92800.5B, Exhibit V-6). In VA cases not under LAPP, the lender receives a copy of the appraisal report, along with the Certificate of Reasonable Value (CRV), (VA From 26-1843, Exhibit V-7). The Conditional Commitment or CRV simply establishes a value on which the agency is willing to base insurance or guaranty of the loan. The appraisal report lets the lender see how that value was reached.

HUD-FHA conditional commitments and VA CRVs should be reviewed as soon as they are received for value and for repair conditions. If values seem inadequate, or if apparently unreasonable repair conditions have been imposed, requests for reconsideration of value or waiver of repair conditions should be prepared and submitted immediately.

In the VA's LAPP program, the lender's approved staff appraisal reviewer, after getting the appraisal report back from the VA assigned fee appraiser, reviews the appraisal for completeness, for soundness and conformity with accepted appraisal techniques and practices, and for VA guidelines. The staff appraisal reviewer takes the acceptable appraisal report and determines the reasonable value of the property. This reasonable value determination may not exceed the aggregate of any loan secured by the property *plus* the amount of any assessment resulting from special improvements for which there may be a lien or right to a lien against the property.

Also, the related loan amount cannot exceed the property's reasonable value plus the funding fee if it is to be financed. LAPP lenders must notify the borrower of the reasonable value

EXHIBIT V-6: HUD-FHA CONDITIONAL COMMITMENT—FORM 92800.5B

86,295-A

VMP-426 (9108) 01 VMP MORTGAGE FORMS • (313)293-8100 • (800)521-7291

☐

Conditional Commitment
Direct Endorsement
Statement of Appraised Value

U.S. Department of Housing and Urban Development
Office of Housing
Federal Housing Commissioner

OMB Approval No. 2502-0111 (exp. 2/28/93)

General Commitment Conditions

1. **Maximum Mortgage Amount and Term:**
(a) Occupant Mortgagors: Mortgage amount and terms assume satisfactory owner-occupant mortgagor(s). They may be changed depending upon the rating of borrower, his/her income and credit.
(b) 203(k) NonOccupant Mortgagors: If mortgagor does not occupy house, the law limits the mortgage amount;
(c) Changes: The Commissioner or Direct Endorsement (DE) Underwriter may, after reviewing pertinent information, change the mortgage amount and term.
2. **Approval of Borrower:** A determination for approval will be based upon receipt of acceptable application for mortgage credit analysis.
3. **Validity Period:** This document expires six months from the issue date in the case of an "existing" house or not more than twelve months from its date for "proposed" construction. A shorter period may be imposed by HUD for proposed construction. All cases are classified as "existing" or "proposed" for the purpose of determining expiration date. Accordingly a house, even though still under construction, may be classified as an existing house if it was not approved by HUD, V.A., or a DE Lender prior to beginning of construction. Lower loan-to-value ratios will be applied unless construction exhibits are certified by builder as meeting applicable codes and HUD requirements and are covered by a HUD approved insured 10-year protection (warranty) plan.
4. **Cancellation:** This document may be cancelled after 60 days from the date of issuance if construction has not started.
5. **Property Standards:** All construction, repairs, or alterations proposed in the application or on the construction exhibits returned herewith must equal or exceed applicable codes and HUD requirements.

Information: The estimates of fire insurance and taxes are furnished for mortgagee's and mortgagor's information. They must be used to prepare form HUD-92900, Application for Commitment and Insurance, when a firm commitment is desired.

Commitment Terms

☐ Conditional Commitment for Mortgage Insurance under the National Housing Act, Sec.

☐ See below

By:

Lender ID
Sponsor/Agent
Mortgagee

Action Date
FHA Case No.
INST Case Ref. No.

Est. Value of Prop. $

Property Address:

☐ Existing ☐ Proposed (see gen. cond. 3)

Commitment Issued
Commitment Expires
Improved Living Area Sq. Ft.

Monthly Expense Estimate
Fire Insurance . . . . $
Taxes . . . . $
Condo. Com. Exp. . . . $
Total . . . . $

Specific Commitment Conditions (Applicable when checked)

HUD's commitment to insure a mortgage on this property is dependent on the completion of the conditions listed below.
HUD Does Not Guarantee the work done to comply with the conditions.

Estimated Remaining Economic Life of this property is years.

This property ☐ is, ☐ is not eligible for a high ratio to value loan.

☐ Manufactured Housing

1. ☐ Subdivision Requirements: Comply with Requirements No. from Report dated for Subdivision.
2. ☐ **Section 221(d)(2):** The maximum insurable mortgage for a mortgagor other than a displaced family presenting a Certificate of Eligibility, form FHA-3476, is $
3. ☐ **Assurance of Completion:** If the required repairs cannot be completed prior to submission of closing papers, form HUD-92300 made in the amount of $ (or such additional amount as the lender desires) may be established as the means to ensure completion.

☐ **See indicated additional items on attached:**
☐ **See the following additional conditions on the back:**

Previous editions are obsolete
VMP-426 (9108) 01 VMP MORTGAGE FORMS • (313)293-8100 • (800)521-7291

form **HUD-92800.5B** (2/91)
ref. Handbook 4115.1

MORTGAGEE'S COPY

EXHIBIT V-6—*continued*

Specific Commitment Conditions (Applicable when indicated on the front of this form)

B. Proposed Construction: The builder or mortgagee must notify the assigned Fee Inspector as appropriate (see items 11, 12, and 13 below).

C. Warranty: Forms HUD-92544 and HUD-92544-A shall be executed between the builder and the purchaser.

D. Section 223: This commitment is issued pursuant to Section 223(e).

E. Health Authority Approval: Submit local health authority approval (on a form or letter) indicating the individual water supply and/or sewage disposal system is acceptable.

F. Reserved.

G. Prefabricator's Certificate: The Lender shall provide a prefabrication certificate as required by the related engineering bulletin.

H. Termite Control (Proposed Construction): If soil poisoning is used, the builder shall complete form HUD-92052, Termite Soil Treatment Guarantee, and transmit a copy to HUD or the Direct Endorsement Underwriter. The Mortgagee will deliver the original and a copy to the mortgagor at closing.

I. Lead Paint Notice: This house was constructed before 1978. There is a possibility that it may contain lead paint that was in use before that time. The lender is required to provide information on Lead Paint Poisoning to the buyer.

4. Flood Insurance Requirement: This property is located in a special flood hazard area and must be covered by flood insurance in accordance with HUD regulation 24 CFR 203.16a.

5. Carpet Identification: (as listed in Certified Products Directory) Manufacturer recommended maintenance program must be provided to the homebuyer.

6. Termite Control (Existing Construction): A recognized termite control operator shall furnish certification that the house and other structures within the legal boundaries of the property indicate no evidence of active termite infestation.

7. Code Enforcement: The lender shall submit a statement from the public authority that the property meets local code requirements. If the mortgage on the property is to be insured under Section 221(d)(2), a code compliance inspection is required.

8. Repairs: The lender shall notify the original appraiser upon completion of required repairs, unless otherwise instructed.

9. Lender's Certificate of Completion: The lender shall furnish a certificate that required repairs have been examined and were satisfactorily completed.

10. Manufacturers Warranties must be provided to the homebuyer covering heating/cooling systems, hot water heaters, ranges, etc.

11. Initial Inspection (2 working days) is requested before the "beginning of construction" with forms in place.

12. Frame Inspection (1 working day) is requested when the building is enclosed and framing, plumbing, heating, electrical, and insulation is complete and visible.

13. Final Inspection is requested when construction is completed and the property ready for occupancy.

14. Insulation Certificate must be posted in a conspicuous location in the dwelling.

15. The Insured Protection Plan Warranty Agreement shall be executed between the builder and the homebuyer.

16. Borrower Notification. At the time of the application for a firm commitment, the mortgagee must include a certificate that the borrower was notified that the property was not approved for mortgage insurance prior to the start of construction and Department does not have authority to provide financial relief for any future property repairs under Section 518(a) of the National Housing Act.

17. The lender shall furnish a certificate of occupancy or letter of acceptance from the local building authority.

Public reporting burden for this collection of information is estimated to average 5 minutes per response, including the time for reviewing instructions, searching existing data sources, gathering and maintaining the data needed, and completing and reviewing the collection of information. Send comments regarding this burden estimate or any other aspect of this collection of information, including suggestions for reducing this burden, to the Reports Management Officer, Office of Information Policies and Systems, U.S. Department of Housing and Urban Development, Washington, D.C. 20410-3600 and to the Office of Management and Budget, Paperwork Reduction Project (2502-0111), Washington, D.C. 20503.

Previous editions are obsolete — form HUD-92800.5B

Conditional Commitment
Direct Endorsement
Statement of Appraised Value

U.S. Department of Housing and Urban Development
Office of Housing
Federal Housing Commissioner

OMB Approval No. 2502-0111 (exp. 2/28/93)

Attention Homebuyers This property is not FHA Approved and FHA does not warrant the condition or the value of the property. However, FHA will insure a mortgage on the property if certain conditions are met.

For Existing Houses: If you are buying a house which has been lived in before, be sure the house is in acceptable condition before signing a purchase contract. An appraisal is made only to estimate the value of the property. This appraisal does not guarantee that the house is free from defects. HUD cannot give you money for repairs so you must protect yourself before you buy. **You** should inspect the property carefully. If you need help, a private home inspection service can be hired in many localities. Look in the telephone book for such services.

For New Homes: If you are buying a new home, HUD requires the builder to provide a one-year warranty. Please read carefully the information on the back of this form under the heading "new construction."

Fair Housing & Equal Opportunity Hotline: 800-424-8590

The law requires that borrowers using HUD-insured financing must receive a copy of this form **prior to** the purchase of property. The following definitions refer to phrases used in the "commitment terms" section below.

Estimated Value of Property (Est. Value of Prop.) is the amount HUD considers the property to be worth.

Estimated Closing Cost is the estimated amount that must be paid to complete the mortgage loan transaction. These costs may be paid by the seller or the buyer. They normally include items such as fees for preparing the mortgage documents, title insurance, loan origination fees, and transfer and recording of the deed.

Maximum Mortgage Amount (Max. Mrtg. Amt.) is the highest mortgage amount HUD can insure for a non-veteran and is based on the sum of the "estimated value of the property" and the "estimated closing costs." There is additional information on the back of this form which you should also read carefully.

Commitment Terms

☐ Conditional Commitment for Mortgage Insurance under the National Housing Act, Sec.

☐ See below

By:

Lender ID
Sponsor/Agent
Mortgagee

Action Date
FHA Case No.
INST Case Ref. No.

Est. Value of Prop. $

Property Address:

☐ Existing ☐ Proposed
(see gen. cond. 3)

Commitment Issued
Commitment Expires
Improved Living Area Sq. Ft.

Monthly Expense Estimate
Fire Insurance . . . . $
Taxes . . . . $
Condo. Com. Exp. . . . . $
Total . . . . $

Specific Commitment Conditions (Applicable when checked)
HUD's commitment to insure a mortgage on this property is dependent on the completion of the conditions listed below.
HUD Does Not Guarantee the work done to comply with the conditions.

Estimated Remaining Economic Life of this property is years.

This property ☐ is, ☐ is not eligible for a high ratio to value loan.

☐ Manufactured Housing

1. ☐ Subdivision Requirements: Comply with Requirements No. from Report dated for Subdivision.
2. ☐ **Section 221(d)(2):** The maximum insurable mortgage for a mortgagor other than a displaced family presenting a Certificate of Eligibility, form FHA-3476, is $
3. ☐ **Assurance of Completion:** If the required repairs cannot be completed prior to submission of closing papers, form HUD-92300 made in the amount of $ (or such additional amount as the lender desires) may be established as the means to ensure completion.

☐ **See indicated additional items on attached:**
☐ **See the following additional conditions on the back:**

Weatherization. Contact your local utility company or other qualified person or firm for home energy audit. If energy-related improvements are required, the value of your property may be increased to include the following: thermostats; insulation wrap for water heaters; insulation of ducts and pipes in unheated spaces of heating/cooling systems; attic insulation; insulation for floors and foundation walls; installation of weather-stripping/caulking; installation of storm windows/doors. The value may be increased by up to: (a) $2,000 without a separate value determination; (b) $3,500 if supported by a value determination by an approved appraiser; or (c) more than $3,500 subject to value determination by the V.A./HUD, as applicable, and subsequent endorsement of the V.A. Certificate of Reasonable Value, HUD Conditional Commitment, or Statement of Appraised Value.

This form must be delivered to the borrower promptly, but no later than at the time of the borrower's signing of the Application for Commitment and Insurance, form HUD-92900.

Previous editions are obsolete
VMP -426 (9108) 01
VMP MORTGAGE FORMS • (313)293-8100 • (800)521-7291
form **HUD-92800.5B** (2/91)
ref. Handbook 4115.1

HOMEBUYER'S COPY

EXHIBIT V-6—*continued*

Specific Commitment Conditions (Applicable when indicated on the front of this form)

B. Proposed Construction: The builder or mortgagee must notify the assigned Fee Inspector as appropriate (see items 11, 12, and 13 below).

C. Warranty. Forms HUD-92544 and HUD-92544-A shall be executed between the builder and the purchaser.

D. Section 223: This commitment is issued pursuant to Section 223(e).

E. Health Authority Approval. Submit local health authority approval (on a form or letter) indicating the individual water supply and/or sewage disposal system is acceptable.

F. Reserved.

G. Prefabricator's Certificate: The Lender shall provide a prefabrication certificate as required by the related engineering bulletin.

H. Termite Control (Proposed Construction). If soil poisoning is used, the builder shall complete form HUD-92052, Termite Soil Treatment Guarantee, and transmit a copy to HUD or the Direct Endorsement Underwriter. The Mortgagee will deliver the original and a copy to the mortgagor at closing.

I. Lead Paint Notice: This house was constructed before 1978. There is a possibility that it may contain lead paint that was in use before that time. The lender is required to provide information on Lead Paint Poisoning to the buyer.

4. Flood Insurance Requirement: This property is located in a flood hazard area and must be covered by flood insurance in accordance with HUD regulation 24 CFR 203.16a.

5. Carpet Identification: (as listed in Certified Products Directory) Manufacturer recommended maintenance program must be provided to the homebuyer.

6. Termite Control (Existing Construction). A recognized termite control operator shall furnish certification that the house and other structures within the legal boundaries of the property indicate no evidence of active termite infestation.

7. Code Enforcement: The lender shall submit a statement from the public authority that the property meets local code requirements. If the mortgage on the property is to be insured under Section 221(d)(2), a code compliance inspection is required.

8. Repairs: The lender shall notify the original appraiser upon completion of required repairs, unless otherwise instructed.

9. Certificate of Completion: The lender shall furnish a certificate that required repairs have been examined and were satisfactorily completed.

10. Manufacturers Warranties must be provided to the homebuyer covering heating/cooling systems, hot water heaters, ranges, etc.

11. Initial Inspection (2 working days) is requested before the "beginning of construction" with forms in place.

12. Frame Inspection (1 working day) is requested when the building is enclosed and framing, plumbing, heating, electrical, and insulation is complete and visible.

13. Final Inspection is requested when construction is completed and the property ready for occupancy.

14. Insulation Certificate must be posted in a conspicuous location in the dwelling.

15. The Insured Protection Plan Warranty Agreement shall be executed between the builder and the homebuyer.

16. Borrower Notification. At the time of the application for a firm commitment, the mortgagee must include a certificate that the borrower was notified that the property was not approved by HUD prior to the start of construction and Department does not have authority to provide financial relief for any future property repairs under Section 518(a) of the National Housing Act.

17. The lender shall furnish a certificate of occupancy or letter of acceptance from the local building authority.

Advice to Homebuyers

Prepaid Items. These are charges that normally will be paid at closing and are recurring in nature. They include such items as funds for real estate taxes and hazard insurance. The amount of these items will vary depending upon the closing date. No estimate is provided with this statement.

Escrow Account: This is a special account that your lender will keep on your behalf to save the necessary funds to pay certain future bills. Your mortgage payment will include, in addition to an amount for interest and principal, amounts to cover such items as property taxes, hazard insurance, and, for certain FHA programs, the mortgage insurance premium. These charges are collected in advance so that your lender will have enough money in the account to apply the charge when it comes due. Generally, 1/12 of the next year's estimated charges will be the amount collected with each of your monthly mortgage payments. Bear in mind that in most communities taxes and other operating costs are increasing. The estimates should give some idea of what you can expect the costs to be at the beginning. In some areas the estimate of taxes may also include charges such as sewer charges, garbage collection fee, water rates, etc.

Mortgage Insurance Premium: The amount for insuring your mortgage. The premium may be in the form of a one time charge or a monthly charge depending upon the section of the Housing Act under which your mortgage is insured. Your lender can provide you with specific information about your transaction.

Estimated Monthly Expenses: These are costs associated with homeownership which HUD believes the home-owners will have to pay when living in the property. Two examples of "estimated monthly expenses" are fire insurance and taxes, which are paid your lender each month as part of your mortgage payment. These are put into your escrow account.

Other Costs of Homeownership: Utilities are usually paid monthly to whomever provides the service. Also, you should save a certain amount each month to cover repair and maintenance costs which will come up while you own your home.

Late Payments: If you do not pay your mortgage payment within 15 days from the 1st day of the month, you can be charged a penalty. This may be 4 cents for each dollar of your payment.

New Construction: After specifications are accepted by HUD or a direct endorsement lender before construction, the builder is required to warrant that the house substantially conforms to approved plans and specifications. This warranty is for 1 year following the date on which title is transferred to the original buyer or the date on which the house was first lived in, whichever happens first. If, during the warranty period, you notice defects for which you believe the builder is responsible, ask him in writing to fix them. If he does not fix them, write the HUD Field Office. Include your FHA case number. If inspection shows the builder to be at fault, HUD will try to persuade him to fix the defect. If he does not, you may be able to obtain legal relief under the builder's warranty. Where a structural defect is involved, HUD can provide money for corrections under certain conditions. You cannot expect the builder to fix damage caused by ordinary wear and tear or by poor maintenance. Keeping the house in good condition is your responsibility.

If you signed your sales contract prior to receiving this statement of appraised value, the sales contract must include, or be changed to include, the following language:

It is expressly agreed that notwithstanding any other provisions of this contract, the purchaser shall not be obligated to complete the purchase of the property described herein or to incur any penalty by forfeiture of earnest money deposits or otherwise unless the mortgagee has delivered to the purchaser a written statement issued by the Federal Housing Commissioner, Veterans Administration or a Direct Endorsement lender setting forth the appraised value of the property of not less than $ which statement the mortgagee hereby agrees to deliver to the purchaser promptly after such appraised value statement is made available to the mortgagee. The purchaser shall, however, have the privilege and option of proceeding with consummation of the contract without regard to the amount of the appraised valuation. The appraised valuation is arrived at to determine the maximum mortgage the Department of Housing and Urban Development (HUD) will insure. HUD does not warrant the value nor the condition of the property. The purchaser should satisfy himself/herself that the price and condition of the property are acceptable.

Amount to be Borrowed

When you borrow to buy a home, you pay interest and other charges which add to your cost. A larger downpayment will result in a smaller mortgage. Borrow as little as you need and repay in the shortest time.

Previous editions are obsolete

form **HUD-92800.5B**

EXHIBIT V-7: VA CERTIFICATE OF REASONABLE VALUE

Department of Veterans Affairs

CERTIFICATE OF REASONABLE VALUE

1. CASE NUMBER

2. PROPERTY ADDRESS *(Include ZIP code and county)*

3. LEGAL DESCRIPTION

4. TITLE LIMITATIONS AND RESTRICTIVE COVENANTS:

☐ CONDOMINIUM ☐ PLANNED UNIT DEVELOPMENT

5. NAME AND ADDRESS OF FIRM OR PERSON MAKING REQUEST *(Include ZIP code)*

6. REMAINING ECONOMIC LIFE OF PROPERTY IS ESTIMATED TO BE NOT LESS THAN *(Enter number of years)* YEARS

7. ESTIMATED REASONABLE VALUE OF PROPERTY $

8. EXPIRATION DATE

9. SECRETARY OF VETERANS AFFAIRS BY *(Signature of authorized agent)*

10. DATE ISSUED

11. V.A. OFFICE

GENERAL CONDITIONS

(NOTE: THE DEPARTMENT OF VETERANS AFFAIRS DOES NOT ASSUME ANY RESPONSIBILITY FOR THE CONDITION OF THE PROPERTY, THE CORRECTION OF ANY DEFECTS NOW EXISTING OR THAT MAY DEVELOP WILL BE THE RESPONSIBILITY OF THE PURCHASER.)

1. This certificate will remain effective as to any written contract of sale entered into by an eligible veteran within the validity period indicated.
2. This dwelling conforms with the Minimum Property Requirements prescribed by the Secretary of Veterans Affairs.
3. The aggregate of any loan secured by this property plus the amount of any assessment consequent on any special improvements as to which a lien or right to a lien shall exist against the property, except as provided in Item 13 below, may not exceed the reasonable value in Item 7 above.
4. Proposed construction shall be completed in accordance with the plans and specifications identified below, relating to both onsite and offsite improvements upon which this valuation is based and shall otherwise conform fully to the V.A. Minimum Property Requirements. Satisfactory completion must be evidenced by either
   A. V.A. Final Compliance Inspection Report (V.A. Form 26-1839), or
   B. V.A. Acceptance of FHA Compliance Inspection Reports or other evidence of completion under FHA supervision applicable to proposed construction.
5. By contracting to sell property, as proposed construction or existing construction not previously occupied, to a veteran purchaser who is to be assisted in the purchase by a loan made, guaranteed, or insured by V.A., the builder or other seller agrees to place any downpayment received by the seller or agent of the seller in a special trust account as required by Section 1806 of title 38, U.S. Code.
6. The V.A. guaranty is subject to and conditioned upon the lending institution's compliance, at the time of the making, increasing, extending or renewing of the proposed loan, with Section 102 of P.L. 93-234, "Flood Disaster Protection Act of 1973."

12. PURCHASER'S NAME AND ADDRESS *(Complete mailing address. Include ZIP code)*

13. EXCEPTIONS TO GENERAL CONDITION NUMBER 3 ABOVE

☐ ENERGY CONSERVATION IMPROVEMENTS - The buyer may wish to contact the local utility company or a qualified person or firm for a home energy audit. If energy-related improvements are suggested, your mortgage may be increased to include the following: Thermostats, water heaters, heating/cooling systems, attic insulation, insulation for floors and foundation walls, weather-stripping/caulking, storm windows and storm doors. The mortgage may be increased by (a) up to $2,000 without a separate determination of the value of the energy-related improvements; (b) up to $3,500 if supported by a value determination by a designated appraiser; or (c) more than $3,500 subject to a value determination by V.A. or HUD, as applicable, and subsequent endorsement of the certificate of reasonable value or HUD conditional commitment.

☐ OTHER *(Cite and explain in Item 26 below)*

SPECIFIC CONDITIONS *(Applicable when checked or completed)*

14. THE REASONABLE VALUE ESTABLISHED HEREIN FOR THE RELATED PROPERTY IS

☐ BASED UPON OBSERVATION OF THE PROPERTY IN ITS "AS IS" CONDITION

☐ PREDICATED UPON COMPLETION OF PROPOSED CONSTRUCTION *(If checked, complete Item 15)*

☐ PREDICATED UPON COMPLETION OF REPAIRS LISTED IN ITEM 17

15. PROPOSED CONSTRUCTION TO BE COMPLETED *(Identify plans, specifications and exhibits)*

16. INSPECTIONS REQUIRED

☐ FHA COMPLIANCE INSPECTIONS FOR PROPOSED CONSTRUCTION

☐ V.A. COMPLIANCE INSPECTIONS ☐ LENDER TO CERTIFY

17. REPAIRS TO BE COMPLETED

18. NAME OF COMPLIANCE INSPECTOR

19. HEALTH AUTHORITY APPROVAL - Execution of Health Authority form or letter indicating approval of the individual:

☐ WATER SUPPLY ☐ SEWAGE DISPOSAL SYSTEM

20. ☐ This document is subject to the provisions of Executive Orders 11246 and 11375, and the Rules and Regulations of the Secretary of Labor in effect on this date, and 38 CFR 36.4390 through 36.4393, and also the provisions of the certification executed by the builder, sponsor or developer named herein which is on file in this office.

21. ☐ WOOD DESTROYING INSECT INFORMATION - EXISTING CONSTRUCTION - The seller shall, at no cost to the veteran-purchaser, prior to settlement, obtain a written statement from a qualified pest control operator reporting wood destroying insect information using V.A. Form 26-8850 or other form acceptable to V.A. The veteran-purchaser will acknowledge receipt of a copy of the statement in Item 14 of V.A. Form 26-8850 or other form acceptable to V.A. PROPOSED CONSTRUCTION - V.A. Form 26-8375, Termite Soil Treatment Guarantee, is required.

22. WARRANTY ☐ *(If checked, complete Item 23)*

23. NAME OF WARRANTOR

24. ☐ Since this property is located in a Special Flood Hazard Area as established by FEMA, flood insurance will be required in accordance with 38 CFC 36.4326.

25. SAFE DRINKING WATER ACT

☐ Certification required that in construction, any solders and flux did not contain more than 0.2 percent lead and any pipes and pipe fittings did not contain more than 8.0 percent lead.

26. OTHER REQUIREMENTS

V.A. FORM DEC 1991 **26-1843**

VMP-427 (9205)

SUPERSEDES V.A. FORM 26-1805, SEP 1987, WHICH WILL NOT BE USED.

VA FILE COPY 4

VMP MORTGAGE FORMS • (313)293-8100 • (800)521-7291

determination and provide him or her with a copy of the reviewed appraisal report as soon as possible; however, the lender may not issue a CRV.

HUD-FHA direct endorsement and conventional appraisals work much the same way. The lender must decide whether the property is acceptable security for the loan under consideration. An underwriter or review appraiser should review the appraisal report for its professional acceptability: that is, whether it is complete and supports the appraiser's value determination.

In some cases there will be a full review of the appraiser's work in the field, including visits to the property and the comparables. In most cases, however, a desk review will suffice: The underwriter or review appraiser simply looks at the submitted report and determines its accuracy and completeness.

Reconsideration

Anytime the value indicated by the appraiser appears low, the lender is free to request reconsideration. Doing so will, of course, take time and effort, but in many cases, there will be no loan without an increase in value.

It is usually helpful if the lender can provide detailed data on at least three comparable properties that have been sold recently where the sales data support a higher value than that assigned by the original appraiser. In conventional cases, the lender may go back to the original appraiser who did the property, or choose another. In HUD-FHA cases, reconsiderations are done by the same appraiser who did the original appraisal. If, after the first reconsideration, the lender is still dissatisfied, HUD-FHA may assign a staff appraiser to handle a second reconsideration request.

VA follows a similar system, but some of its original reconsiderations are assigned to staff appraisers and fee appraisers who are assigned to do reconsiderations; that is, they are not necessarily given to the original appraiser. VA lenders may not process an appeal of any amount under LAPP authority if they will be using an appraisal report from an appraiser they selected to support the appeal. When the lender wishes to use an additional appraisal report, the case must be forwarded to VA for processing and final determination.

Repair Requirements

VA appraisals are generally of "as is" value, although some requirements may be imposed as conditions of guaranty. The CRV should be checked for this. If the appraisal is as is, but the seller anticipates making improvements before closing that might affect value and the selling price, VA may be asked to reconsider its value determination based on those improvements.

In most cases, however, VA will simply identify defects in the property, establish the as is value and require that the veteran acknowledge the condition of the property before closing. If such a CRV is used to support an application to HUD-FHA, care should be taken to ensure that the value is adequate to support the HUD-FHA loan and that none of the repair requirements are such that they would disqualify the property, according to HUD-FHA standards. This is especially true of existing properties—the problem almost never is encountered in new construction cases.

HUD-FHA appraisals, on the other hand, usually assume that any repairs required by the appraiser have been completed. Instructions to HUD-FHA appraisers provide that only repairs of defects that potentially affect the health or safety of the occupants should be required. This is sometimes a difficult line to draw, however. HUD-FHA can waive repair requirements if the lender requests it.

Thus, if a HUD-FHA conditional commitment includes repair conditions the lender believes are unreasonable, waivers should be requested immediately, while the other processing of the application continues. If the lender waits until the firm commitment is ready for submission, delays will be encountered. The loan will not be insured or guaranteed until all of these conditions have either been met or waived, and work should start immediately on those that will not be waived.

The form these requests take will vary from office to office. Where there are repair conditions that are not likely to be waived, the seller should be notified immediately.

While the selling broker usually notifies the sellers of repair requirements, it is not mandatory that the seller pay for the repairs. They may be paid by either party in accordance with his or her contract. However, as repairs will almost always have to be completed before loan closing, it is unlikely the buyer will be prepared to pay for repairs to a property he or she does not yet own.

It is possible, of course, to arrange for the buyer to pay for repairs initially completed at the seller's expense as a part of the closing transaction, but this will usually require that the buyer have additional assets available to close.

Depending on the condition of the property, the lender's certification of acceptable completion is usually acceptable. In some cases, HUD-FHA or VA might require that inspections be performed by staff inspectors. After the property is completed and ready for occupancy in proposed construction cases, HUD-FHA or VA must always perform the final inspection.

Interim inspections may be conducted by local authorities or, in the case of properties constructed subject to approved insured warranty programs, by anyone acceptable to the warrantor. Any requirement that inspections be performed by HUD-FHA or VA staff should be included as a part of the appraisal report that imposed the commitment. If it is not, it can usually be assumed that mortgagee inspections and certifications are acceptable.

Lender Responsibility for Appraisals

Increasingly, lenders are taking responsibility for appraisal management, whether they originate HUD-FHA, VA, or conventional loans. It may be convenient for processors, underwriters, and others to rely strictly on the appraiser's judgment when evaluating an appraisal report; however, remember that the ultimate responsibility for the appraisal remains with the lender. The lender also has responsibility to borrowers. It is now a federal requirement that lenders provide borrowers with a copy of the appraisal.

It is important for those on the front lines of mortgage loan origination, especially processors, to be familiar with the appraisal guidelines published by investors and agencies. Open communication with the appraiser and borrowers is the first step.

Many experts feel that negligently or fraudulently prepared appraisals account for a substantial percentage of losses for mortgage lenders. While most loan processors feel they are unqualified to review and pass judgment on the appraisal, there are many problems you can spot easily—you need only use common sense. Also, if possible, become familiar with the appraisers in your area and with their appraisal techniques.

Finally, know the real estate in your area and ask yourself such questions as, "Is the value consistent with market condition?" and "Has the appraiser allowed for depreciation in a stable or declining area?"

Warning Signals

Here are some warning signals for troublesome appraisals:

- The appraisal was ordered by a party to the transaction (buyer, seller, real estate broker).
- Comparables cannot be verified as recorded or submitted by potentially biased party (seller, real estate broker).
- The tenant is shown to be the occupant on owner-occupant application.
- The income approach has not been used on tenant-occupied single-family residences.
- There have been excessive adjustments in an urban or suburban area where marketing time is under six months.
- There are large, unjustified adjustments.

- The distance between comparables is significant.
- The comparison of square footage to value seems off.
- Photos do not match the description of property.
- There is an unidentified appraiser.
- Appreciation in occurring in a stable or declining area.
- "For sale" or "for rent" signs in the yard or windows (in refinance loans).
- The appraiser is from outside of subject property county.
- Photographs look familiar from other appraisals.
- Comparables look familiar from other appraisals.
- Information is missing: name of borrower, client, occupant, etc.
- The appraisal was ordered before the sales contract was written.
- The occupant is unknown.
- Photos reveal items that are not disclosed in the appraisal, such as commercial property next door, railroad tracks, or another structure on the premises.
- Despite old comparables (nine to 12 months), the lender is in a "hot" market.
- Potential problems are identified on the appraisal's notes.
- Land constitutes a large percentage of value.

Case Examples

1. In a case in new Jersey, an appraiser increased the property value by 10 percent because of the view. However, a backup appraisal revealed that the property was located in the downtown area of an economically distressed part of a city, where many homes and businesses had been boarded up. In this case, the loan processor should have required further justification for why such an adjustment was warranted.
2. Reading the notes to the appraisal report is essential. In a recent case in New York, a lender failed to do so—

a costly mistake. In this case, the appraiser clearly indicated that while there were no problems with the property, it had been and was presently being used as a real estate office by the prospective mortgagor.

3. In a case in Florida, a lender failed to look at the picture contained in an appraisal report for a refinance transaction. Had the lender done so, he would have seen over the top of the front door a large wooden sign with Greek letters. This so-called single-family residence was being used a fraternity house.

Clearly, the appraisal is an important tool for the lender. Now, however, we turn our attention to another critical factor: verifying the application data.

6

Verifying Application Data

Investors, HUD-FHA, VA, and private mortgage insurers insist on third-party, independent verifications of almost every statement on the application. No investor, guarantor, or insurer evaluates the creditworthiness of a prospective borrower solely on unverified statements.

While most applicants don't intentionally falsify application information, they commonly overstate income and understate obligations. Thus, the verifications of credit history, income, and obligations are important to the overall loan evaluation.

There are three basic questions that must be answered regarding each applicant:

- Does the applicant have enough cash or liquid assets to pay the balance of the down payment and the cost of closing this loan?
- Is the applicant's income stable, and is it adequate to meet this new monthly obligation, along with the added costs likely to be associated with it?
- Does the credit history reasonably establish that the applicant will pay monthly obligations on time, assuming he or she can pay them at all?

The basic sources of information about the borrower are: verifications of deposit (to determine whether assets are available to close); verifications of income (to determine if income is both adequate and stable when related to the mortgage requirements); and the credit report or other verifications of credit (to determine whether the applicant has a history of paying bills as agreed). They serve as the basis for making the ultimate underwriting decision related to the borrower.

In this chapter, we will review the various ways of securing verifications of income, credit history, and liquid assets for closing, and we will look at the meaning of the information included in those verifications. We will also discuss the problems encountered when information from independent supporting documentation conflicts with the information the borrower has provided in the application.

During this period, it is essential that processors stay abreast of changes in the circumstances on which the loan is being evaluated. If the sales price changes, perhaps because of the addition of options to a new house or an agreement that the buyer will pay for repairs, the conditions of approval change. If the contract calls for repairs not required by the appraisal, their completion must be monitored, along with those required by the appraisal.

In condominiums or planned unit developments (PUDs), the underlying documents governing the appropriate association must be reviewed. Sometimes applicants will change their minds about the type of loan they want if market conditions change.

As we have noted before, time is important in processing any application. The more time that passes between application and the lender's final approval of the loan, the more likely it is that there will be problems. If, for example, market conditions change for the worse and an applicant who was pre-qualified as being eligible at the application time is rejected by the time the application is ready for approval, the processor's effort will be wasted.

If the verification process is not started as soon as possible after the application is taken, loan approval can be delayed. Since third-party verifications are provided by entities with no personal interest in whether the loan is granted or not, securing them is one of the most time-consuming aspects in processing mortgage applications. Some employers take a personal interest and help speed the process, but they in the minority.

Guidelines vary for how old verifications of employment and deposit may be at the time the loan is approved and at the time the note is executed. Generally, if there are any verifications over 90 days old, processors should check to be sure the date of verification still falls within investor guidelines. On new loans for new construction, the guidelines may differ from those for existing construction or refinance.

Thus, if it appears that there will be an extensive delay before the application can be submitted for final approval, the requests for verification should be updated accordingly. If there are complications—and there may be significant delays in securing some verifications—those requests should be sent early. A follow-up telephone call may help get the forms back quickly.

Because most applications require full documentation, we will start this chapter with discussion of the complete verification process.

Ordering Verifications

All requests for verification should be sent directly to the person or firm being asked to provide the verification. They then should be returned directly to the lender without passing through the hands of the applicant or any other third party. Although this is time-consuming, the convenience of asking the applicant to secure verifications is just not worth it.

HUD-FHA, VA and conventional investors regularly audit lender originations to ensure that lenders are getting verifications through appropriate channels. If their reviewers discover verifications handled by someone other than the lender and the source of verifying information, the lender might be required to agree to indemnify HUD-FHA, VA, or the investor against loss in specific cases and may even find its approval as a HUD-FHA mortgagee withdrawn.

Further, requests should not be sent to an individual by name if the only source of the name is the applicant. If the applicant is asked to provide the name of someone at his or her place of employment who should complete the verification, for example, there is nothing to prevent him or her from providing the name of someone completely out of the proper chain who has been prompted to provide a false verification.

This is not to say that verification requests should never be addressed to individuals by name. Whenever the identity of the proper person is known from an independent source, in fact, it is probably better to use that name to speed up the process.

Having verification requests signed by the applicant as a part of the application process is important, because requiring the borrowers to come in a second time is inconvenient and time-consuming for both the applicant and the processor. HUD-FHA and VA no longer object, as they once did, to having applicants sign verification forms in blank, as long as certain additional information is provided as part of the application process.

The person taking the application should consider having the applicant sign more copies of verification requests than are likely to be needed, in case the verification is lost or misplaced.

Verification of Cash for Down Payment and Closing

Nearly all loan programs, government as well as conventional, prohibit the applicant from borrowing closing costs. Most lenders expect borrowers to come up with money on their own so that they have some stake, or equity, in the property. The VA allows borrowers to buy houses with no money down but requires that the loan be within the veteran's repayment ability. If the veteran needs money to close, it must come from his or her own sources and not from borrowed funds.

The verification process has two steps. First, you must determine that the applicant actually has the funds required, or has liquid assets that could readily be converted. Second, if there appears to have been a recent substantial increase in liquid assets, you must ensure that the increase was the result of some logical occurrence, and that the "new" money was not borrowed (or, if it was borrowed, that the loan is acceptable). In transactions where a secondary loan to finance the property is allowed, it may be adequate simply to verify the existence of the loan and its terms, and then establish its repayment as a recurring obligation.

Verifications of deposit are used to establish that the applicant has, or will have by closing, sufficient cash to meet settlement requirements. The applicant listed the source of the funds in the basic application, and the verification of deposit is used to establish that they actually exist.

"Deposits" may be something of a misnomer, because there are sources of funds for settlement other than deposits in banks, credit unions, or savings banks. Borrowers may own stocks, have vested interest in retirement funds, plan to sell other real estate in which they have equity, hold U.S. Savings Bonds, plan to use the cash value of life insurance policies, or rely on a gift. Following are ways in which each of these sources of funds can be verified.

Earnest Money Deposits

Generally, sellers of real estate require that a portion of the purchase price, sometimes called earnest money, be put down as a deposit when the sales contract is signed. If the transaction cannot be completed, and it isn't the buyer's fault, the deposit is returned. If the buyer decides not to complete the transaction, the deposit is forfeited. If the transaction is completed, the deposit is applied to settlement costs.

It is important to determine that the deposit was actually paid in cash. (Fannie Mae, Freddie Mac, and HUD-FHA may require verification of payment in cash only when the deposit exceeds a certain percentage of the sale price.) The sales contract sometimes answers this question. If, however, the contract indicates that the deposit was made by check or note, or is unclear on the manner of payment, further verification is needed.

If the deposit was paid by check, the best and simplest form of verification is a copy of the canceled check, secured from the applicant at the time of application. If the check has not yet cleared the bank when the application is taken, the verification of deposit sent to the bank on which the check was drawn should ask specifically for verification that the check has been paid.

This can be done with a form that verifies that earnest money has been paid in cash (Exhibit VI-1) or be an entry in the Remarks section on the verification of deposit. This entry might read "Please verify payment of check number ________________ for $________________, including date of payment." Alternatively the applicant could furnish the canceled check prior to underwriting of the loan.

If the deposit was by note, verification may be through an affidavit from the seller that the note has been redeemed, a copy of the canceled note indicating receipt of the cash by the seller, or an affidavit from the real estate agent to the effect that the cash is being held in escrow for the account of the buyer.

Exhibit VI-1 can also serve this purpose.

Bank Deposits

The most common sources of funds are deposits in a bank, savings bank, credit union, or other financial institution. These funds are readily verified through the use of a form similar to FNMA Form 1006 (Exhibit VI-2.) Both HUD-FHA and VA accept FNMA Form 1006.

As part of the HUD-FHA application process, a copy of the current bank statements should be secured at the time of application. For loans to be sold to Fannie Mae and Freddie Mac, copies of statements for three months may substitute for a verification of deposit.

EXHIBIT VI-1: SAMPLE VERIFICATION THAT EARNEST MONEY DEPOSIT HAS BEEN PAID IN CASH

(LENDER'S LETTERHEAD)
(Date)

Applicant ________________

Case Number ______________

TO: (Builder, Broker, or Other Party, as Appropriate)

In order to complete processing of the loan identified above, it is necessary that we verify the amounts already paid in cash by the applicant. Please check the appropriate statement or statements below, sign where indicated, and return this letter to me at the address indicated above.

Sincerely,

Loan Processor

☐ I am holding no funds on behalf of the applicant, other than those for which receipt in cash is acknowledged in the sales contract.

☐ The note identified in the sales contract has been redeemed, and (as the seller) I have received $_______ from the applicant in cash, in addition to any deposit paid in cash and acknowledged in the sales contract.

☐ As the seller, I hereby acknowledge receipt of $______ from the applicant in cash, in addition to the amount for which receipt in cash is acknowledged in the sales contract. There was no note requiring payment of these funds.

☐ The real estate firm of _______________________ has received a deposit of $______ from the applicant in cash, which is being held for application to the applicant's account at the time of closing.

____________	____________________________	_______________
Date	Signature	Title

EXHIBIT VI-2: REQUEST FOR VERIFICATION OF DEPOSIT

VMP MORTGAGE FORMS • (313)293-8100 • (800)521-7291

VMP-24 (9007).02

INSTRUCTIONS TO LENDER:
1. FILL OUT PART I - REQUEST
2. HAVE APPLICANT(S) SIGN EACH COPY (No Carbon Signatures)
3. PULL YELLOW COPY AND FILE FOR FOLLOW-UP
4. FORWARD OTHER 2 COPIES (CARBON INTACT) TO DEPOSITORY

Printed on Recycled Paper

INSTRUCTIONS TO DEPOSITORY:
1. COMPLETE PART II
2. RETURN BOTH COMPLETED COPIES TO LENDER

FannieMae — Request for Verification of Deposit

Privacy Act Notice: This information is to be used by the agency collecting it or its assignees in determining whether you qualify as a prospective mortgagor under its program. It will not be disclosed outside the agency except as required and permitted by law. You do not have to provide this information, but if you do not your application for approval as a prospective mortgagor or borrower may be delayed or rejected. The information requested in this form is authorized by Title 38, USC, Chapter 37 (if VA); by 12 USC, Section 1701 et. seq. (if HUD/FHA); by 42 USC, Section 1452b (if HUD/CPD); and Title 42 USC, 1471 et. seq., or 7 USC, 1921 et. seq. (if USDA/FmHA).

Instructions: **Lender** - Complete items 1 through 8. Have applicant(s) complete item 9. Forward directly to depository named in item 1.
Depository - Please complete items 10 through 18 and return directly to lender named in item 2.
The form is to be transmitted directly to the lender and is not to be transmitted through the applicant(s) or any other party.

Part I - Request

1. To (Name and address of depository)	2. From (Name and address of lender)

I certify that this verification has been sent directly to the bank or depository and has not passed through the hands of the applicant or any other party.

3. Signature of Lender	4. Title	5. Date	6. Lender's No. (Optional)

FOLD

7. Information To Be Verified

Type of Account	Account in Name of	Account Number	Balance
			$
			$
			$
			$

To Depository: I/We have applied for a mortgage loan and stated in my financial statement that the balance on deposit with you is as shown above. You are authorized to verify this information and to supply the lender identified above with the information requested in items 10 through 13. Your response is solely a matter of courtesy for which no responsibility is attached to your institution or any of your officers.

8. Name and Address of Applicant(s)	9. Signature of Applicant(s)
	X
	X

To Be Completed by Depository

Part II - Verification of Depository

10. Deposit Accounts of Applicant(s)

Type of Account	Account Number	Current Balance	Average Balance For Previous Two Months	Date Opened
		$	$	
		$	$	
		$	$	
		$	$	

11. Loans Outstanding To Applicant(s)

FOLD

Loan Number	Date of Loan	Original Amount	Current Balance	Installments (Monthly/Quarterly)		Secured By	No. of Late Pymts.
		$	$	$	per		
		$	$	$	per		
		$	$	$	per		

12. Please include any additional information which may be of assistance in determination of credit worthiness. (Please include information on loans paid-in-full in item 11 above.)

13. If the name(s) on the account(s) differ from those listed in item 7, please supply the name(s) on the account(s) as reflected by your records.

Part III — Authorized Signature - Federal statutes provide severe penalties for any fraud, intentional misrepresentation, or criminal connivance or conspiracy purposed to influence the issuance of any guaranty or insurance by the VA Secretary, the USDA, FmHA/FHA Commissioner, or the HUD/CPD Assistant Secretary.

14. Signature of Depository Representative	15. Title (Please print or type)	16. Date

17. Please print or type name signed in item 14

18. Phone No.

Fannie Mae
Form 1006 Mar. 90

VMP-24 (9007).02 VMP MORTGAGE FORMS • (313)293-8100 • (800)521-7291

DEPOSITORY-RETURN BOTH COPIES TO LENDER
LENDER-DETACH THIS COPY AND FILE FOR FOLLOW-UP

VMP-24

If the account is recently opened, or if the current balance is considerably larger than the average balance over the last three months, the source of the funds must be established.

If there is any indication that the funds have been borrowed, make sure that the loan has not been secured by the property under consideration but by another asset. The payments on that loan must also be included as an obligation, and if monthly payments are not required, a monthly payment schedule must be developed for underwriting purposes by amortizing the loan on a monthly basis over its term.

Retirement Funds

Individual retirement accounts (IRAs) and Keogh retirement plans can be verified in the same manner as deposits and stocks and bonds, depending on where the funds are being held. However, the applicant may claim a vested interest in an employer-managed retirement fund, with the intention of using a portion of those funds for closing.

If so, a letter should be sent to the employer asking if the employee does, in fact, have the vested interest and, most importantly, if the rules of the fund permit withdrawal of all or a part of the interest at this time. Most plans prohibit withdrawals while the employee is still employed and for a certain period after employment is terminated, but there are exceptions. Most recently the federal government has allowed individuals to borrow against their vested funds.

If a loan is granted by the employer, this is counted as a recurring debt at underwriting and a copy of the executed note must be provided as proof. See Exhibit VI-3 for an example of a letter that might be used for this purpose.

Where the source of funds is an IRA or a Keogh account, the withdrawal is subject to significant penalties. Ten percent of the amount withdrawn will be paid as a federal tax penalty, and the institution managing the account may add additional penalties. In addition, the full amount withdrawn is considered as ordinary income in the year of withdrawal.

EXHIBIT VI-3: SAMPLE LETTER REQUESTING VERIFICATION OF VESTED INTEREST IN RETIREMENT FUND

(LENDER'S LETTERHEAD)
(Date)

Applicant ________________
Case Number ______________
Employee Number ___________

TO: (Administrator of
Retirement Fund
Named by Applicant)

Dear __________________:

The applicant named above has applied for a mortgage loan and claims a vested interest in a retirement fund under your control. The applicant has also indicated an intention to withdraw funds in order to meet some of the costs of closing on the mortgage loan. We would appreciate your responses to the questions below.

Sincerely,

Loan Processor

Release of the requested information is authorized.

____
Applicant

Does the applicant have a vested interest in a fund? ______________

What is the extent of that interest? $______________________________

What is the maximum which could be withdrawn today? $______________

Is the applicant's current employment covered by the fund? ________

If so, could the withdrawal be made without leaving that current employment? ____

____ ______________________
Date Signature Title

The applicant should be required to acknowledge understanding of these penalties, and the new amount remaining after applying the penalties should be all that is considered available for closing. (Since this is a one-time income item, however, the amount of the withdrawal should not be added to income for the purpose of computing tax obligations or ability to make payments.)

Equity in Other Real Estate

It is common for purchasers of homes to sell their former homes and use all or part of the equity proceeds of the sale to pay settlement costs of the new home. If such a sale has already taken place, the old mortgage should have been satisfied and the residual proceeds of the sale are on deposit. A copy of the HUD-1 settlement statement (Exhibit VI-4) showing the terms of the sale is required in the file to establish the source of these funds. They are verified in the routine course of processing.

If the other property has not yet been sold, however, the application should show an outstanding mortgage, and the funds will not yet appear in any verified deposits. When this happens, the mortgage obligation should be verified. The probable proceeds of the sale can be verified in several ways, but approval of the application is conditioned on providing a copy of the settlement statement at or before closing, to establish that the transaction actually funded. This requirement is lifted when a bridge (or swing) loan is involved, as we will show.

The most common means of establishing equity is a combination of a copy of a sales contract between the lender's applicants and the purchasers of the former property and an analysis by the applicants' real estate agent of the costs and proceeds of the sale. Exhibit VI-5 is a sample form for requesting this information.

If there is not yet a sales contract, the real estate agent's analysis will probably be the only verification available. It is important in such cases, though, to establish that the estimate is realistic, not only in terms of the dollar amounts included, but with respect to the general marketability of the property. The

EXHIBIT VI-4: SETTLEMENT STATEMENT HUD-1

VMP-501 (8811) 01 Page 1 1 ply

VMP (8811) 01 VMP MORTGAGE FORMS • (313)293-8100 • (800)521-7291

A. Settlement Statement

U.S. Department of Housing and Urban Development

OMB No. 2502-0265

B. Type of Loan

	6. File Number	7. Loan Number	8. Mortgage Insurance Case Number
1. ☐ FHA 2. ☐ FmHA 3. ☐ Conv. Unins. 4. ☐ VA 5. ☐ Conv. Ins.			

C. NOTE: *This form is furnished to give you a statement of actual settlement costs. Amounts paid to and by the settlement agent are shown. Items marked "(p.o.c.)" were paid outside the closing; they are shown here for informational purposes and are not included in the totals.*

D. NAME AND ADDRESS OF BORROWER:

E. NAME AND ADDRESS OF SELLER:

F. NAME AND ADDRESS OF LENDER:

G. PROPERTY LOCATION:

H. SETTLEMENT AGENT:
PLACE OF SETTLEMENT:

I. SETTLEMENT DATE:

J. SUMMARY OF BORROWER'S TRANSACTION		K. SUMMARY OF SELLER'S TRANSACTION	
100. GROSS AMOUNT DUE FROM BORROWER:		**400. GROSS AMOUNT DUE TO SELLER:**	
101. Contract sales price		401. Contract sales price	
102. Personal property		402. Personal property	
103. Settlement charges to borrower: *(from line 1400)*		403.	
104.		404.	
105.		405.	
ADJUSTMENTS FOR ITEMS PAID BY SELLER IN ADVANCE:		**ADJUSTMENTS FOR ITEMS PAID BY SELLER IN ADVANCE:**	
106. City/town taxes to		406. City/town taxes to	
107. County taxes to		407. County taxes to	
108. Assessments to		408. Assessments to	
109.		409.	
110.		410.	
111.		411.	
112.		412.	
120. GROSS AMOUNT DUE FROM BORROWER: ►		**420. GROSS AMOUNT DUE TO SELLER:** ►	
200. AMOUNTS PAID BY OR IN BEHALF OF BORROWER:		**500. REDUCTIONS IN AMOUNT DUE TO SELLER:**	
201. Deposit or earnest money		501. Excess deposit *(see instructions)*	
202. Principal amount of new loan(s)		502. Settlement charges to seller *(line 1400)*	
203. Existing loan(s) taken subject to		503. Existing loan(s) taken subject to	
204.		504. Payoff of first mortgage loan	
205.		505. Payoff of second mortgage loan	
206.		506.	
207.		507.	
208.		508.	
209.		509.	
ADJUSTMENTS FOR ITEMS UNPAID BY SELLER:		**ADJUSTMENTS FOR ITEMS UNPAID BY SELLER:**	
210. City/town taxes to		510. City/town taxes to	
211. County taxes to		511. County taxes to	
212. Assessments to		512. Assessments to	
213.		513.	
214.		514.	
215.		515.	
216.		516.	
217.		517.	
218.		518.	
219.		519.	
220. TOTAL PAID BY/FOR BORROWER: ►		**520. TOTAL REDUCTIONS IN AMOUNT DUE SELLER:** ►	
300. CASH AT SETTLEMENT FROM/TO BORROWER:		**600. CASH AT SETTLEMENT TO/FROM SELLER:**	
301. Gross amount due from borrower *(line 120)*		601. Gross amount due to seller *(line 420)*	
302. Less amount paid by/for borrower *(line 220)*	( )	602. Less total reductions in amount due seller *(line 520)*	( )
303. CASH (☐ *FROM*) (☐ *TO*) BORROWER: ►		**603. CASH (☐ *TO*) (☐ *FROM*) SELLER:** ►	

HUD-1 (3-86)
RESPA, HB 4305.2

VMP (8811) 01 VMP MORTGAGE FORMS • (313)293-8100 • (800)521-7291

PAGE 1

EXHIBIT VI-4—*continued*

VMP-502 (8811) 01 Page 2 1 ply — VMP (8811) 01 — VMP MORTGAGE FORMS • (313)293-8100 • (800)521-7291

HUD-1 (Rev. 3/86) OMB No. 2502-0265

L. SETTLEMENT CHARGES

	PAID FROM BORROWER'S FUNDS AT SETTLEMENT	PAID FROM SELLER'S FUNDS AT SETTLEMENT
700. TOTAL SALES / BROKER'S COMMISSION: BASED ON PRICE $ @ % =		
DIVISION OF COMMISSION (LINE 700) AS FOLLOWS:		
701. $ to		
702. $ to		
703. Commission paid at settlement		
704.		
800. ITEMS PAYABLE IN CONNECTION WITH LOAN:		
801. Loan origination fee %		
802. Loan discount %		
803. Appraisal fee to:		
804. Credit report to:		
805. Lender's inspection fee		
806. Mortgage insurance application fee to		
807. Assumption fee		
808.		
809.		
810.		
811.		
900. ITEMS REQUIRED BY LENDER TO BE PAID IN ADVANCE:		
901. Interest from to @ $ /day		
902. Mortgage insurance premium for mos. to		
903. Hazard insurance premium for yrs. to		
904. *Flood Insurance Premium for* yrs. to		
905.		
1000. RESERVES DEPOSITED WITH LENDER:		
1001. Hazard Insurance months @ $ per month		
1002. Mortgage insurance months @ $ per month		
1003. City property taxes months @ $ per month		
1004. County property taxes months @ $ per month		
1005. Annual assessments months @ $ per month		
1006. *Flood insurance* months @ $ per month		
1007. months @ $ per month		
1008. months @ $ per month		
1100. TITLE CHARGES:		
1101. Settlement or closing fee to		
1102. Abstract or title search to		
1103. Title examination to		
1104. Title insurance binder to		
1105. Document preparation to		
1106. Notary fees to		
1107. Attorney's fees to *(includes above items Numbers:*)		
1108. Title insurance to *(includes above items Numbers:*)		
1109. Lender's coverage $		
1110. Owner's coverage $		
1111.		
1112.		
1113.		
1200. GOVERNMENT RECORDING AND TRANSFER CHARGES:		
1201. Recording fees: Deed $; Mortgage $; Releases $		
1202. City/county tax / stamps: Deed $; Mortgage $		
1203. State tax / stamps Deed $; Mortgage $		
1204.		
1205.		
1300. ADDITIONAL SETTLEMENT CHARGES:		
1301. Survey to		
1302. Pest inspection to		
1303.		
1304.		
1305.		
1306.		
1307.		
1400. TOTAL SETTLEMENT CHARGES *(Enter on line 103, Section J-and-line 502, Section K)* ▶		

I have carefully reviewed the HUD-1 Settlement Statement and to the best of my knowledge and belief, it is a true and accurate statement of all receipts and disbursements made on my account or by me in this transaction. I further certify that I have received a copy of the HUD-1 Settlement Statement.

Borrower: ______________________ Date: ____________ Seller: ______________________ Date: ____________

Borrower: ______________________ Date: ____________ Seller: ______________________ Date: ____________

The HUD-1 Settlement Statement which I have prepared is a true and accurate account of this transaction. I have caused or will cause the funds to be disbursed in accordance with this statement.

______________________ Date: ____________ Settlement Agent: ______________________ Date: ____________

WARNING: It is a crime to knowingly make false statements to the United States on this or any other similar form. Penalties upon conviction can include a fine and imprisonment. For details see: Title 18 U.S. Code Section 1001 and Section 1010.

PAGE 2

EXHIBIT VI-5: SAMPLE ANALYSIS OF EXPECTED PROCEEDS FROM SALE OF REAL ESTATE (UNDER CONTRACT)

(LENDER'S LETTERHEAD)
(Date)

Applicant __________________
Case Number _______________

TO: (Real Estate Broker
Identified by the Applicant)

Dear ___________________:

The applicant named above has applied for a mortgage loan and has reported that you have placed a contract for the sale of the property identified below. We would appreciate it if you would provide the information requested, based on that contract and your best professional judgment.

Sincerely,

Loan Processor

Release of the requested information is authorized.

____
Applicant

____
Applicant

Property Address: _______(Completed by Lender)_____________________________

Holder of Outstanding Mortgage ________________________ Unpaid Balance: $____________

Contract Sales Price: $__________ Your Commission: ___%, $_____ Anticipated Discount: $______

Anticipated Seller Share of prorations: $___________ Other Anticipated Costs to Seller: $______________

Anticipated Closing Dated: ____________________ Anticipated Net to Seller: $____________________

____________________ __________________________________
Date Signature

request (see Exhibit VI-6 for an example) should also ask for information about general market conditions in the area, the condition of the property being sold, how long it has been on the market, if the asking price has been reduced, and so on. It is not improper in such cases to require that the applicant secure a formal appraisal of the property to support the claim. The detail necessary in these verifications depends to a large degree on the extent to which the applicant needs the funds to complete the transaction the lender is processing.

In most conventional transactions, the listing price must be reduced by at least 10 percent in computing the probable proceeds in these cases. While neither HUD-FHA nor VA impose specific requirements in this regard, a 10 percent minimum reduction is reasonable and should probably be applied in all cases. This allows for a sales commission.

A bridge loan provides funds to the home buyer who is between the purchase of a new home and closing the sale of another property. Investors as well as HUD-FHA and VA consider bridge loans an acceptable source of funds for closing, provided the applicant has the capacity to make the payments on the bridge loan in addition to other obligations. If the bridge loan does not incorporate a monthly payment schedule, one must be developed based on the terms of the loan. Generally, there are no restrictions on the terms of such a loan.

U.S. Savings Bonds

The lender need not actually see the bonds claimed as assets, unless there is some question about them based on information the applicant has provided. At minimum, a lender should ask for a list of the bonds, including the dates on which they were purchased, their face value, and their purchase price. To be more accurate (and, incidentally, add to the cash available), the lender might also establish their current redemption value.

Because redemption value tables are probably more readily available to lenders than to applicants—especially when the lender is a depository institution or associated with one—

EXHIBIT VI-6: SAMPLE ANALYSIS OF EXPECTED PROCEEDS FROM SALE OF REAL ESTATE (NOT YET UNDER CONTRACT)

(LENDER'S LETTERHEAD)
(Date)

Applicant ________________
Case Number ______________

TO: (Real Estate Broker
Identified by the
Applicant)

Dear __________________:

The applicant named above has applied for a mortgage loan and has reported owning the property identified below, which is to be sold as a part of this transaction. We understand the property has been listed with you, but that there is not yet a firm buyer under contract. We would appreciate it if you would provide the information requested, based on your best professional judgment.

Sincerely,

Loan Processor

Release of the requested information
is authorized.

____
Applicant

____
Applicant

Property Address: _______(Completed by Lender)_______________________
Holder of
Outstanding Mortgage: ______________________________________

Outstanding Balance: $________________________		Date Property Offered for Sale: _____________	
Date of Purchase: _________	Purchase Price: $______	Asking Price: $______	Anticipated Discount $_______
Your Commission: _______ %, $__________		Anticipated Seller Share of Prorations: $__________	
Other Anticipated Costs to Seller: $________________		Anticipated Net to Seller: $________________	
Is this an active market?____________________		Anticipated Sale Date: ___________________	

Your best estimate of a realistic sale price: $____________________

lenders might choose to provide calculations as a customer service. If current redemption value is unknown, purchase price must be used. Exhibit VI-7 is a sample form for obtaining the information from the borrower on savings bonds.

Cash Value of Life Insurance Policies

Cash value of life insurance policies can be accrued in two ways: cash value guaranteed by the basic contract or produced by the accumulation of interest and dividends. To verify the basic cash value, a copy of the policy itself is needed. It will include a table of cash surrender values at various times during the life of the policy.

Dividends and interest are reported to the policyholder periodically on a statement that usually also shows whether there are any outstanding loans against the policy. (These reduce both available cash and the insurance value of the policy.) A copy of both the basic policy and a recent statement of dividends and interest should be required.

A letter from the insurance agent responsible for servicing the policy can also serve this purpose, but any such letter should be requested by and sent to the lender, not the applicant, just as with any other verification. Agents, by the way, generally have access to current data about dividend and loan accounts, but they often do not have information from the cash value tables of specific policies sold in the past. Initially agreeing to accept a letter from an agent could prove unnecessarily time-consuming if the agent must first do the same thing you could do yourself—look at the policy.

Gifts

Gifts are generally acceptable to satisfy all or part of the cash settlement requirements if:

- it is established that the donor has a bona fide relationship with the applicant, to lend credence to the claim that the funds are actually a gift;

EXHIBIT VI-7: SAMPLE LIST OF SAVINGS BONDS OWNED

I HEREBY CERTIFY THAT I HAVE THE FOLLOWING U.S. SAVINGS BONDS IN MY POSSESSION:

Series	*Serial Number*	*Face Amount*	*Mo. & Yr. Purchased*	*Current Value*
			Total:	

Date ______________________

Signature ______________________

- there is a statement from the donor attesting that tha money is indeed a gift and clearly stating that no repayment is required or expected;
- there is verification that the funds are actually available to the donor or a cancelled check is provided; and
- verification of receipt of gift funds is available.

On HUD-FHA loans, the funds must have been received prior to underwriting. The gift letter (Exhibit VI-8) serves only to support the source of the funds. On conventional loans, an appropriate verification form should be sent to the place where the funds are held.

The gift letter serves primarily as a verification of the source of funds. If the funds are needed for closing in conventional cases and VA cases, they must have been transferred to the applicant before closing.

In HUD-FHA cases, evidence of deposit of gift funds must accompany the application, along with the gift letter. This evidence can be a verification of deposit showing a significant increase in an account balance—approximately the size of the gift—at a time coincidental with the gift letter and application.

In most Fannie Mae and Freddie Mac cases, the applicant must make a cash investment of at least 5 percent of the sales price. For Fannie Mae loans, unless the gift is at least 20 percent of the sales price, the 5 percent requirement is in addition to the gift funds. If the gift funds are at least 20 percent of the sales price (in effect making loan-to-value 80 percent or lower), Fannie Mae does not require additional verified funds. Check current guidelines to ensure compliance.

Fannie Mae has introduced a community home buyer program, available on a negotiated basis, which permits a minimum 3 percent down payment by the borrowers with the remaining 2 percent contributed by a family member, a nonprofit organization, or a public entity.

EXHIBIT VI-8: SAMPLE GIFT LETTER

DATE: ____________________

TO WHOM IT MAY CONCERN:

I, ______________________________, OF ______________________________,
(DONOR'S NAME) (DONOR'S ADDRESS)

______________________________, DO HEREBY CERTIFY THAT I HAVE GIVEN / WILL GIVE A GIFT
(DONOR'S TELEPHONE NUMBER)

OF $__________ TO MY ________________________, TO BE APPLIED TOWARD
(RELATIONSHIP)
THE PURCHASE OF THE PROPERTY LOCATED AT ________________________.
(ADDRESS)
I FURTHER CERTIFY THAT THERE IS NO REPAYMENT EXPECTED OR IMPLIED ON THIS GIFT EITHER IN THE FORM OF CASH OR FUTURE SERVICES FROM

______________________________ OR ______________________________.
(RECIPIENT) (RECIPIENT)

NOTE: If the gift has not yet been given to the recipient, provide verification that the donor has sufficient assets to do so. If the recipient has received funds, please assure that they are included in Verification of Deposit.

WARNING: Section 1010 of Title 18, U.S.C. "Department of Housing and Urban Development Transactions," provides, "Whoever, for the purpose of influencing in any way the action of such Department...makes, passes, utters, or publishes any statement, knowing the same to be false...shall be fined not more than $5,000 or imprisoned not more than two years or both."

SIGNED: ______________________________ ______________________________
(DONOR'S SIGNATURE) (RECIPIENT'S SIGNATURE)

______________________________ ______________________________
(DONOR'S SIGNATURE) (RECIPIENT'S SIGNATURE)

VERIFICATION OF DEPOSIT
(To be filled out by bank or depository)

I hereby verify that the above-named donor does have the funds available to give as a gift if he (or she) so desires.

Name and address of bank or other depository ______________________________

Signature and title of official or other depository: ______________________________
(SIGNATURE)
____
(TITLE)
____
(DATE)

Stocks and Bonds

Ownership of stocks and bonds, including such investments as mutual funds, can be verified with the verification of deposit form if the investment is in a depository institution or if, for example, stocks are held by a broker in a deposit-type account. In other situations, however, a letter or current statement of the account, showing the number of shares held and the market value on the date of the statement, is acceptable.

If the statement does not show current market value, or if stock certificates are held by the applicant, ask the applicant to copy the certificates (when appropriate) and then check the financial section of a newspaper to determine the per-share value of the holding. If information on value cannot be readily obtained, the lender should insist that the applicant provide some evidence of the current value of the holdings.

Cash Settlements and Inheritances

Sometimes an applicant indicates that cash settlement of a lawsuit or a substantial inheritance is pending. This should be treated carefully for several reasons. First, precise amounts are seldom known in advance; second, the exact date of payment is usually unknown. If the funds are not actually received before loan closing, they will not be available.

Where such funds are needed for closing, the applicant should provide information from his or her attorney, the insurance agent responsible, the executor of the estate, or other reliable individuals. Specifics must be furnished about the amount of settlement expected, the probability that the amount will actually be received, and the date when payment can be expected. In some cases the processor may do this; if so, a sample letter is provided in Exhibit VI-9.

In general, all investors and agencies look on settlements and inheritances with a jaundiced eye. Verify these sources, however, and the funds will likely prove acceptable.

EXHIBIT VI-9: SAMPLE VERIFICATION OF PENDING CASH SETTLEMENT, INHERITANCE, ETC.

(LENDER'S LETTERHEAD)
(Date)

Applicant ________________
Case Number ______________

TO: (Attorney or Other Party
Named by Applicant)

The applicant named above has applied for a mortgage loan and has identified you as the attorney (insurance adjustor, executor, etc.) best able to verify the potential outcome of (Identify the lawsuit, pending insurance settlement, estate from which an inheritance is expected, etc.). In order to complete processing of this loan, it is essential that we have the answers to the questions below. Would you please respond briefly, sign this form, and return it to me?

Sincerely,

Loan Processor

Release of the requested information is authorized.

____
Applicant

1. When can settlement of the matter identified above be expected?
   ____
2. What amount can the applicant expect to realize as a result of settlement? ____
3. How will the amount be paid (lump sum, _______ installments of $__________ each, etc)?________________________________
4. How certain are the answers above as they relate to the applicant? ____

________________________ ________________________________
Date Signature

Verification of Employment

The processor must verify the applicant's employment for two reasons. First these verifications establish the applicant's income at the time of application and probable income in the immediate future. Second, they establish the stability of that income.

Lenders should look at an applicant's employment record going back at least two years to establish an employment history. If the applicant has been employed at the same place (not necessarily in the same job) for at least two years, the process is simple. If, however, the applicant has recently changed jobs, is self-employed, or has recently started a first job after finishing school, it becomes more complicated.

As with the verification of deposits, HUD-FHA and VA use a joint form to verify income (HUD Form 92004G/VA Form 26-8497). Fannie Mae has its own form—FNMA Form 1005 (Exhibit VI-10). HUD-FHA and VA accept the FNMA Form 1005. Most lenders use these forms to verify the employment of applicants even if the loans will not be Freddie Mac, Fannie Mae, HUD-FHA, or VA loans.

Fannie Mae, Freddie Mac, and HUD-FHA sometimes accept simplified methods of employment verification. This usually involves obtaining W-2 forms covering the most recent two full years, plus pay stubs covering the most recent 30 day period. Telephone confirmations of this information, with proper documentation in the file as to the specifics of the call, are required.

When there has been more than one employer in the past two years, the telephone conversation should also establish the reason for the change. If an employer is unwilling to provide that information by telephone, the lender must usually revert to the standard verification form. The VA is using this simplified documentation in certain VA field offices.

Regardless of the source of income, continuity is important. If there are significant gaps in the application, the applicant should be asked to explain them in writing as soon as possible. If part of the two-year period was spent as a full-time

EXHIBIT VI-10: REQUEST FOR VERIFICATION OF EMPLOYMENT

VMP MORTGAGE FORMS • (313)293-8100 • (800)521-7291

VMP-23 (9007).01

INSTRUCTIONS TO LENDER:
1. FILL OUT PART I - REQUEST
2. HAVE APPLICANT(S) SIGN EACH COPY (No Carbon Signatures)
3. PULL YELLOW COPY AND FILE FOR FOLLOW-UP
4. FORWARD OTHER 2 COPIES (CARBON INTACT) TO EMPLOYER

Printed on Recycled Paper

INSTRUCTIONS TO EMPLOYER:
1. COMPLETE PART II - VERIFICATION
2. RETURN BOTH COMPLETED COPIES TO LENDER

FannieMae — Request for Verification of Employment

Privacy Act Notice: This information is to be used by the agency collecting it or its assignees in determining whether you qualify as a prospective mortgagor under its program. It will not be disclosed outside the agency except as required and permitted by law. You do not have to provide this information, but if you do not your application for approval as a prospective mortgagor or borrower may be delayed or rejected. The information requested in this form is authorized by Title 38, USC, Chapter 37 (if VA); by 12 USC, Section 1701 et. seq. (if HUD/FHA); by 42 USC, Section 1452b (if HUD/CPD); and Title 42 USC, 1471 et. seq., or 7 USC, 1921 et. seq. (if USDA/FmHA).

Instructions: **Lender** - Complete items 1 through 7. Have applicant complete item 8. Forward directly to employer named in item 1.
Employer - Please complete either Part II or Part III as applicable. Complete Part IV and return directly to lender named in item 2.
The form is to be transmitted directly to the lender and is not to be transmitted through the applicant or any other party.

Part I - Request

1. To (Name and address of employer)

2. From (Name and address of lender)

I certify that this verification has been sent directly to the employer and has not passed through the hands of the applicant or any other interested party.

3. Signature of Lender | 4. Title | 5. Date | 6. Lender's Number (Optional)

FOLD

I have applied for a mortgage loan and stated that I am now or was formerly employed by you. My signature below authorizes verification of this information.

7. Name and Address of Applicant (include employee or badge number)

8. Signature of Applicant

X

Part II - Verification of Present Employment

9. Applicant's Date of Employment | 10. Present Position | 11. Probability of Continued Employment

12A. Current Gross Base Pay (Enter Amount and Check Period)

$ ______ ☐ Annual ☐ Weekly ☐ Other (Specify) ☐ Monthly ☐ Hourly

12B. Gross Earnings

Type	Year To Date	Past Year 19____	Past Year 19____
Base Pay	Thru____ 19____ $	$	$
Overtime	$	$	$
Commissions	$	$	$
Bonus	$	$	$
Total	$	$	$

13. For Military Personnel Only

Pay Grade

Type	Monthly Amount
Base Pay	$
Rations	$
Flight or Hazard	$
Clothing	$
Quarters	$
Pro Pay	$
Overseas or Combat	$
Variable Housing Allowance	$

14. If Overtime or Bonus is Applicable, Is Its Continuance Likely?
Overtime ☐ Yes ☐ No Bonus ☐ Yes ☐ No

15. If paid hourly — average hrs. per wk.

16. Date of applicant's next pay increase

17. Projected amount of next pay increase

18. Date of applicant's last pay increase

19. Amount of last pay increase

20. Remarks (If employee was off work for any length of time, please indicate time period and reason)

FOLD

Part III — Verification of Previous Employment

21. Date Hired

22. Date Terminated

23. Salary/Wage at Termination Per (Year) (Month) (Week)
Base______ Overtime______ Commissions______ Bonus______

24. Reason for Leaving | 25. Position Held

Part IV — Authorized Signature - Federal statutes provide severe penalties for any fraud, intentional misrepresentation, or criminal connivance or conspiracy purposed to influence the issuance of any guaranty or insurance by the VA Secretary, the USDA, FmHA/FHA Commissioner, or the HUD/CPD Assistant Secretary.

26. Signature of Employer | 27. Title (Please print or type) | 28. Date

29. Print or type name signed in Item 26

30. Phone No.

Fannie Mae
Form 1005 Mar. 90

VMP-23 (9007).01 VMP MORTGAGE FORMS • (313)293-8100 • (800)521-7291

EMPLOYER-RETURN BOTH COPIES TO LENDER
LENDER-DETACH THIS COPY AND FILE FOR FOLLOW-UP

student, this needs to be verified as though it were employment, ideally via copies of transcripts or diplomas.

Fannie Mae requires explanation of gaps of employment lasting more than one month. Other investors might require explanation of any gap at all. Generally speaking, part-time employment is significant only if there is a history of such employment for at least 12 months. Judgment can be applied, however, if the lender believes that the part-time employment is likely to continue. If part-time income is relatively recent, it is a good idea to verify on the standard verification of employment form, so it may be used as a compensating factor.

Self-Employed Persons

For processors, those applicants who operate their own business concerns can require more paperwork, because the applicant's ability to repay the loan depends upon the success of the business. Most investors and insurers define a self-employed borrower as someone who has a 25 percent or greater ownership in a business. Fannie Mae has such detailed requirements for verifying income from self-employment that many investors rely on its guidelines.

Because self-employed persons present special problems in verification of income, they are usually asked to supply additional documentation, principally federal income tax returns and accounting statements. A profit-and-loss statement covering the current year to date, as well as financial statements and profit-and-loss statements for the previous two full years, may also be required. Profit-and-loss statements and financial statements should be audited and certified, although most HUD-FHA and VA offices, and some investors, accept unaudited statements for smaller business owners.

In the particular case of these smaller businesses, audited statements are seldom available because of their cost. Similarly, tax returns should be professionally prepared, but this is not always required.

If the applicant has been self-employed for less than two full years and the self-employment is not directly related to former employment, it is difficult to establish an adequate pattern of income to support approval of the loan.

Fannie Mae specifically states that a borrower who has been self-employed for less than two years must have had at least two years of previous successful employment in the same occupation in order to be eligible for financing. Also, Fannie Mae discourages lenders from using maximum financing if a borrower has been self-employed for less than two years, that is, making loans where the loan-to-value ratio is within five percent of the maximum for the loan type.

While decisions of this nature depend largely on company policy, it may not be worthwhile to continue processing cases where the lending decision hinges on income from self-employment and there is no firm way to substantiate that income.

Self-employed borrowers are sometimes hesitant to provide all the information that a lender requires to make a decision. They will say that their copy of the tax return has been lost or destroyed. The IRS will send the borrower a copy of any previous tax return that has been filed. This will cause delays in processing but is the only option available.

There are four types of self-employed businesses: sole proprietorship, partnership, corporation, and S corporation. Each of these basic business structures is explained below with a list of the tax returns usually required from that borrower. Processors should be familiar with investor documentation requirements.

Sole Proprietorship

A sole proprietorship is a business owned by one person. It is the least expensive and the simplest form of business to establish. The owner is personally liable for all debts of the business, and therefore has unlimited liability. No distinction is made between the owner's personal assets and the assets used in the business, so that either may be taken by creditors. Business income or loss is reported on Schedule C, IRS Form 1040, which is included with the owner's tax return. Two years' federal income tax returns, which include Schedule C, are required for analysis.

Partnership

A partnership is formed when two or more individuals form a business and share not only profits and losses but responsibility for running the business. There are two types of partnerships: general and limited. For both types, qualifying income will be found on Schedule K-1, IRS Form 1065. It is important to obtain a full set of tax returns, as some information on the IRS Form 1040 may be required.

Corporation

A corporation is a state-chartered business owned by stockholders. The stockholder is not personally responsible for the debts of the corporation. Borrowers may be shareholders and officers in closely held corporations, that is, be one of a select few who both own and manage the corporation. Qualifying income should be determined by W-2 forms in conjunction with the compensation of officers section of IRS Form 1120.

S Corporation

An S corporation is generally a small, start-up business that is taxed like a partnership. Because of the entrepreneurial nature of an S corporation, it is difficult to substantiate a track record of earnings and income to the borrower.

Qualifying income should be determined with W-2 forms in conjunction with an analysis of IRS Form 1120-S, especially the compensation of officers line. Additionally, income should be taken from Schedule K-1, IRS Form 1120-S. Again, it is important to obtain a full set of tax returns, as some information on the IRS Form 1040 may be used.

Interest, Dividends, and Trust Funds

Verification of employment forms do not substantiate income from sources such as interest, dividends, real estate, trust funds, alimony, and child support. This income must be established in other ways.

The types of verification for interest, dividends, and trust funds vary widely. For example, stockbrokers often provide periodic statements of the status of client accounts, including dividends and the manner in which they were handled. Savings accounts are generally accompanied either by periodic statements or a passbook showing deposits (including deposits of interest) and withdrawals. Letters from the source of income are also acceptable, as are copies of tax returns can also be used. In any event, continued receipt of the income over at least two years must be verified, and the amounts received must be averaged over the entire period to produce an estimate of future income.

In the case of trust income, there also should be a statement from the trustee that the income will continue for at least three (conventional) to five (HUD) years. Be careful not to include these amounts as both income and assets. If the account shows a history of regular withdrawals, the withdrawals can be considered income. If not, the total account balance represents an asset.

Retirement Benefits and Social Security

Recipients of Social Security and other retirement income receive periodic notices from the sources of income advising them of their current benefits and of the expiration date of those benefits. Copies of letters that reflect current benefits are acceptable verification. If such notices are not issued automatically, the administrator of the retirement fund should be asked for verification. Exhibit VI-11 also serves this purpose.

EXHIBIT VI-11: SAMPLE REQUEST FOR VERIFICATION OF RETIREMENT OR OTHER INCOME

Date:____________

Re: Name ________________________________
Address ______________________________
Your Identifying Number _____________

Gentlemen:

We are processing a mortgage loan application for the above-mentioned applicant(s), and they have indicated that they received income on a regular basis from you (or through you).

Your cooperation in furnishing the information requested below and promptly returning this form to us will sincerely be appreciated.

Very truly yours,

____

I/WE AUTHORIZE RELEASE OF THE INFORMATION REQUESTED BELOW:

____
(Signature of Applicant)

____
(Signature of Co-Applicant)

VERIFICATION OF OTHER INCOME

Amount of Income Received: $_____ per month/year/other:________

Source (Reason) for Income:_____________________________________

____

To your knowledge, is this income taxable to the recipient?
________ Yes ________ No
(If income is partly taxable, please explain on reverse.)

When will payment of this income stop?
___ Upon death of recipient
___ Other: (Explain and give approximate date payment will stop) ____

Information furnished by:

_________________________ _________________ _______________
(Signature) (Title) (Date)

Real Estate

Net income for real estate consists of gross rents minus an allowance for vacancies, maintenance costs, utilities included in the rent, mortgage payments, taxes, and insurance premiums.

Where there are mortgages, the verifications of those obligations generally include information on costs related to the mortgage, and the lender can estimate maintenance and vacancy deductions based on company policy or, for HUD-FHA or VA loans, quotes from the local offices. Copies of current leases should be secured to establish rental income and whether utilities are included in the rent. Schedule E of the tax return may also be required.

Several forms can be used to organize data substantiating income from real estate holdings. One is illustrated in Exhibit VI-12. Investors and agencies may not recognize income from rental properties unless the properties are shown on Schedule E, Supplemental Income Schedule, of a federal income tax return or unless current leases are provided.

Some underwriters do not require copies of leases where several properties are involved, but Schedule E has important information about mortgage interest paid on the holdings and depreciation. Not substantiating mortgage interest and depreciation may penalize the borrower when calculating income and qualification ratios.

Alimony, Child Support, and Separate Maintenance

The applicant does not have to use alimony, child support, or separate maintenance as qualifying income. Unless he or she has stated positively that it should be used, no effort needs to be made to verify it. If the applicant does intend to rely on it, however, the verification must prove not only that the applicant is entitled to receive it, but also that it is being paid.

EXHIBIT VI-12: SAMPLE SCHEDULE OF REAL ESTATE OWNED

Applicant: ____________________ Case Number: ____________

Property Address	Lender and Account Number	No. of Units	Mtge. Balance	Gross Rent	Monthly Payment*
1					
2					
3					
4					
5					
6					

*Monthly Payment includes Principal, Interest, Taxes and Insurance, taxes and insurance are included in the payment to the lender.

Will any of the above properties be sold? ______ If yes, which ones(s)?

Do not consider properties being sold: Total Gross Rent: $________

Total Net Rental Income (Gross Rent–Payments–Expenses) $____________________

Total Mortgage Payments: $________

Total Utilities, Maintenance, etc.

It is easy to verify alimony because it must be reported on tax forms as income. For other types of payment, verification is more complicated. If payments are made through a court, the court will usually verify them. If they are not, copies of canceled checks or some other evidence of payment should be requested. Deposit slips or tax returns may also be acceptable.

It must also be established that the income will continue for a reasonable time. Fannie Mae requires three years, HUD-FHA five years. Others establish no precise limits. This can be verified through a copy of the divorce decree or settlement agreement, although it is best not to insist on copies of these documents, since they contain personal information not related to eligibility for the loan.

If the applicant refuses to provide a copy of the basic document, some other form of verification is required. A certification by an attorney that he or she has seen the basic document—and that it includes specific provisions relating to the amount of the award and the term it will be paid—is one example of a substitute for the document itself.

HUD-FHA and VA sometimes accept income that is received regularly and will continue for at least five years. VA sometimes requires that income such as aid to dependent children be received for at least one-third of the life of the loan. Some private investors are more restrictive. Fannie Mae, for example, will not consider certain allowances as income if they are offset by an expense, as if the case of automobile allowances, since the cost of operating the automobile usually exceeds the allowance provided.

Regardless of investor or agency, if such income is to be used for qualification, documentation will be needed to support its amount and likelihood of continuance.

Credit History

Even if it is established that the applicant has cash to settle and sufficient income to support mortgage payments and household expenses, it is important also to establish a credit history. The applicant must have a reasonable record of paying his or her bills as agreed. This information can come directly from the lenders involved, or it can come from a consumer reporting agency bureau via a credit report.

Credit information is very sensitive, and there are laws to protect the consumer. Before doing anything with credit reports, origination personnel must be thoroughly familiar with the Fair Credit Reporting Act.

Consumer reporting agencies specialize in obtaining records on the credit history of almost everyone who has ever borrowed money. They contact national repositories of accumulated credit records for each area of the country where the applicant has lived during the most recent two-year period and prepares a credit report (Exhibit VI-13).

Each credit report must include all available public records information and must disclose whether any judgments, foreclosures, tax liens, or bankruptcies were discovered. In addition, for each debt listed, it must provide the creditor's name, the date the account was opened, the amount of the highest credit, the current status of the account, the required payment amount, the unpaid balance, and a payment history.

The consumer reporting agency must present all data in a format that is easy to read, without the need of code translations. The credit report must contain all discovered credit and legal information that is not considered obsolete under the Fair Credit Reporting Act—or at least a seven-year history for all credit and public record information.

When co-borrowers have individually obtained credit, separate repository inquiries are necessary. The results of both reports may be combined in one residential mortgage credit report if the report clearly indicates that this has been done.

If the applicant is self-employed, investors or agencies may require that a business credit report be ordered. For the most part, the same requirements that apply for personal credit reports also apply to business credit reports.

EXHIBIT VI-13: SAMPLE CREDIT REPORT (CREDCO)

CREDCO

FILE NO	REPORT TYPE	PREPARED FOR		CREDCO CONTROL NO
200120	RESIDENTIAL MORTGAGE	X Y Z MORTGAGE COMPANY	9999-9999	DD CN 072090640

RECEIVED	COMPLETED	REVISED	ATTENTION / ADDITIONAL INFORMATION
07-05-90	07-05-90		

CHARGES	CREDIT AND PUBLIC RECORDS SOURCES
NO CHARGE	TRANS UNION, TRW

BORROWER	DOE, JOHN E.	SOCIAL SECURITY NO	123-95-6698 DOB: 05-23-60
CO-BORROWER	DOE, SAMANTHA B.	SOCIAL SECURITY NO	555-33-6789 DOB: 03-09-60
ADDRESS	77 TARRYTOWN ROAD SILVER SPRING, MD 20902	MARITAL STATUS	MARRIED
		DEPENDENTS	03 CHILDREN
LENGTH	01 YEAR - OWN		

BORROWER		CO-BORROWER	
EMPLOYER	IBM CORPORATION	EMPLOYER	SAMANTHA'S SILK FLOWERS
POSITION	SYSTEMS ANALYST	POSITION	PRESIDENT/OWNER
LENGTH	18 MONTHS	LENGTH	05 YEARS
INCOME	DECLINED	INCOME	N/A
VERIFIED	07-05-90/JOHN SMITH	VERIFIED	07-05-90/NOT VER/SELF-EMP

CREDITOR ACCOUNT NUMBER	ECOA	DATE OPEN	HIGH CREDIT	PAYMENT TERMS	APPROXIMATE BALANCE	CURRENT STATUS		PAST DUE 30	60	90+	DATE LAST PAST DUE	MOS. REV.
UNITED SAVINGS												
8347398784774	J	04-89	127000	1285	126452	M-3 DEL 60	04-90	0	1	0		12
		PROP ADDR: 1092 COMMODORE COURT										
ACADEMIC FINANCIAL SERVICES												
123956698	I	05-86	10000	116	5098	I-1 CURRENT	03-90	0	0	0		24
		STUDENT LOAN										
GECC												
2349990096092	J	02-88	1000	50	750	R-1 CURRENT	06-90	0	0	0		12
CHEMICAL BANK MASTERCARD												
521178993422	I	04-88	500	0	-0-	R-1 CURRENT	06-90	0	0	0		12
DISCOVER CARD												
6111390004093	J	03-88	1000	0	-0-	R-1 CURRENT	06-90	0	0	0		24
HARRIS BANK/VISA												
4400394721724	J	04-89	-0-	0	-0-	R-U *	N/A	-	-	-		-
		NEVER USED										
BARTONVILLE BANK												
993394657	I	09-83	6686	0	CLOSED	I-1 CLOSED	09-85	0	1	0	09-84	24
NEIMAN MARCUS												
871234	U	03-80	156	0	CLOSED	R-9 CLOSED	04-89	-	-	-		-
		CHARGED TO LOSS IN 04-85 PAID 09-85										
Accounts under co-borrower:												
CITIBANK VISA												
42713399033	I	02-87	500	10	200	R-2 DEL 30	06-90	1	0	0		12
GANTOS												
N/A	I	07-89	500	10	200	R-1 CURRENT	06-90	1	0	0	03-90	12

Inquiries made in the 90 days prior to 07-05-90:
06-23-90 CHEMICAL BANK

Collections:
1. CO-BORROWER'S ACCOUNT SUBMITTED TO I.C. SYSTEMS, INC. IN 01-88 BY DR. PAUL JONES FOR $258; PAID 01-89.

Borrower's previous residence:
109 MICHAEL MANOR, SILVER SPRING, MD - 03 YEARS

Borrower's previous employment:
CATERPILLAR TRACTOR COMPANY - ELECTRICAL ENGINEER - 04 YEARS

Public records:
1. CIVIL JUDGEMENT FILED AGAINST BORROWER BY CHASE MANHATTAN ON 12-14-83 FOR $138; SATISFACTION ENTERED 02-20-84. (#81M1128855 SMITH COUNTY, ST)

2. FEDERAL TAX LIEN FILED AGAINST BORROWER IN 06-85 FOR $100. PAID 01-86. (#56100234 SMITH COUNTY, ST)

Prepared by: CREDCO INC.,
850 EAST HIGGINS ROAD #125, SCHAUMBURG, IL 60173 (800)492-8460
** END OF REPORT **

B009270

THIS CREDIT REPORT IS ISSUED ONLY TO PERMISSIBLE USERS AS DEFINED BY THE FAIR CREDIT REPORTING ACT (PUBLIC LAW 91-508) AND IS DONE SO IN THE STRICTEST OF CONFIDENCE. THIS REPORT IS FURNISHED AT THE JOINT REQUEST OF THE USER AND THE SUBJECT OF THE REPORT WHO BOTH AGREE TO INDEMNIFY CREDCO FOR INCORRECT INFORMATION OR MISUSE OF THIS REPORT. A GOOD FAITH EFFORT HAS BEEN MADE TO OBTAIN ALL INFORMATION FROM SOURCES CREDCO DEEMS AS RELIABLE BUT CREDCO CANNOT GUARANTEE THE ACCURACY OF THIS INFORMATION. CREDCO CERTIFIES THAT OUR RESIDENTIAL MORTGAGE CREDIT REPORTS COMPLY WITH THE STANDARDS SET FORTH BY FNMA, FHLMC, FmHA, FHA AND VA.

Member Associated Credit Bureaus, Inc.

EXHIBIT VI-13—*continued*

CREDCO

HOW TO INTERPRET YOUR CREDIT REPORT

FILE NO.	REPORT TYPE	PREPARED FOR	CREDCO CONTROL NO. ❶
505832	RESIDENTIAL MORTG.	THE MORTGAGE COMPANY 8888	DD CN 095225720

RECEIVED	COMPLETED	REVISED ❷	ATTENTION / ADDITIONAL INFORMATION
01-07-91	01-09-91		SHARON/LOAN #09-10-66754

CHARGES	CREDIT AND PUBLIC RECORDS SOURCES ❸
NO CHARGE	TUC, TRW, CBI/CSC, DIRECT

BORROWER	SAMPLE, SAM	SOCIAL SECURITY NO.	234-56-7891 AGE: 33
CO-BORROWER	SAMPLE, SAMANTHA	SOCIAL SECURITY NO.	567-89-1234 AGE: 32
ADDRESS	6789 MAIN STREET	MARITAL STATUS	MARRIED
	OPPORTUNITY, US 99999	DEPENDENTS	02 CHILDREN
LENGTH	01 YEAR 06 MONTHS		

BORROWER		CO-BORROWER	
EMPLOYER	ABC MANUFACTURING	EMPLOYER	SAMANTHA'S SILK FLOWERS
POSITION	MARKETING REPRESENTATIVE	POSITION	OWNER
LENGTH	03 YEARS	LENGTH	01 YEAR
INCOME	3000	INCOME	N/A
VERIFIED ❹	R. SMITH/01-08-91	VERIFIED	ALICE/01-08-91

	❺	❻	❼ (Ⓐ Ⓑ Ⓒ)	❽	❾	❿
SAMPLE CITY BANK 232427638	J	06-89 75950 724 75393	M-1 CURRENT 12-90	0 0 0		18

❶ CREDCO CONTROL NO. is a unique security control number to insure authenticity.

❷ REVISED date indicates when we last changed the original report.

❸ REPOSITORIES ACCESSED displays all sources used for credit and public record information.

CBI/CSC	The Credit Bureau, Inc./Computer Science Corporation
STW	Statewide Information Systems/Prentice Hall
TRW	TRW Information Systems
TUC	Trans Union Credit Information Corporation
DIRECT	Direct searches by CREDCO personnel

❹ VERIFIED field is used to indicate the manner in which employment was verified.

❺ ECOA code indicates who is responsible for each account and the type of participation for that account, as follows:

U	UNDESIGNATED	Not designated by the creditor.
I	INDIVIDUAL	Individual account.
J	JOINT	Joint account.
A	AUTHORIZED USER	Authorized to use someone else's account.
S	SHARED	Joint account.
C	CO-MAKER	Joint responsibility for the account.
B	CO-SIGNER	Responsibility only in case of default on the account.
M	MAKER	Individual account.
T	TERMINATED	Closed account.

❻ PAYMENT TERMS displays the monthly liability on each account. Optionally, "REV" can be displayed on revolving accounts.

❼ CURRENT STATUS describes the current status of the account as of the date reported and, optionally, the type of account.

Column 7A displays the universal rating code or, alternatively, a three letter account type designation.
Column 7B displays the current status in our own "English" format.
Column 7C displays the date each account was last reported by the creditor.

Account type:			Universal Rating Code:			English version of the ratings:
R or REV	means	Revolving	0	means	Too new to rate	CURRENT
I or INS	means	Installment	1	means	Current	CURRENT
O or OPN	means	Open, 30 day	2	means	30 days late	DEL 30
M or MTG	means	Mortgage	3	means	60 days late	DEL 60
C or CRL	means	Line of Credit	4	means	90 days late	DEL 90
			5	means	120 days late	DEL 120
			6	means	150 days late	DEL 150
			7	means	Wage earner plan or bankruptcy	WEP/BKRP or footnoted
			8	means	Repossession or foreclosure	REPO/FCL or footnoted
			9	means	Collection or charge-off	COL/P&L or footnoted
			U	means	Unrated	footnoted

❽ PAST DUE displays number of payments received 30, 60 and 90+ days late, as reported by the creditor.

❾ DATE LAST PAST DUE displays the date of the most recent delinquency. If this information is not provided by the creditor, a footnote will be added to the tradeline indicating the most specific delinquency information we can obtain.

❿ MOS. REV. (months reviewed) is the number of months of credit history the creditor has provided.

Any debt appearing on the credit report that was not revealed at the time of application must be explained. This explanation has to be sufficiently strong to overcome the assumption that the applicant was trying to conceal the debt. Where there is a history of slow payment or problems with credit, a written explanation from the borrower of what caused the problem and how it was resolved will smooth the evaluation process.

Also, ideally every account should be brought current before the file goes to the underwriter or at least before closing. This requirement applies generally in the case of judgments or liens. Few underwriters accept assurance that these will be resolved before closing; they must be cleared before underwriting.

If there has been a bankruptcy, it must be fully discharged. The applicant must have re-established satisfactory credit since the bankruptcy. Re-establishing credit is usually thought of as renewed use of credit and the maintenance of a satisfactory record over a period of at least two years.

Families that have not used credit since a bankruptcy will be able to meet the "re-establish credit" requirement only through evidence that they have maintained a satisfactory record of paying utility and telephone bills, rent, and personal property taxes, and have been able to maintain reasonable financial reserves. The same requirements apply when no credit history has been established, although the evaluation is usually more liberal than in the case of bankrupt applicants.

Evidence of previous mortgage foreclosure is also a strong negative credit factor. Some investors will not purchase or securitize a new mortgage if the mortgagors were involved in foreclosure proceedings completed within the past three years. If, however, the foreclosure was the result of extenuating circumstances beyond the applicant's control, such as serious illness, loss of employment due to factory shutdown, and so on, it is possible for the lender to make the loan provided it meets other underwriting criteria.

Credit reports generally include information about inquiries during the past 90 days. An inquiry is simply a request for credit information from a potential creditor. The lender's request for a report to use in processing the mortgage application itself will appear as an inquiry on credit reports provided by the same reporting agency in the future.

Because an inquiry indicates that the applicant has asked for credit from some other source, it can be significant, depending on when the inquiry was made and whether or not credit was granted. This is especially true where there are inquiries from other mortgage lenders, for obvious reasons. Also, any case of rejected credit is potentially significant. Why was the application rejected?

Direct Verification

When the processor receives the credit report (which will probably arrive earlier than verifications from other sources), it should be reviewed immediately to see if includes any entries such as "information refused." Direct verifications of those accounts should be requested immediately. This may require, of course, that the applicant be contacted and asked to sign additional verification authorizations, unless the loan officer anticipated the requirement at application time.

When mortgage information is not included in the credit report, however, the processor may seek it in other ways. As with other verifications, time is important, so the request should be made as early as it is deemed necessary. Sometimes a special verification form is used, such as Exhibit VI-14.

The requirement for mortgage companies to report to credit repositories that maintain national files should help solve any problem associated with mortgage verification.

It may be necessary to secure the verification of mortgage payments information directly from the mortgagee. Fannie Mae and Freddie Mac, as well as other investors and insurers,

EXHIBIT VI-14: SAMPLE REQUEST FOR VERIFICATION OF MORTGAGE INDEBTEDNESS

(LENDER'S LETTERHEAD)
(Date)

TO: Holder of Existing Mortgage

Applicant(s) ______________
____
Case Number ______________

Gentlemen:

The applicant named above has applied for a mortgage loan and indicated a present or past mortgage with you firm on the property and with the account number shown below. Would you please furnish us the following information and make any additional comments which you believe might be helpful?

Sincerely,

Loan Processor

Release of the requested information is authorized:

______________ Applicant

______________ Applicant

Account Number ______________

Property Address ______________
____
____
____

Type of mortgage ☐ VA ☐ FHA ☐ Conventional

Date of Mortgage ______________

Date of Maturity ______________

Original Amount $______________

Present Balance $______________

Terms of Payment ______________

installments of $______________

Is the account current? ☐ Yes ☐ No

Remarks:

______________ Date

______________ Signature

______________ Title

may accept copies of canceled checks covering the past 12 months of mortgage payments as verification of payment.

Likewise, rental history is an important indication about how first-time borrowers handle their housing costs. Lenders look at future housing expense in relation to previous housing expense, especially in borderline case. If the applicant has paid rent regularly and on time in the past, it is likely he or she will make the mortgage payments regularly and on time. So it is important to verify not only how the rent was paid but whether the borrower was responsible for any utilities and maintenance costs.

Exhibit VI-15 is a form that can be used for this purpose; however, copies of canceled checks covering the most recent 12 months may are acceptable in lieu of direct verification from the landlord.

Processors frequently find that they cannot rely on the credit report for information on credit union accounts and thus must seek direct verification. Credit union accounts can be verified with the standard request for verification of deposit (VOD). You may get this information automatically when requesting deposit account information, since there is space on the VOD for loan information. However some lenders use a special form such as Exhibit VI-16 to get credit union loan balances.

Many lenders verify child care expenses to establish the amount of the obligation. While it can be assumed that child care expenses have been paid regularly if there is an obligation, it should also be verified to establish the amount of the obligation. Exhibit VI-17 is one example of a form that can be used for this purpose.

Alternative, "Low Doc" programs

Alternate documentation or so-called "low doc" programs are fairly common in mortgage lending. They can sometime be less work for the borrower and the lender, but processors must use care to follow the correct guidelines.

EXHIBIT VI-15: SAMPLE REQUEST FOR VERIFICATION OF PAYMENT OF RENT

(MORTGAGEE LETTERHEAD)
(Date)

Re: (Name of Applicant) ________
(Address) ________
____

(Name and Address of Landlord)

Dear ________________________:

The individual or family named above has applied for a mortgage loan and stated that the property identified has been rented from you.

Please provide the information requested below so that the application can be processed.

Your cooperation is appreciated.

Sincerely,

Loan Processor

RELEASE OF THE INFORMATION
IS AUTHORIZED

____
Applicant

The applicant has been a tenant since ________________________.

Total monthly rent: $____________.

Are utilities included? Yes No (Circle One)

If utilities are not included, what do you estimate the monthly utility bill to be? $____________.

Has payment of rent been satisfactory? Yes No (Circle one)

Do you have any complaints about the tenancy in general?

____

Information provided by ________________________ (Signature) ____________ (Date)

EXHIBIT VI-16: SAMPLE REQUEST FOR CREDIT UNION VERIFICATION

(LENDER'S LETTERHEAD)
(Date)

Applicant ________________
Case Number ______________

TO: Credit Union

Gentlemen:

The applicant identified above has applied for a mortgage loan and supplied the information below. We would appreciate your cooperation in providing the requested verifications and returning this letter to me at your earliest convenience.

Sincerely,

Loan Processor

☐ I am now a member of the credit union named above. My account numbers follow:

☐ I am not now a member of the credit union named above, but I am a former member and continue to maintain the following accounts:

Savings # ___________ Checking #___________ Loan(s) #___________
Other (specify)____

I hereby authorize the credit union to provide the information requested below.

____
Applicant

Present Balances: Savings $____________ Checking: $____________

Outstanding Loan Balance: $__________ Date Loan Opened:___________

Original Loan Amount: $_____________ Monthly Payment: $__________

Date	Signature	Title

EXHIBIT VI-17: SAMPLE REQUEST FOR VERIFICATION OF CHILD CARE EXPENSES

(MORTGAGEE LETTERHEAD)
(Date)

Re: (Name of Applicant) ______
(Address) ______
______

(Name and Address of person or institution providing child care)

Dear ______________________:

The individual or family named above has applied for a mortgage loan and stated that you provide child care for members of the family. Please answer the questions below and return this letter to me as soon as possible.

Your cooperation is appreciated.

Sincerely,

Loan Processor

RELEASE OF THE INFORMATION IS AUTHORIZED

____
Applicant

Name and ages of children cared for:

Name	Age	Name	Age
______	____	______	____
______	____	______	____
______	____	______	____

Total cost of care: $_______ per Day Week Month (Circle)
Enter "0" if care is provided at no cost to the parent(s).

Information provided by ______________________ (Signature) __________ (Date)

Business name or relationship to parent(s)______________________

On HUD-FHA loans, for example, employment may be verified with two years of original W-2 forms and original pay stubs covering the most recent 30-day period. The original of the W-2 form can be any of the copies of the form that the borrower did not otherwise use to attach to his or her income tax returns.

Pay stubs must contain, at a minimum, the borrower's name and social security number. The lender is required to verify by telephone all employment for the last two years. Similarly, deposit verification may be in the form of original bank statements for the most recent three-month period.

Through a few selected field offices, the VA is testing a program where the verification of employment and deposit are not required. Instead of pay stubs, there is a telephone call to the employer and bank statements are provided. Certain conventional products can also be approved with limited documentation or alternative documentation. The details vary from program to program, from company to company, and from time to time. Check agency, insurer, or investor guidelines before embarking on any low or no-doc loan applications.

In so-called "rate reduction" refinance situations, it is usually unnecessary to verify income and assets. In the HUD-FHA program, if the old mortgage is an FHA-insured mortgage and is current at closing, no verifications are needed unless the borrower will need substantial cash to close. Practically speaking, only verification of adequate closing funds is necessary. In the VA rate reduction program, even this documentation is not required if the old mortgage is current.

In summary, verification of an applicant's income, assets, and credit history is one of the processor's most important jobs. Processors who can guarantee that the completed verifications make up a true picture of the borrower's resources can be sure that they have performed their tasks with professionalism and integrity.

Fraud Prevention

Loan origination abuses frequently revolve around the applicant's income, assets, and liabilities. Inflated income creates the illusion that an applicant who would otherwise be considered a poor risk has the financial capability to meet monthly financial obligations. As such, it is critical that the verification of employment (VOE) form does not pass through the hands of interested third parties such as the applicant, seller, broker, or builder. Ultimately, the loan processor should always compare the VOE to other available data sources (such as credit report, W-2 forms, and original application) to reconcile any differences.

Other income sources are not as easy to verify. The most notoriously troublesome include income from assets (rental, dividends, and interest), alimony or child support receipts, and income generated from a self-owned business. Where such income types are reported, the loan processor should carefully evaluate supporting documentation for accuracy and simply to determine if it makes sense.

Too often, loan processors and underwriters feel they are not sophisticated enough to analyze this type of data and err by taking it on face value. You need be an expert to spot the majority of inconsistencies and problems discussed in this section. Often the fraud is simple and unsophisticated. If you apply common sense and raise the right questions, you will find the problems.

Warning Signals

Numerous warning signals can alert you to fraudulent information on a credit application.

Verification of Employment (VOE)

- There are similarities in names of seller and applicant.
- VOE is not submitted on letterhead.
- There is an out-of-town employer.

- Current and prior employment overlap.
- The date of hire is a weekend or holiday.
- Income is primarily commissions (self-employed).
- The employer uses a mail drop or post office box address.
- The borrower changed profession between the previous and current employer.
- There is an illegible signature with no further identification.
- The business entity is not in good standing or is not registered with applicable regulatory agencies.
- The co-borrower's maiden name is the same as the signature of the employer (self-employed).
- VOE was completed the same day as ordered, indicating it was hand-carried.
- VOE says there is a company car but the application shows an auto loan.
- There are deletions and crossouts.
- Numbers have been "squeezed-in."
- VOE is uncreased or unfolded, such that it may have been hand-carried.
- Income is not commensurate with the type of employment.
- The verification source (secretary or relative) is inappropriate. Verification should come from the personnel department.
- The employee is paid monthly instead of weekly or biweekly.
- There are no prior earnings on the VOE.
- The borrower is a business professional (may be self-employed).
- There is an answering machine or answering service at the place of business (may indicate self-employed).

Payroll Check Stub

- The company name is not printed on the stub.
- The employee name is not printed.

- The stub is handwritten, even though it's a large company.
- Pay is in round dollar amounts.
- Debts are reflected as a deduction from pay (credit union loans, etc.) that were not disclosed on the loan application.
- The sequence of payroll check numbers does not jibe with payroll dates.

W-2 Form

- The employer identification number is formatted other than as xx-xxxxxxx or other than numeric (could be invalid).
- FICA wages/taxes and local taxes (where applicable) exceed ceilings or set percentages.
- The copy submitted is not the employee's copy (copy C).
- There are different typefaces within the form.
- The form is handwritten or clumsily typed—even though the employer is a large company.
- Pay is shown as a round dollar amount—especially suspicious for applicants paid on an hourly basis.

Tax Return Form 1040

- Tax returns are not signed and dated by borrower.
- The address or profession does not agree with other information submitted on the loan application.
- There are no estimated tax payments for a self-employed borrower (Schedule SE required).
- A paid preparer signs all copies of the 1040 form, including the taxpayer's copy. Generally a paid preparer will not do this.
- A paid preparer hand-writes the tax return.
- A different paid preparer is used each year.

- The borrower files Schedule G (showing income averaging), which is for taxpayers with income that fluctuates from year to year.
- Type or handwriting varies within the return.
- There is evidence of ink eradication or other alterations.
- Self-employment income is shown as wages and salaries.
- Income or deductions are shown in an even dollar amount.
- A high-bracket taxpayer does not use a professional tax preparer. A high-bracket taxpayer shows few or no deductions or tax shelters.

Schedule A, Itemized Deductions

- Real estate taxes have been paid but no property is owned.
- No mortgage interest has been paid, yet the borrower shows ownership of property (or vice versa).
- A large amount of interest was paid, but few creditors are shown on the loan application or credit report.

Schedule B, Interest and Dividend Income

- The amount or source of income does not agree with information submitted on the loan application.
- No dividends were earned on stocks owned.
- A borrower with substantial cash in the bank shows little or no related interest income.

Schedule C, Profit/Loss from Business Owned

- Gross income does not agree with total income on Form 1099.
- The borrower shows interest expense but no related loan (business loans with personal liability).

- The borrower takes a depreciation deduction for real estate not disclosed (or vice versa).
- There is no IRA or Keogh deduction.
- No salaries were paid in the case of a non-commission company.
- No cost of goods is shown for retail or similar operations.
- No Schedule SE was filed (computation of self-employed tax).

Schedule E, Rents and Royalties

- Net income from rents plus depreciation does not equal cash flow submitted by the borrower.
- Additional properties were listed but not shown on the loan application.
- The borrower shows partnership income. (He or she may be liable as a general partner for the partnership's debts).

Case Examples

1. A recent case in Virginia clearly illustrates the need to use common sense when evaluating income documentation. Study the inconsistencies in this file:

- The employer's copy of the W-2 form was submitted.
- The submitted W-2 form lacked the employer's ID number.
- No applicant's name or account number was provided on the VOD.
- The credit report did not verify the applicant's employment.
- The VOE was returned stating that no such person worked for that company.

Despite the above problems, all the lender did was call the real estate broker to inquire about the returned VOE. The broker replied, "I will take care of it." And he did.

A few days later, the lender received a written verification (not a VOE) from the employer (a medical center) that was not on letterhead, contained numerous grammatical errors, lacked a phone number, was dated on a Sunday, and had a printed signature for the doctor/employer.

The applicant was actually an unemployed straw buyer. A simple phone call to the medical center would have easily detected fraud.

2. A case in Texas emphasizes the need to be alert to post office box addresses for employers. In this case the false VOE was sent to a post office box owned by the investor-mortgagor. The employer was a national airline company known to be headquartered in another state. This fraud was discovered during a post-closing reverification, but the loan had gone into default and a claim had been paid.
3. In Chicago, the W-2 forms submitted for a certain applicant were typed out, not machine-printed (i.e., computer-generated). The purported employer was at that time one of the ten largest companies in the U.S. The insurer of this loan tagged this case for a reverification of employment check, which revealed that the original VOE was falsified in the same manner as the W-2 form.
4. In New York, payroll check stubs for cases submitted by the same broker showed inconsistencies. These incongruities would have been easy to spot had the loan processor taken a few extra seconds to review the submitted exhibits. In one case, the check number sequence differed from the payroll dates. For example, the check stub for June 1 was numbered 100, and the check stubs for July and August were numbered 83 and 78, respectively. In the second case, the check

numbers were consecutive; however, the employer had many employees.

The following cases are good illustrations of how mortgage finance fraud is often crude, basic, and easy to spot by simply comparing information such as numbers and dates.

5. A VOE was for an out-of-town employer and was signed by a secretary instead of the personnel or payroll section. While having the applicant's employers in a different city is plausible for a sales position, this particular applicant was salaried. Since it would have meant a long-distance phone call, the lender decided not to make a telephone check. The lender should have followed his original hunch—the VOE was falsified.
6. Do not let tax returns overwhelm you. Some of the fraud found in reviewing the 1040 form is easy to recognize. Consider the case in California where the submitted tax return contained the following discrepancies:

- It was handwritten by a self-employed doctor who earned over $275,000 per year.
- He was indebted to various finance companies.
- No interest income was shown on a reported $125,000 savings account.
- In determining net income, there was no cost identified for salaried employees (receptionist, etc.).
- There were no estimated tax payments.
- The 1040 form showed real estate taxes paid but no real estate was owned.
- There were no dividends on a substantial amount of claimed stock ownership.
- Office rent was $300 per month (much too low for a doctor's office).

- The doctor was actually a plumber who was paid to be a straw buyer for this fraudulently originated loan. The lender could have confirmed the existence of the doctor's office by checking the phone book for the "doctor"—he wasn't listed. Also, the applicant should have been called in to explain the problems with the 1040.

In short, you need not be a tax expert to recognize such mistakes as these.

Down Payment/Assets to Close

Perhaps the most prevalent type of fraud committed in a loan transaction relates to assets needed to close. Potential mortgagors commonly have insufficient monies for the required down payment or want to save whatever assets they do have. You must use care in determining the availability and adequacy of the necessary funds to close.

Take a step back and see if there is any "funny money" involved in the transaction. Typically, if the mortgagor cannot or will not make the down payment, there are others involved in the transaction willing to provide the necessary monies—namely the seller, builder, or real estate broker.

Warning Signals

Several games are commonly played in an attempt to hide the true source of the down payment. Identifying such charades is fairly simple in most cases.

- Unusual source of funds, such as sale of personal property (e.g., a coin collection); promissory notes on other real estate; or repayment of a debt.
- Substantial cash on deposit. (Most mortgagors will put only the minimum down.)
- No bank account.
- A small employer has a credit union.

- An escrow receipt is used as a verification of funds.
- There is an equity trade or exchange (the mortgagor exchanging his or her current residence for the down payment).
- There is substantial cash on hand.
- Sweat equity has been claimed.
- There are gift letters.

Verification of Deposit (VOD)

- VODs have their own complement of warning signals:
- Cash in the bank is insufficient to close.
- The bank account is new (so verify the previous one.
- There is a round dollar amount (especially on interest-bearing accounts.
- The closing check is drawn on a different bank.
- The buyer has no accounts ("I don't believe in banks"), but there is a VOD in the file.
- The loan is secured by a checking or savings account.
- There is an illegible signature with no further identification.
- There were significant changes in the balance from two months prior to the date of verification.
- There is an excessive balance in the checking account versus the savings account.
- The date of verification by the bank is a weekend or holiday (per a perpetual calendar).
- The VOD was completed the same day as ordered.
- There are deletions and crossouts.
- Numbers have been "squeezed-in."
- The VOD is not creased or folded, suggesting it may have been hand-carried.
- Use of a post office box for depository is not typical for the area or company.
- Checking accounts show an average two-month balance exactly equal to the present balance.

- Funds for the down payment have been on deposit for a short period.
- Young borrowers show substantial cash in the bank.
- Type or handwriting is identical throughout the VOD form.
- A low-income borrower shows large cash on deposit.
- The account is not in the borrower's name or is in a joint account with a third party.

Case Examples

1. The source of funds for the down payment in a case in Atlanta was the mortgagor's employer's credit union. However, the employer was a small church located in a rural area outside of Atlanta, and the address was a post office box number. An investigation revealed that while the employer (the church) existed, the credit union did not. Small employers typically do not have either credit unions or a post office box address for a depository. Both occurrences should raise your concern.
2. In a case in Georgia involving a joint bank account, it was discovered that that account was actually the real estate broker's account. The broker simply added each prospective mortgagor's name to it to show sufficient assets to close. At one point this joint account had 17 different mortgagor names on it. While the account, when verified by the lender, reflected only the applicant/mortgagor's name, it also indicated "joint account." The lender should have determined the identity of the other depositor.
3. In a case in Texas, the mortgagor stated that the monies to be used for low down payment ". . .will come from monies buried in his flower bed." The loan processor called and asked for the source of these monies. The mortgagor confirmed that the real estate broker advised him first to borrow it, then bury it in his flower

bed, and finally, advise the lender of where his down payment was located.

4. In a case in Tennessee, the mortgagor's down payment was to come from "sweat equity" performed on the subject property for an amount equal to $1,500. The required repair items for the sweat equity included replacing roof shingles, replacing a bathtub, and regrading the backyard. The information the loan processor missed was that the mortgagor was a 71 year-old widow. In this case, the seller completed all the repairs and the mortgagor was used as a straw buyer.
5. A recent case in Michigan revealed a VOD that showed a new, unsecured loan. When questioned about this loan, the mortgagor claimed it was for new furniture, a TV, and a stereo. The source of funds for closing was a gift letter from an aunt. When the bank was called for more information about the unsecured loan, it advised that the purpose of the loan was a down payment on the subject property.
6. In a case in California, an applicant was to sell some expensive jewelry to raise the necessary down payment. The submitted financial statement reflected the existence and value of the jewelry; however, there was no insurance coverage for these "valuable" assets. When asked to provide an independent appraisal of the jewelry, the applicant withdrew his application.
7. A large percentage of gift letters are actually seller-assisted financing or a borrowed down payment. In a recent case in Washington, the original application stated that the source of closing funds was an impending sale of stock. This reference was then crossed through and the words "gifts from cousin" were inserted. When the cousin was called to confirm the gift's legitimacy, he replied that the mortgagor was not related to him and, in fact, he didn't even know him.

8. Soft market areas provide an abundance of examples of unethical financing practices. In Denver, a builder having trouble unloading its housing inventory started taking mortgagors' second trusts on other real estate for down payment. Unfortunately, the mortgagors either didn't own any other real estate or had insufficient equity in the real estate.

To conclude, whenever there is a selling, pledging, or trading of an asset or assets for the down payment, the loan processor must verify that the assets exist (title evidence), verify their value (appraisal), and verify the mortgagor's equity position.

Credit Report

Like the lender application, the credit report lists many items you can compare with other credit documents for consistency and accuracy. If adverse credit is reported, review carefully any explanations by the mortgagor and, if any questions develop, call the mortgagor again.

Warning Signals

- Here are some warning signals for the credit report:
- The mortgagor's employment cannot be confirmed.
- Employment information and history varies on the loan application and VOE.
- There is no credit (possible use of alias).
- Employment or residence data varies from other sources.
- Recent inquiries are on record from other mortgage lenders.
- The Social Security number is invalid or inconsistent.
- "AKA" or "DBA" is indicated.

- All accounts were paid in full recently—possibly the result of a new, undisclosed consolidation loan.
- Indebtedness disclosed on the loan application varies from that on the credit report.
- The date of the credit report doesn't jibe with the loan application.
- The length of time on file is inconsistent with the buyer's age.
- The applicant is over 25 but has no credit history.
- Personal data is not consistent with the handwritten application.
- Late payments are attributed to unemployment because of illness/layoff, but VOE income does not appear to be less during this period.
- Nicknames have no relation to the real name; Buddy, Ace, Lefty, and so on.
- The borrower cannot be reached at the stated place of business.
- There are multiple Social Security numbers or names.
- All trade lines were opened at the same time, for no apparent reason.
- Spouse claims no credit (note the ECOA).
- All trade line balances end in zero.
- The pattern of delinquency is inconsistent with the letter of explanation.

Case Examples

1. Beware of falsified Social Security numbers. A case in Texas involved a credit report that stated "new to file since 1/90." This date was just a month before the date of the credit report. The broker and mortgagor were setting up a new credit history based on a different Social Security number.
2. In a case in Kansas City, the credit report reflected no credit for the 45-year-old mortgagor, who had been married for 20 years and who lived in the same area

for over 30 years. While he had supposedly worked for the same company for 17 years, the credit report could not confirm employment. Further, the lender application revealed that the mortgagor owned two late-model cars, a boat, and a motorcycle.

This scenario sounded too good to be true, and when the employer and mortgagor were called, it was discovered that the mortgagor did not exist—at least not under his given name. This transaction was actually a scam developed by a real estate broker to set up a false identity and a straw buyer.

3. Sometimes the explanations of poor credit can raise more questions and problems that they correct. In Maryland, a mortgagor explained that the reason he has some late payments was because he had fallen behind in his child support and alimony payments. While this may or may not be a legitimate excuse, the obligation for support and alimony was not mentioned or included in the overall application as a liability or debt, which would, of course, adversely affect the income-to-debt ratio.
4. In another case involving a letter of explanation, the mortgagor claimed that the late payments were due to being laid off for six months during the prior year. However, both the VOE and W-2 form for that year showed no reduction in income. The mortgagor's explanation was accurate: the VOE and W-2 form were both falsified.

Now that we've considered the various types of documentation that help evaluate the buyer, we'll turn our attention to the work of the underwriter.

7

The Final Application and Submission to Underwriting

Previous chapters have discussed taking the application, ordering and evaluating the appraisal of property, and ordering the documentation to support evaluation of the borrower. When all of that is done, the underwriter can evaluate the loan.

Actually, underwriting is a continuous process. At each of the stages described, someone has evaluated the accuracy and completeness of material being collected and made preliminary decisions about eligibility. By now, however, there should be nothing obvious in the file that makes the loan ineligible.

Many conventional investors will accept the handwritten initial application, so final underwriting may begin immediately after all the information is in the file—provided there have been no changes as a result of the verification process.

In most conventional loan situations there is no need to copy the initial application if it was signed by every applicant when it was taken and there have been no changes. However, if there have been any changes, or if a handwritten application is being converted to a typewritten or computer generated final one, new signatures will be needed. Conventional financing permits signing of the final, updated application at closing.

If the application is to be submitted HUD-FHA for insurance, HUD will permit the final URLA and the final Addendum to the URLA (HUD-92900-A) (Exhibit VII-1) to be signed by the borrowers anytime before or at closing provided an initial addendum and URLA are signed by the borrower before the loan is underwritten. The underwriter may condition the loan approval for the final URLA and final addendum to be signed and dated by the borrowers. In any case the underwriter must have the final URLA (singed or unsigned) before underwriting the loan application.

Addendum to the URLA

The VA will allow the borrower to sign the URLA and the addendum anytime prior to closing or submission to VA.

This section will discuss the addendum and the documentation that goes to HUD-FHA or VA with the application and how it should be put together. Various HUD-FHA and VA offices have their own local requirements. Our discussion is based on national requirements, which may sometimes be modified in the field. Lenders need to ensure that local variations are observed.

The addendum itself is a five-page form. Pages 1 and 2 contain statutory and regulatory information and certifications. Pages 3 and 4 contain the direct endorsement lender's approval/certifications and the borrower certification. Page 5 contains the VA Commitment for Guaranty. The following summarizes procedures in different programs.

In general, for HUD-FHA loans:

- Page 1 of the initial Addendum should be signed by the interviewer. Page 1 of the final addendum must be signed by an officer of the company.
- Page 3 (interview information) of the final URLA does not have to be completed and signed by the interviewer

EXHIBIT VII-1: HUD-FHA ADDENDUM—FORM 92900-A

OMB Approval Nos. V.A.: 2900-0144
HUD: 2502-0059

HUD/V.A. Addendum to Uniform Residential Loan Application

Part I - Identifying Information (mark the type of application)

1. ☐ **V.A.** Application for Home Loan Guaranty ☐ **HUD/FHA** Application for Insurance under the National Housing Act

2. Agency Case Number (include any suffix):

3. Lender's Case Number:

4. Section of the Act: (for HUD cases)

5. Borrower's Name & Present Address (include zip code)

6. Property Address (including name of subdivision, lot & block no. & zip code):

7. Loan Amount (include the UFMIP if for HUD or Funding Fee if for V.A.) $

8. Interest Rate: %

9. Proposed Maturity: yrs. mos.

10. Discount Amt.: (only if borrower is permitted to pay)

11. Amount of Up Front Premium: $

12a. Amount of Annual Premium: $ /month

12b. Term of Annual Premium: months

13. Lender's I.D. Code:

14. Sponsor/Agent I.D. Code:

15. **Lender's Name & Address (include zip code)**

16. Name & Address of Sponsor/Agent:

17. Lender's Telephone Number:

(Type or Print all entries clearly)

V.A.: The veteran and the lender hereby apply to the Secretary of Veterans Affairs for Guaranty of the loan described here under Section 3710, Chapter 37, Title 38, United States Code, to the full extent permitted by the veteran's entitlement and severally agree that the Regulations promulgated pursuant to Chapter 37, and in effect on the date of the loan shall govern the rights, duties, and liabilities of the parties.

18. First Time Homebuyer?
a. ☐ Yes
b. ☐ No

19. **V.A. Only:** Title will be Vested in:
☐ Veteran
☐ Veteran & Spouse
☐ Other (specify):

20. Purpose of Loan (blocks 9 - 12 are for V.A. loans only)
1) ☐ Purchase Existing Home Previously Occupied
2) ☐ Finance Improvements to Existing Property
3) ☐ Refinance (Refi.)
4) ☐ Purchase New Condo. Unit
5) ☐ Purchase Existing Condo. Unit
6) ☐ Purchase Existing Home Not Previously Occupied
7) ☐ Construct Home (proceeds to be paid out during construction)
8) ☐ Finance Co-op Purchase
9) ☐ Purchase Permanently Sited Manufactured Home
10) ☐ Purchase Permanently Sited Manufactured Home & Lot
11) ☐ Refi. Permanently Sited Manufactured Home to Buy Lot
12) ☐ Refi. Permanently Sited Manufactured Home/Lot Loan

Part II - Lender's Certification

21. The undersigned lender makes the following certifications to induce the Department of Veterans Affairs to issue a certificate of commitment to guarantee the subject loan or a Loan Guaranty Certificate under Title 38, U.S. Code, or to induce the Department of Housing and Urban Development - Federal Housing Commissioner to issue a firm commitment for mortgage insurance or a Mortgage Insurance Certificate under the National Housing Act.

A. The loan terms furnished in the Uniform Residential Loan Application and this Addendum are true, accurate and complete.

B. The information contained in the Uniform Residential Loan Application and this Addendum was obtained directly from the borrower by a full-time employee of the undersigned lender or its duly authorized agent and is true to the best of the lender's knowledge and belief.

C. The credit report submitted on the subject borrower (and co-borrower, if any) was ordered by the undersigned lender or its duly authorized agent directly from the credit bureau which prepared the report and was received directly from said credit bureau.

D. The verification of employment and verification of deposits were requested and received by the lender or its duly authorized agent without passing through the hands of any third persons and are true to the best of the lender's knowledge and belief.

E. The Uniform Residential Loan Application and this Addendum were signed by the borrower after all sections were completed.

F. This proposed loan to the named borrower meets the income and credit requirements of the governing law in the judgment of the undersigned.

G. To the best of my knowledge and belief, I and my firm and its principals: **(1)** are not presently debarred, suspended, proposed for debarment, declared ineligible, or voluntarily excluded from covered transactions by any Federal department or agency; **(2)** have not, within a three-year period preceding this proposal, been convicted of or had a civil judgment rendered against them for (a) commission of fraud or a criminal offense in connection with obtaining, attempting to obtain, or performing a public (Federal, State or local) transaction or contract under a public transaction; (b) violation of Federal or State antitrust statutes or commission of embezzlement, theft, forgery, bribery, falsification or destruction of records, making false statements, or receiving stolen property; **(3)** are not presently indicted for or otherwise criminally or civilly charged by a governmental entity (Federal, State or local) with commission of any of the offenses enumerated in paragraph G(2) of this certification; and **(4)** have not, within a three-year period preceding this application/proposal, had one or more public transactions (Federal, State or local) terminated for cause or default.

Items "H" through "J" are to be completed as applicable for V.A. loans only.

H. The names and functions of any duly authorized agents who developed on behalf of the lender any of the information or supporting credit data submitted are as follows:

Name & Address:

Function: (e.g. obtained information on the Uniform Residential Loan Application, ordered credit report, verifications of employment, deposits, etc.)

If no agent is shown above, the undersigned lender affirmatively certifies that all information and supporting credit data were obtained directly by the lender.

I. The undersigned lender understands and agrees that it is responsible for the omissions, errors, or acts of agents identified in item H as to the functions with which they are identified.

J. The proposed loan conforms otherwise with the applicable provisions of Title 38, U.S. Code, and of the regulations concerning guaranty or insurance of loans to veterans.

Signature & Title of Officer of Lender:

Date:

X

V.A. Form **26-1802a** Dec. 1991 form **HUD-92900-A (12/91)**

VMP -475R (9203).01 Page 1 of 5

VMP MORTGAGE FORMS • (313)293-8100 • (800)521-7291

EXHIBIT VII-1—*continued*

PART III — Notices to Borrowers Public Reporting Burden for this collection of information is estimated to average 0.10 hours per response, including the time for reviewing instructions, searching existing data sources, gathering and maintaining the data needed, and completing and reviewing the collection of information. Send comments regarding this burden estimate or any other aspect of this collection of information, including suggestions for reducing this burden, to the Office of Information Policies and Systems, U.S. Department of Housing and Urban Development, Washington D.C. 20410-3600; and to the Office of Information and Regulatory Affairs, Office of Management and Budget, Washington, D.C. 20503.

Privacy Act Information The information requested on the Uniform Residential Loan Application and this Addendum is authorized by 38 U.S.C. 3710 (if for DVA) and 12 U.S.C. 1701 et seq. (if for HUD/FHA). The Debt Collection Act of 1982, Pub. Law 97-365, and HUD's Housing and Community Development Act of 1987, 42 U.S.C. 3543, require persons applying for a federally insured or guaranteed loan to furnish his/her social security number (SSN). You must provide all the requested information, including your SSN. HUD and/or V.A. may conduct a computer match to verify the information you provide. HUD and/or V.A. may disclose certain information to Federal, State and local agencies when relevant to civil, criminal, or regulatory investigations and prosecutions. It will not otherwise be disclosed or released outside of HUD or V.A., except as required and permitted by law. The information will be used to determine whether you qualify as a mortgagor. Any disclosure of information outside V.A. or HUD/FHA will be made only as permitted by law. Failure to provide any of the requested information, including SSN, may result in disapproval of your loan application.

This is notice to you as required by the Right to Financial Privacy Act of 1978 that V.A. or HUD/FHA has a right of access to financial records held by financial institutions in connection with the consideration or administration of assistance to you. Financial records involving your transaction will be available to V.A. and HUD/FHA without further notice or authorization but will not be disclosed or released by this institution to another Government Agency or Department without your consent except as required or permitted by law.

Caution Delinquencies, defaults, foreclosures and abuses of mortgage loans involving programs of the Federal Government can be costly and detrimental to your credit, now and in the future. The lender in this transaction, its agents and assigns as well as the Federal Government, its agencies, agents and assigns, are authorized to take any and all of the following actions in the event loan payments become delinquent on the mortgage loan described in the attached application: (1) Report your name and account information to a credit bureau; (2) Assess additional interest and penalty charges for the period of time that payment is not made; (3) Assess charges to cover additional administrative costs incurred by the Government to service your account; (4) Offset amounts owed to you under other Federal programs; (5) Refer your account to a private attorney, collection agency or mortgage servicing agency to collect the amount due, foreclose the mortgage, sell the property and seek judgment against you for any deficiency; (6) Refer your account to the Department of Justice for litigation in the courts; (7) If you are a current or retired Federal employee, take action to offset your salary, or civil service retirement benefits; (8) Refer your debt to the Internal Revenue Service for offset against any amount owed to you as an income tax refund; and (9) Report any resulting written-off debt of yours to the Internal Revenue Service as your taxable income. All of these actions can and will be used to recover any debts owed when it is determined to be in the interest of the lender and/or the Federal Government to do so.

PART IV - Borrower Certification

22. **Complete the following for a HUD/FHA Mortgage.** 22**a**. Do you own or have you sold **other** real estate within the past 60 months on which there was a HUD/FHA mortgage? ☐ Yes ☐ No	Is it to be sold? ☐ Yes ☐ No	22**b**. Sales Price $	22**c**. Original Mortgage Amount $

22**d**. Address:

22**e**. If the dwelling to be covered by this mortgage is to be rented, is it a part of, adjacent or contiguous to any project subdivision or group of concentrated rental properties involving eight or more dwelling units in which you have any financial interest? ☐ Yes ☐ No If "Yes" give details.

22**f**. Do you own more than four dwellings? ☐ Yes ☐ No If "Yes" submit form HUD-92561.

23. **Complete for V.A. - Guaranteed Mortgage.** Have you ever had a V.A. home Loan? ☐ Yes ☐ No

24. **Applicable for Both V.A. & HUD.** As a home loan borrower, you will be legally obligated to make the mortgage payments called for by your mortgage loan contract. The fact that you dispose of your property after the loan has been made **will not relieve you of liability for making these payments. Payment of the loan in full is ordinarily the way liability on a mortgage note is ended.** Some home buyers have the mistaken impression that if they sell their homes when they move to another locality, or dispose of it for any other reasons, they are no longer liable for the mortgage payments and that liability for these payments is solely that of the new owners. Even though the new owners may agree in writing to assume liability for your mortgage payments, this assumption agreement will not relieve you from liability to the holder of the note which you signed when you obtained the loan to buy the property. Unless you are able to sell the property to a buyer who is acceptable to V.A. or to HUD/FHA and who will assume the payment of your obligation to the lender, you will not be relieved from liability to repay any claim which V.A. or HUD/FHA may be required to pay your lender on account of default in your loan payments. **The amount of any such claim payment will be a debt owed by you to the Federal Government.** This debt will be the object of established collection procedures.

25. **I, the Undersigned Borrower(s) Certify that:**

(1) I have read and understand the foregoing concerning my liability on the loan and Part III Notices to Borrowers.

(2) **Occupancy:** (for V.A. only - mark the applicable box)

☐ **(a)** I now actually occupy the above-described property as my home or intend to move into and occupy said property as my home within a reasonable period of time or intend to reoccupy it after the completion of major alterations, repairs or improvements.

☐ **(b)** My spouse is on active military duty and in his or her absence, I occupy or intend to occupy the property securing this loan as my home.

☐ **(c)** I previously occupied the property securing this loan as my home. (for interest rate reductions)

☐ **(d)** While my spouse was on active military duty and unable to occupy the property securing this loan, I previously occupied the property that is securing this loan as my home. (for interest rate reduction loans)

Note: If box **2b** or **2d** is checked, the veteran's spouse must also sign below.

(3) Mark the applicable box (not applicable for Home Improvement or Refinancing Loan) I have been informed that ($) is:

☐ the reasonable value of the property as determined by V.A. or;

☐ the statement of appraised value as determined by HUD/FHA.

Note: If the contract price or cost exceeds the V.A. "Reasonable Value" or HUD/FHA "Statement of Appraised Value," mark either item (a) or item (b), whichever is applicable.

☐ **(a)** I was aware of this valuation when I signed my contract and I have paid or will pay in cash from my own resources at or prior to loan closing a sum equal to the difference between the contract purchase price or cost and the V.A. or HUD/FHA established value. I do not and will not have outstanding after loan closing any unpaid contractual obligation on account of such cash payment;

☐ **(b)** I was not aware of this valuation when I signed my contract but have elected to complete the transaction at the contract purchase price or cost. I have paid or will pay in cash from my own resources at or prior to loan closing a sum equal to the difference between contract purchase price or cost and the V.A. or HUD/FHA established value. I do not and will not have outstanding after loan closing any unpaid contractual obligation on account of such cash payment.

(4) Neither I, nor anyone authorized to act for me, will refuse to sell or rent, after the making of a bona fide offer, or refuse to negotiate for the sale or rental of, or otherwise make unavailable or deny the dwelling or property covered by his/her loan to any person because of race, color, religion, sex, handicap, familial status or national origin. I recognize that any restrictive covenant on this property relating to race, color, religion, sex, handicap, familial status or national origin is illegal and void and civil action for preventive relief may be brought by the Attorney General of the United States in any appropriate U.S. District Court against any person responsible for the violation of the applicable law.

(5) All information in this application is given for the purpose of obtaining a loan to be insured under the National Housing Act or guaranteed by the Department of Veterans Affairs and the information in the Uniform Residential Loan Application and this Addendum is true and complete to the best of my knowledge and belief. Verification may be obtained from any source named herein.

(6) **For HUD Only** (for properties constructed prior to 1978) I have received information on lead paint poisoning. ☐ Yes ☐ Not Applicable

(7) **I am aware that neither HUD/FHA nor V.A. warrants the condition or value of the property.**

Signature(s) of Borrower(s) - **Do not sign** unless this application is fully completed. Read the certifications carefully & review accuracy of this application. | Date:

X

V.A. Form **26-1866a** Federal statutes provide severe penalties for any fraud, intentional misrepresentation, or criminal connivance or conspiracy purposed to influence the issuance of any guaranty or insurance by the V.A. Secretary or the HUD/FHA Commissioner. form **HUD-92900-A**

Page 2 of 5

EXHIBIT VII-1—*continued*

U.S. Department of Housing and Urban Development

Direct Endorsement Approval for a HUD/FHA - Insured Mortgage

1. ☐ **HUD/FHA** Application for Insurance under the National Housing Act	2. Agency Case Number (include any suffix):	3. Lender's Case Number:	4. Section of the Act:

5. Borrower's Name & Present Address (include zip code)	7. Loan Amount (include the UFMIP): $	8. Interest Rate: %	9. Proposed Maturity: yrs. mos.
6. Property Address (including name of subdivision, lot & block no. & zip code):	10. Discount Amt.: (only if borrower is permitted to pay)	11. Amount of Up Front Premium: $	12a. Amount of Annual Premium: $ /month
			12b. Term of Annual Premium: months
	13. Lender's I.D. Code:	14. Sponsor/Agent I.D. Code:	

15. **Lender's Name & Address (include zip code)**	16. Name & Address of Sponsor/Agent:
(Type or Print all entries clearly)	17. Lender's Telephone Number:

☐ **Approved:** Approved subject to the additional conditions stated below, if any.

☐ **Modified & Approved as follows:**	Loan Amount (include UFMIP): $	Interest Rate: %	Proposed Maturity: yrs. mos.	Monthly Payment: $	Amount of Up Front Premium: $	Amount of Annual Premium: $	Term of Annual Premium: months

Additional Conditions:

☐ Form HUD-92544, Builder's Warranty is required.

☐ Owner-Occupancy **Not** required (delete item b of the borrower's Certification on the back of this sheet).

☐ The property is to be insured under Section 221(d)(2); a code compliance inspection is required.

This certifies, in compliance with the Right to Financial Privacy Act of 1978, that, in connection with any subsequent request for access to financial records for the purpose of considering or administering assistance to this applicant, the Department of Housing and Urban Development is in compliance with the applicable provisions of said act.

Date of Approval:	Direct Endorsement Underwriter: (signature & typed or printed name & CHUMS ID number)
Date Approval Expires:	X

VMP-475R (9203).01 — Page 3 of 5 — form **HUD-92900-A**

VMP MORTGAGE FORMS • (313)293-8100 • (800)521-7291

EXHIBIT VII-1—*continued*

Borrower's Certificate The undersigned certifies that:

(a) I will not have outstanding any other unpaid obligations contracted in connection with the mortgage transaction or the purchase of the said property except obligations which are secured by property or collateral owned by me independently of the said mortgaged property, or obligations approved by the Commissioner;

(b) One of the undersigned intends to occupy the subject property, (note: delete this item if owner-occupancy is not required by the commitment);

(c) All charges and fees collected from me as shown in the settlement statement have been paid from my own funds, and no other charges have been or will be paid by me in respect to this transaction;

(d) Neither I, nor anyone authorized to act for me, will refuse to sell or rent, after the making of a bona fide offer, or refuse to negotiate for the sale or rental of, or otherwise make unavailable or deny the dwelling or property covered by this loan to any person because of race, color, religion, sex, handicap, familial status or national origin. I recognize that any restrictive covenant on this property relating to race, color, religion, sex, handicap, familial status or national origin is illegal and void and any such covenant is hereby specifically disclaimed. I understand that civil action for preventative relief may be brought by the Attorney General of the United States in any appropriate U.S. District Court against any person responsible for a violation of this certificate.

Borrower'(s) Signature(s) & Date:

X

Lender's Certificate The undersigned certifies that to the best of its knowledge:

(a) The statements made in its application for insurance and in this Certificate are true and correct;

(b) The conditions listed above or appearing in any outstanding commitment issued under the above case number have been fulfilled;

(c) Complete disbursement of the loan has been made to the borrower, or to his/her creditors for his/her account and with his/her consent;

(d) The security instrument has been recorded and is a good and valid first lien on the property described;

(e) No charge has been made to or paid by the borrower except as permitted under HUD regulations;

(f) The copies of the credit and security instruments which are submitted herewith are true and exact copies as executed and filed for record;

(g) It has not paid any kickbacks, fees or consideration of any type, directly or indirectly, to any party in connection with this transaction except as permitted under HUD regulations and administrative instructions.

Lender's Name	Note: If the approval is executed by an agent in the name of lender, the agent must enter the lender's code number and type.	
Signature & Title of Lender's Officer & Date: X	Code Number (5 digits)	Type

form **HUD-92900-A**

EXHIBIT VII-1—*continued*

Certificate of Commitment for V.A. Home Loan Guaranty

1. ☐ V.A. Application for Home Loan Guaranty	2. Agency Case Number (include any suffix):	3. Lender's Case Number:	
5. Borrower's Name & Present Address (include zip code)	7. Loan Amount (include Funding Fee): $	8. Interest Rate: %	9. Proposed Maturity: yrs. mos.
6. Property Address (including name of subdivision, lot & block no. & zip code):	10. Discount Amt.: (only if borrower is permitted to pay)		
	13. Lender's I.D. Code:		
15. Lender's Name & Address (include zip code)		17. Lender's Telephone Number:	

(Type or Print all entries clearly)

This part is to be completed by V.A. and returned to the lender.	☐ If this box is marked, certification of active duty status as of date of note is required.	Percent of Guaranty: %

Terms of Commitment The documents submitted in connection with the loan described above on this Certificate have been examined and the loan has been determined to be eligible under Chapter 37, Title 38, U.S.C., and Regulations effective thereunder.

Upon receipt of a duly executed Certificate of Loan Disbursement* showing full compliance with the applicable regulations, the Secretary will issue a Loan Guaranty Certificate as indicated above on this Certificate, subject to any adjustment necessary under Section 36.4303(g) of the regulations upon ascertainment of the exact principal amount of the loan, or upon submission of the loan disbursement report under Section 36.4305 thereof.

In the case of a joint loan as defined in Section 36.4307 of the Regulations, the portion of such loan eligible for guaranty shall be as provided therein.

This Certificate of Commitment will expire and will be invalid 6 months from the date hereon, unless the loan described herein is closed prior to such expiration date.

* If the loan described above on this Certificate is made by the lending institution named herein, this Certificate need not be returned to V.A. Otherwise this Certificate or a copy of the agreement assigning this Certificate must accompany the Certificate of Loan Disbursement.

Secretary of Veterans Affairs, by (authorized agent): X	Issuing Office:	Date:

V.A. Form Sept. 1991 **26-1866a**

Page 5 of 5

VMP MORTGAGE FORMS • (313)293-8100 • (800)521-7291

VMP -475R (9203).01

provided the initial application contains the information and signature of the interviewer.

HUD Processed Cases

Completed, signed, and dated Pages 1 and 2 of the addendum must be included in the case binder at the time of submission for firm commitment processing. Omit pages 3 and 4; in lieu of them, the HUD field office executes a firm commitment.

Preclosing Direct Endorsement and Coinsurance Cases

Completed, signed, and dated pages 1 through 3 must be included in the case binder at time of submission for firm commitment processing. Omit page 4 of the addendum. The HUD field office executes a firm commitment on preclosing cases.

Direct Endorsement and Coinsurance Cases

Completed, signed, and dated pages 1 through 4 must be included in the case binder at the time of submission for insurance endorsement.

The applications and the addendum do not have to be signed on the same date. It is possible that a borrower would start a case as a conventional mortgage and convert the application to a government case by signing the addendum, and this would result in signatures with different dates. However, the lender's certification on the first page, part II of the addendum, must be the same date or after the date of the borrower's certification on the second page, part IV. Lenders must give the borrower a copy of the addendum.

The Worksheet

After the application is completed, the processor and the underwriter usually complete a worksheet together. In HUD-FHA cases, this is the Mortgage Credit Analysis Worksheet, HUD

Form 92900-WS (Exhibit VII-2). In VA cases, it is the VA Form 26-6393, Loan Analysis (Exhibit VII-3).

In conventional cases, investors do not generally specify worksheets, but something similar to the Fannie Mae Transmittal, FNMA Form 1008, Exhibit VII-4, serves the purpose of the credit worksheet and helps the underwriter make an orderly analysis.

HUD-FHA and VA Worksheets

For both HUD-FHA and VA, the application and addendum will be accompanied by a worksheet the underwriter uses to evaluate the application. A few sections of the HUD-FHA and VA worksheets can create frequent errors and delays.

Agency Case Number

For government loans, this is the agency case number assigned by HUD-FHA or VA. In the case of HUD-FHA it will be the same first 10 digits as the case number on the conditional commitment.

HUD-FHA assigns a 13-digit case number to properties and, with the possible exception of the last three digits, that case number stays with the property until the mortgage is paid in full or foreclosed. If a buyer is unable to complete the transaction, even after a firm commitment has been issued, an application submitted for another buyer of the same property will carry the same case number.

All 13 digits should be included. The last three digits are an ADP/Suffix code identifying the exact National Housing Act section under which you want the mortgage to be insured, including any variations. These last three digits may differ from the last three digits in the case number under which the conditional commitment was issued.

A list of the most commonly used suffixes tied to the program variations they identify is Exhibit VII-5. It includes a brief synopsis of three HUD-FHA insurance funds, at Exhibit VII-6.

EXHIBIT VII-2: MORTGAGE CREDIT ANALYSIS WORKSHEET (HUD)—FORM 92900-WS

VMP-45 (9210) VMP MORTGAGE FORMS • (313)293-8100 • (800)521-7291

Mortgage Credit Analysis Worksheet

U.S. Department of Housing and Urban Development
Office of Housing

All numbered entries in $ except where noted. OMB Approval No. 2502-0059

Case number:	Sec. of the Housing Act:	Check one: ☐ Existing Construction ☐ Proposed Construction		
1a. Borrower's name:	2a. Social Security No.:	3a. Age ▲:	4. Dependents: a. No. ▲: b. Ages:	5. Marital Status ▲ a. ☐ Married b. ☐ Separated c. ☐ Unmarried
1b. Co-Borrower's name:	2b. Social Security No.:	3b. Age ▲:		

6a. Mortgage without Up-front MIP ▲:	6b. Total UFMIP ▲:	6c. Mortgage with UFMIP ▲:	7. Appraised Value ▲: (without CC)	8. a. Total CC ▲: – b. Paid by Seller ▲: = c. Borrower's CC ▲:

9. Current housing expenses ▲:	10. Term of loan (years):	11. Interest rate (%):	12. First-time Homebuyer? ▲ ☐ Yes ☐ No	13. Adj. buy-down interest rate▲: %

14. Settlement requirements / Mortgage calculation
• For refinances, see instructions on reverse

a. Contract Sales Price ▲	
b. Repairs & Improvements ▲	
c. Borrower-paid Closing Costs (from line 8c)	
d. Sales Concessions (Subtract) ▲	
e. Mortgage Basis (Sum of Lines 14a+b+c minus 14d) ▲	
f. (1) Multiply Mort. Basis (line 14e) by 97/95/90%. [if $50,000 or less, multiply by 97%.] ▲	
(2) Multiply the Value (line 7) by 97.75%. [if $50,000 or less, multiply by 98.75%.] ▲	
g. **Mortgage (without UFMIP) Note: this may not exceed the lesser of line 14f(1) or 14f(2).** ▲	
h. Required investment (line 14e minus line 14g) ▲	
i. Discounts ▲	
j. Prepayable expenses ▲	
k. MIP paid in cash ▲	
l. Non-Realty and other items (see 14d)	
m. **Total requirements (sum of lines 14h-14l)** ▲	
n. Amount paid in ☐ cash ☐ other (explain)	
o. Amount to be paid in ☐ cash ☐ other ▲	
p. Assets available ▲	
q. 2nd mortgage proceeds (if applicable)	

15. Monthly Effective Income

a. Borrower's base pay ▲	
b. Borrower's other earnings (explain) ▲	
c. Co-borrower's base pay ▲	
d. Co-borrower's other earnings (explain) ▲	
e. Net income from real estate ▲	
f. **Gross monthly income** ▲	

16. Debts & Obligations	Monthly Payment	Unpaid Balance
a. Total installment debt	▲	▲
b. Child support, etc.		
c. Other		
d. **Total monthly payments**		

17. Future monthly payments

a. Principal & interest — 1st mortgage	
b. Monthly MIP ▲	
c. Homeowners Association Fee ▲	
d. Ground rent	
e. Principal & interest — 2nd mortgage	
f. Hazard insurance ▲	
g. Taxes & special assessments ▲	
h. **Total mortgage payment** ▲	
i. Recurring expenses (from line 16d) ▲	
j. **Total fixed payment** ▲	

18. Ratios

a. Loan-to-value (line 14g / line 7)	%
b. Mortgage Payment-to-income (line 17h / line 15f)	%
c. Total fixed payment-to-income (line 17j / line 15f)	%

19. Borrower rating (enter "A" for acceptable or "R" for reject)

a. Credit characteristics ▲	
b. Adequacy of effective income ▲	
c. Stability of effective income ▲	
d. Adequacy of available assets ▲	

20. Borrower's CAIVR #:

Co-borrower's CAIVR #:

Remarks (attach additional paper if needed):

Total Amount of Gifts: $

21. Final application decision ▲ ☐ approve ☐ reject	**22. Examiner's signature & date:** X	**23. Underwriter's signature & date:** X	**CHUMS ID#**

Previous editions are obsolete. form **HUD-92900-WS** (10/92) ref. handbook 4155.1

HUD Staff — retain the original in the case binder, and send a copy to the Headquarters Data Center, Room 4135.

VMP-45 (9210) VMP MORTGAGE FORMS • (313)293-8100 • (800)521-7291

EXHIBIT VII-2—*continued*

Public reporting burden for this collection of information is estimated to average 0.1 hour per response, including the time for reviewing instructions, searching existing data sources, gathering and maintaining the data needed, and completing and reviewing the collection of information. Send comments regarding this burden estimate or any other aspect of this collection of information, including suggestions for reducing this burden, to the Reports Management Officer, Office of Information Policies and Systems, U.S. Department of Housing and Urban Development, Washington, D.C. 20410-3600 and to the Office of Management and Budget, Paperwork Reduction Project (2502-0059), Washington, D.C. 20503. Do not send this form to either of the above addressees.

Sensitive Information: The information collected on this form is considered sensitive and is protected by the Privacy Act. The Privacy Act requires that these records be maintained with appropriate administrative, technical, and physical safeguards to ensure their security and confidentiality. In addition, these records should be protected against any anticipated threats or hazards to their security or integrity which could result in substantial harm, embarrassment, inconvenience, or unfairness to any individual on whom the information is maintained.

The **Mortgage Credit Analysis Worksheet** has been revised to reflect changes to the percentage of financeable closing costs. Several of the more important changes are discussed below:

Line 8 **Closing Costs:** On line 8a, show the total buyer's closing costs of the transaction. On line 8b, subtract any amount of buyer's closing costs paid by the seller. Line 8c is the total amount of borrower-paid financeable closing costs. Borrower-paid closing costs will be added on line 14c.

Line 14d **(Subtract Sales Concessions):** Refers to seller-paid prepaid items, personal property items, seller concessions exceeding 6% from Attachment A, etc. This does not include seller-paid closing costs from line 8b. This amount should also appear on line 14l to correctly determine total cash requirements.

Line 14f(1) **Multiply Mortgage Basis:** Multiply the amount on line 14e by 97% on the first $25,000, 95% on the amount between $25,000 and $125,000, and 90% on the remainder. (However, if line 14e is $50,000 or less, multiply the entire amount by 97%.) Note: If the value is less than sales price, then multiply the value plus closing costs by the amounts described above.

Certain types of loans (e.g., 90% new construction loans, loans to Veterans, etc.), may require alternative calculations on line 14f(1). Such variations must be indicated in the "remarks" section of the worksheet.

Line 14f(2) Do not complete for loans to Veterans under Section 203(b)(2)

* **Notes on Refinances:** The following instructions should be substituted on the appropriate lines for refinance transactions.

Line 14a. Unpaid Principal Balance
Line 14b. (Repairs not allowable on streamline refinances.)
Line 14c. Add borrower's closing costs and discount points.
Line 14d. (Subtract MIP Refund, if appropriate)
Line 14f(1) Add Appraised Value and Closing Costs; then multiply by appropriate LTV Ratio (i.e., 97/95, 85% for cash-out refinances, etc.)
Line 14g. Mortgage (without UFMIP) Note: This may not exceed lowest of lines 14e, 14f(1) or 14f(2).

---

form HUD 92900—WS
ref. handbook 4155.1

EXHIBIT VII-3: LOAN ANALYSIS (VA)—FORM 26-6393

OMB No. 2900—0523
Respondent Burden: 30 minutes

Department of Veterans Affairs — **LOAN ANALYSIS**

LOAN NUMBER

PRIVACY ACT INFORMATION: The information requested on this form is authorized by 38 U.S.C. 3710. The information will be used to determine whether a veteran-borrower qualifies for a V.A.-guaranteed loan and the lenders adherence to V.A. credit standards. Responses may be disclosed outside V.A. only if the disclosure is authorized under the Privacy Act, including the routine uses identified in the V.A. system of records, 55VA26, Loan Guaranty Home, Condominium and Manufactured Home Loan Applicant Records, Specially Adapted Housing Applicant Records, and Vendee Loan Applicant Records—V.A., published in the Federal Register.

RESPONDENT BURDEN: Public reporting burden for this collection of information is estimated to average 30 minutes per response, including the time for reviewing instructions, searching existing data sources, gathering and maintaining the data needed, and completing and reviewing the collection of information. Send comments regarding this burden estimate or any other aspect of this collection of information, including suggestions for reducing this burden, to the V.A. Clearance Officer (723), 810 Vermont Ave., NW, Washington, DC 20420; and to the Office of Management and Budget, Paperwork Reduction Program (2900-0523), Washington, DC 20503. Do NOT send requests for benefits to these addresses.

SECTION A — LOAN DATA

1. NAME OF BORROWER	2. AMOUNT OF LOAN	3. CASH DOWN PAYMENT ON PURCHASE PRICE
	$	$

SECTION B — BORROWER'S PERSONAL AND FINANCIAL STATUS

4. APPLICANT'S AGE	5. OCCUPATION OF APPLICANT	6. NUMBER OF YEARS AT PRESENT EMPLOYMENT	7. LIQUID ASSETS *(Cash, savings, bonds, etc.)*	8. CURRENT MONTHLY HOUSING EXPENSE
			$	$

9. UTILITIES INCLUDED	10. SPOUSE'S AGE	11. OCCUPATION OF SPOUSE	12. NUMBER OF YEARS AT PRESENT EMPLOYMENT	13. AGE OF DEPENDENTS
☐ YES ☐ NO				

NOTE: ROUND ALL DOLLAR AMOUNTS BELOW TO NEAREST WHOLE DOLLAR

SECTION C — ESTIMATED MONTHLY SHELTER EXPENSES *(This Property)*

	ITEMS	AMOUNT
14.	TERM OF LOAN: YEARS	
15.	MORTGAGE PAYMENT *(Principal and Interest)* @ %	$
16.	REALTY TAXES	
17.	HAZARD INSURANCE	
18.	SPECIAL ASSESSMENTS	
19.	MAINTENANCE	
20.	UTILITIES *(Including heat)*	
21.	OTHER *(HOA, Condo fees, etc.)*	
22.	TOTAL	$

SECTION D — DEBTS AND OBLIGATIONS *(Itemize and indicate by (✓) which debts considered in Section E, Line 41)*

	ITEMS	(✓)	MO. PAYMENT	UNPAID BAL.
23.			$	$
24.				
25.				
26.				
27.				
28.				
29.				
30.	JOB RELATED EXPENSE *(e.g., child-care)*			
31.	TOTAL		$	$

SECTION E — MONTHLY INCOME AND DEDUCTIONS

	ITEMS		SPOUSE	BORROWER	TOTAL
32.	GROSS SALARY OR EARNINGS FROM EMPLOYMENT		$	$	$
33.	DEDUCTIONS	FEDERAL INCOME TAX			
34.		STATE INCOME TAX			
35.		RETIREMENT OR SOCIAL SECURITY			
36.		OTHER *(Specify)*			
37.		TOTAL DEDUCTIONS	$	$	$
38.	NET TAKE-HOME PAY				
39.	PENSION, COMPENSATION OR OTHER NET INCOME *(Specify)*				
40.	TOTAL *(Sum of lines 38 and 39)*		$	$	$
41.	LESS THOSE OBLIGATIONS LISTED IN SECTION D WHICH SHOULD BE DEDUCTED FROM INCOME				
42.	TOTAL NET EFFECTIVE INCOME				$
43.	LESS ESTIMATED MONTHLY SHELTER EXPENSE *(Line 22)*				
44.	BALANCE AVAILABLE FOR FAMILY SUPPORT			GUIDELINE $	$
45.	RATIO *(Sum of items 15, 16, 17, 18, 21 and 41 ÷ sum of items 32 and 39)*				%

46. PAST CREDIT RECORD ☐ SATISFACTORY ☐ UNSATISFACTORY

47. DOES LOAN MEET V.A. CREDIT STANDARDS? *(Give reasons for decision under "Remarks," if necessary, e.g., borderline case)* ☐ YES ☐ NO

48. REMARKS *(Use reverse, if necessary)*

CRV DATA (V.A. USE)

49a. VALUE	49b. EXPIRATION DATE	49c. ECONOMIC LIFE
		YRS.

SECTION F — DISPOSITION OF APPLICATION AND UNDERWRITER CERTIFICATION

☐ Recommend that the application be approved since it meets all requirements of Chapter 37, Title 38, U.S. Code and applicable V.A. Regulations and directives.

☐ Recommend that the application be disapproved for the reasons stated under "Remarks" above.

The undersigned underwriter certifies that he/she personally reviewed and approved this loan. *(Loan was closed on the automatic basis.)*

50. DATE	51. SIGNATURE OF EXAMINER/UNDERWRITER

52. FINAL ACTION	53. DATE	54. SIGNATURE AND TITLE OF APPROVING OFFICIAL
☐ APPROVE APPLICATION ☐ REJECT APPLICATION		

V.A. FORM JAN 1992 **26-6393**

EXISTING STOCK OF V.A. FORM 26-6393, JAN 1991, WILL BE USED.

VMP-406 (9207)
VMP MORTGAGE FORMS • (313)293-8100 • (800)521-7291

EXHIBIT VII-4: TRANSMITTAL SUMMARY—FORM 1008

Uniform Underwriting and Transmittal Summary

I. Borrower and Property Information

Borrower Name ______ SSN: ______
Co-Borrower Name ______ SSN: ______
Property Address ______

Property Type
☐ Detached Housing
☐ Attached Housing
☐ Condominium
☐ PUD ☐ CO-OP

Project Classification
☐ A/III Condo ☐ E PUD ☐ 1 CO-OP
☐ B/II Condo ☐ F PUD ☐ 2 CO-OP
☐ C/I Condo ☐ III PUD
Project Name ______

Occupancy Status
☐ Primary Residence
☐ Second Home
☐ Investment Property

Number of Units ______
Sales Price $ ______
Appraised Value $ ______

II. Mortgage Information

Loan Type
☐ Conventional
☐ FHA
☐ VA
☐ FmHA

Amortization Type
☐ Fixed-Rate—Monthly Payments
☐ Fixed Rate—Bi-Weekly Payments
☐ Balloon
☐ ARM (type) ______
☐ Other (specify) ______

Loan Purpose Type
☐ Purchase
☐ Cash-Out Refinance
☐ No Cash-Out Refinance
Purpose of Refinance: ______

Lien Position
☐ First Mortgage
☐ Second Mortgage
Amount of Subordinate Financing
$ ______

Note Information
Original Loan Amount $ ______
Initial P&I Payment $ ______
Initial Note Rate ______ %
Note Date ______
Term (in months) ______

Mortgage Originator
☐ Seller
☐ Third Party
Third Party Name: ______

Buydown
☐ Yes
☐ No

If Second Mortgage
Owner of First Mortgage
☐ Fannie Mae ☐ Freddie Mac
☐ Seller/Other
Original Loan Amount of First Mortgage
$ ______

III. Underwriting Information

Underwriter's Name ______
Appraiser's Name/License # ______
Appraisal Company Name ______

Stable Monthly Income

	Borrower	Co-Borrower	Total
Base Income	$ ______	$ ______	$ ______
Other Income	$ ______	$ ______	$ ______
Positive Cash Flow (Subject Property)	$ ______	$ ______	$ ______
Total Income	$ ______	$ ______	$ ______

Qualifying Ratios	
Primary Housing Expense/Income	______ %
Total Obligations/Income	______ %

Loan-to-Value Ratios	
LTV	______ %
Total LTV	______ %

Qualifying Rate
☐ Note Rate ______ %
☐ ____ % Above Note Rate ______ %
☐ ____ % Below Note Rate ______ %
☐ Bought Down Rate ______ %
☐ Other ______ %

Proposed Monthly Payments

Borrower's Primary Residence:

First Mortgage P&I	$ ______
Second Mortgage P&I	$ ______
Hazard Insurance	$ ______
Taxes	$ ______
Mortgage Insurance	$ ______
Homeowners Association Fees	$ ______
Lease/Ground Rent	$ ______
Other	$ ______
Total Primary Housing Expense	$ ______

Other Obligations:

Negative Cash Flow (subject property)	$ ______
All Other Monthly Payments	$ ______
Total All Monthly Payments	$ ______

Underwriter Comments (If more space is needed, use page two) ______

IV. Seller, Contract, and Contact Information

Seller Name ______
Seller Address ______
Seller No. ______ Investor Loan No. ______
Seller Loan No. ______
Master Commitment No. ______
Contract No. ______

Contact Name ______
Contact Title ______
Contact's Phone Number ______ ext. ______
Contact's Signature ______
Date ______
Type of Commitment ☐ Standard ☐ Negotiated

V. Delivery Data (Completion of this section is optional; however, the data must be transmitted on the applicable Fannie Mae or Freddie Mac delivery form when the mortgage is delivered for sale.) (See FNMA 1008A/FHLMC 1077A for a list of valid codes.)

Borrower Information
Number of Borrowers ______
Borrower Age ______
Co-Borrower Age ______
Are any of the occupant borrowers first-time homebuyers? ☐ Yes ☐ No

Property Information

Number of Bedrooms	Gross Monthly Rents
Unit 1 ______	Unit 1 $ ______
Unit 2 ______	Unit 2 $ ______
Unit 3 ______	Unit 3 $ ______
Unit 4 ______	Unit 4 $ ______

Year Built ______

Information for Government Monitoring Purposes Only
Borrower Race Code ______ Borrower Gender Code ______ Co-Borrower Race Code ______ Co-Borrower Gender Code ______

Mortgage Insurance
Mortgage Insurer (MI) Code ______
Certificate Number ______
Percentage of Coverage ______ %
Adjustor Coverage ☐ Yes ☐ No

Special Feature/Characteristics Codes
Code 1 ______ Code 3 ______ Code 5 ______
Code 2 ______ Code 4 ______ Code 6 ______

Freddie Mac Form 1077 11/92
Fannie Mae Form 1008 11/92

EXHIBIT VII-5: LIST OF HUD-FHA CASE NUMBER SUFFIXES

In this list, the first number in the left-hand column is the section of the National Housing Act under which, for purposes of applications and submissions for mortgage insurance, the mortgage is insured. Technically speaking, mortgages are never insured under section 245. They are insured under section 203(b), *pursuant* to section 245. For practical purposes, though, HUD-FHA considers that they are insured under section 245, and you should use 245 in the "Section of the Act" entries in applications. There are other codes not included in this list. Some have been left out because they are inactive and lenders need not be concerned with them. Others have been left out because they are very seldom used. If you deal with military impacted areas, coinsurance, or financing sales of HUD-acquired properties using what is known as "FNMA Direct" financing, check with the HUD office for the proper codes.

Section of the Act	*Basic Code*	*Pursuant to 223(e)*	*VA CRV Cases*	*Direct Endorsement Cases*
203(b)	203	303	503	703
203(b) (ARM)	229	—	529	729
203(k) First Lien	202	302	502	702
203(k) (1st Lien ARM)	230	—	530	730
203(k) Second Lien	253	353	553	—
203(m) (Vacation Home)	200	—	500	—
203(n) (Cooperative)	260	360	560	—
213 (Cooperative)	213	313	513	—
220 (Urban Renewal)	220	320	520	—
221(d)(2)	221	321	521	721
222 (Servicemen)	222	322	522	—
234(c) (Condominium)	234	334	534	734
234(c) (ARM)	231	—	531	731
(235(i)REV (Recapture)	266	266	566	—
237 (Counseling)	237	337	537	—
245(a)/203 GPM	270	—	570	770
245(a)/203 Buydown	263	398	563	763
245(a)/203 GEM	241	—	541	741
245(a)/234 Condo GPM	242	—	542	742
245(a)/234 Condo GEM	271	—	571	771
245(b)/203 GPM	261	—	561	761
245(b)/234 Condo	262	—	562	762
All Mutual Mortgage Insurance Fund, except Coinsurance & 245, Buydown	296	398	596	796
All General Mortgage Insurance Fund, Buydown	297	398	597	797

EXHIBIT VII-6: FHA'S THREE INSURANCE FUNDS

Mutual Mortgage Insurance Fund (MMI)

1. Oldest and largest Insurance Program

2. UpFront (UFMIP) and Monthly Mortgage Insurance

3. Includes Sections 203(b)
   203(h) Disaster Assistance
   203(i) rural Areas
   203(n) Cooperatives
   244 Coinsurance
   245 GPM/GEM
   251 ARM - Other than Condominiums

4. Borrower may obtain a refund of UFMIP

General Insurance Fund (GI)

1. Monthly Mortgage Insurance (No upfront)

2. Includes Sections 234(c) Condominiums
   251 Condo - ARM
   203(k) Rehab Loans
   221(d)(2) Low and Moderate Income
   222 Service Members
   240 Fee Simple

3. No refund to borrower

Special Risk Insurance Fund (SRI)

1. Monthly Mortgage Insurance (No Upfront)

2. Includes Sections 223(e) Miscellaneous Housing Insurance
   235/265 Subsidy Loans
   237 Special Credit Risk

3. No refund to borrower

On the other hand, VA assigns the case number to the veteran. If the lender has a certificate of reasonable value (CRV) under a different veteran's name, a request for a new CRV must be prepared and submitted with a new application. On that new VA Form 26-1805, show the new veteran's name, and under it enter "CRV #— previously issued in the name of ____________________." In the blanks, enter the old CRV number and the name of the earlier veteran.

Occasionally, a CRV will be issued without the veteran having been named. When that happens, of course, only the earlier CRV number need be entered. If the appraisal is part of a master CRV, do not enter a number: VA will assign one when it gets the application.

Section of the Act

For HUD/FHA loans, this is the actual section of the National Housing Act under which the mortgage will be insured. It is not always the same as the case number suffix we discussed earlier. In some cases, a letter, or a letter and number, is included. For example, 203(b), 203(k), 221(d)(2), and 245(a) are all sections of the act.

Section 203(b), however, would appear that way in this block, but it would appear in the case number in item 1 as XXX-XXXXXX-703. The number you use here will be the first number, from the left-hand column of Exhibit VII-5. In the case of Adjustable Rate Mortgages, it will be "203(b)," "203(k)," or "234(c)," followed by "/251."

Loan Amount

This is the full loan amount including any upfront mortgage insurance premium (UFMIP) being financed. It may exceed the maximum dollar limit in the area by up to the amount of the UFMIP included.

VA has a national maximum and a funding fee, which may be financed.

Percent

If the HUD-FHA borrower is to pay a discount, enter the percentage. The 1 percent origination fee is not considered a discount; it is included in closing costs. HUD-FHA borrowers are permitted to pay discounts in any transaction, but the amount is limited to what is "reasonable and customary" in the market area at the time for the interest rate involved.

The discount entered here may not increase at closing unless the application has been reprocessed by HUD or the direct endorsement underwriter. Increases without reprocessing are one of the most frequent violations of the regulations found in HUD reviews of approved mortgagees.

For VA loans, the veteran may pay a discount only if the transaction is to refinance an existing mortgage or to build on a lot already owned by the veteran. In the latter case, evidence of ownership must accompany the application.

Signatures

The final application and addendum should be signed by the applicants before the application is submitted to the underwriter.

Submission of HUD-FHA Cases to Underwriting

About 98 percent of HUD-FHA loans are processed under the direct endorsement (DE) program. If the application is processed in the HUD-FHA direct endorsement program, it can be forwarded to the DE underwriter.

If the loan is not under the DE program and HUD is to do the credit underwriting, special procedures must be followed. The special case binder was sent to the HUD-FHA office at the same time as the appraisal request was sent to the appraiser, so the HUD-FHA office already has all the original appraisal exhibits. Now the credit documents are forwarded to HUD-FHA without a folder, in the order specified below.

The documents shown as going on the right side of the case binder go on top of those shown as going on the left side. If a VA CRV is used, however, the folder is prepared and forwarded at this time.

The file folder must meet precise specifications, as described in HUD Mortgagee Letter 87-18 (and revised in HUD Mortgage Letters 87-34 and 92-35). In a CRV case, the documentation is included in the folder as follows.

Right Side

- Copy of the Conditional Commitment (HUD Form 92800.5b)
- VA Certificate of Reasonable Value or Master Certificate of Reasonable Value
- Final Typed/Computer Generated Uniform Residential Loan Application and Addendum
- Initial Application and Addendum
- Mortgage Credit Analysis Worksheet, HUD Form 92900-WS, original
- Good Faith Estimate and Attachment A

Left Side

- Copy of the Uniform Residential Loan Application
- Mortgage Credit Analysis Worksheet, HUD Form 92900-WS, copy
- Copy of Affirmative Fair Housing Marketing Plan (in proposed construction cases)
- Copy of Builder Certification (in proposed construction cases)
- Credit report(s), original—no copies
- Verification(s) of deposit, original
- Copy of bank statement required at time of application
- Verification(s) of employment, original
- Salary or pay stub required at time of application

- Picture identification of applicant(s) (or explanation of why none is included)
- Evidence of Social Security number(s) of applicant(s). This can be another copy of the salary or pay stub already included, a note referring to that stub, or a copy of the Social Security cards(s).
- Sales contract (supplements or amendments affecting value, deposit, sales price, and so on); should be on top, most recent first). Original or certified true copy
- Remaining documents, no particular order. Except for contract supplements or amendments, explanations of other documents should be included with the documents being explained, following the basic document.

Underwriting

Underwriting is the last step in establishing the loan's eligibility. It involves a review of both the property and the borrower's qualifications. Briefly stated, the underwriter is required to answer a series of questions: (1) Is this property acceptable as security for our loan? (2) Does the value of the property support the loan amount being applied for? (3) Does the applicant have sufficient cash (or other liquid assets) to close the transaction? (4) Is the applicant's income adequate to make the mortgage payments and meet other anticipated obligations and is that adequate income likely to continue into the foreseeable future? (5) Assuming all of the other answers are positive, is it likely the applicant will make the payments if the application is approved?

This process involves a largely subjective analysis of the information gathered and refined in the earlier parts of the process. The property has been appraised and the appraisal report reviewed for general acceptability; the borrower has provided basic information which has been verified; and a final application has been prepared. Now the underwriter is charged with reviewing all that information to make possible a final decision.

The underwriter's job is not to eliminate risk, but rather to evaluate it in terms of the company's risk management policies.

Few underwriting decisions are cut and dried. Underwriters often disagree with each other over the interpretation of identical sets of facts.

Experience

In its direct endorsement program, HUD-FHA requires that an approved underwriter have at least three years of underwriting experience. (One year of that requirement can be met through attendance at MBA's Appraisal Techniques Seminar, a one-week course presented annually.)

VA Automatic underwriters must have three years of experience in reviewing credit and underwriting decisions, with at least two recent years in connection with loans submitted to VA for guarantee. The experience requirement will be satisfied if the nominee has been designated an ARU (accredited residential underwriter) by the MBA of America.

Few people have extensive experience in the review of both properties and borrowers. Most underwriters traditionally come from credit analysis backgrounds and are less experienced in reviewing and evaluating appraisal reports. Yet, the property is a significant influence on the ultimate underwriting decision.

In any event, all underwriting decisions should be subject to review by an experienced supervisor as a part of the company's quality control program, and a sampling of decisions should be reviewed automatically as a part of that program. The supervisor should also be available to mediate or even arbitrate underwriting decisions that are questioned by the production staff.

There are two different ideas about the proper relationship between underwriters and loan producers, that is, loan officers and processors.

Some managers question the ability of an underwriter in one state to make informed decisions about applications from another state. They believe that underwriters should be physically located in the areas in which their decisions are being made.

Others take the position that underwriters should be centralized, so they can make independent decisions without being under the influence of loan producers. Even when the underwriter is physically located in a branch, but is under the supervision of a chief underwriter in some other location, they say, the physical proximity to the production-oriented branch manager and loan officers creates unavoidable adverse influences. VA requires that underwriters in the VA automatic program review cases in a central location.

Some larger companies have worked out a compromise between these two positions. They have established regional underwriting centers serving relative large areas but located in reasonable proximity to the properties and applicants being underwritten. These centers are independent of the production managers but still close enough, say the proponents, to be responsive to them.

Review and Control

Whatever organizational structure is adopted, review and control independent of the production process is important. Whenever possible, systems should be established to make both underwriters and producers aware of problems that might exist in the origination and underwriting process.

Certainly a default or foreclosure in the first year after origination might point to such problems. Such defaults and foreclosures, in which circumstances that develop after loan closing cannot be clearly identified as the cause, should trigger a close examination of how the loans were originated and the standards that were applied in documenting and approving the applications. This information is not very useful, however, unless those responsible for the origination and underwriting are made aware of it through feedback.

In some companies, automated systems have been developed to make preliminary underwriting decisions. In the most sophisticated of these systems, information is entered into the system beginning when the application is taken. The information is refined along the line, and the final worksheet is produced automatically when the processor or underwriter is satisfied that it is complete and current.

Some systems even make it possible to print the final application and worksheet using a laser printer that reproduces the entire form, thus eliminating the problems associated with registering forms in a printer. Remember, however, that these systems are no more accurate than the information provided to them. Nothing substitutes for final review of the application and its supporting documents by a human being before the loan is finally approved.

Providing the application passes the review of the underwriter and is approved, it moves on to closing, which is covered in the next chapter.

8

Closing the Loan

Closing involves preparing and assembling the documents that will bring a valid lien and an enforceable debt into being. It also involves meeting with the borrower and the seller to get their respective, formal agreement to the terms of the transaction, and recording those of the resulting documents that require notice to the "whole world" if they are to be enforceable.

How closings are prepared and conducted varies with local custom and practice. Sometimes, the file that has been discussed up to this point is simply forwarded to an attorney, title company, escrow agent, or other firm, and responsibility for the rest of the transaction is assumed by that party.

In other cases the necessary documents are prepared by the originating lender, and the completed documents are forwarded to the closing agent to finish the process. In still others, the originating lender does all the work, including preparation of the documents, conducting the actual closing, and recording the results.

However the work is divided, the lender must make sure the loan was properly closed. Our discussion takes a middle-of-the-road approach, in which the lender prepares the closing package, sends it to an agent for the actual loan closing, and after closing, receives the documents back for packaging and shipping.

Once an application has been approved and a commitment has been issued by an investor, insurer, guarantor, or any combination of the three, the loan is ready for closing.

As with processing the application, time is of the essence. Not only is there pressure to satisfy a customer and get the loan on the books, but the pressure is now intensified because the commitment has an expiration date. That date will vary from 30 days to a year, depending on the type of commitment, but it nevertheless imposes a very real deadline for completion.

Two Related Transactions

The closing is actually comprised of two separate but closely related transactions. In one, the sale of the property is consummated: Title passes from the seller to the buyer, and the seller is paid. In the other, the buyer borrows the money with which to pay the seller and pledges the property as security for repayment of the debt.

It is something of a chicken-and-egg proposition: The two transactions are so closely dependent on each other that it is impossible to say which comes first. It is certain, however, that you can't have one without the other.

There are some preliminary steps that must be completed at or before closing, and the details can vary from area to area. For example, the borrower is required to insure the property against fire and other hazards. Usually, the mortgage or deed of trust provides that both the amount of insurance and the insurance carrier must be acceptable to the lender. Most lenders accept generally recognized insurers and require that the amount of insurance be at least the amount of the mortgage, though others instead allow the amount of coverage to equal the home's replacement cost.

In cases involving low loan-to-value ratios, however, some care must be taken to assure that the coinsurance clause of the insurance policy does not excessively limit recovery in the event of a partial loss. Many lenders require guaranteed replacement coverage.

In most cases, a two-month insurance binder, accompanied by evidence that the premium for the first year has been paid, is required. In some areas the actual insurance policy is required. These situations usually stem from agreements between specific insurance companies and lenders, with the lender relying on assurance from the insurance carriers that binders will be honored.

Title insurance is also essential in certain areas. A title insurance binder should be secured well before closing to make review possible. If the binder reveals unacceptable exceptions to title, such as tax liens, you must clear those exceptions (or waive them) before the actual closing. The actual title policy, issued as of the date of closing or later, should be free of unacceptable exceptions.

HUD-FHA has identified certain title exceptions to which the agency will not object, should a claim for mortgage insurance benefits is filed later. This list incorporates exceptions commonly allowed by lenders and investors. If, however, there are additional exceptions, they should be carefully considered. HUD-FHA will waive additional exceptions in advance, and those waivers should be sought whenever they are appropriate.

While the question of marketable title will never arise as a source of risk to the lender unless there is a subsequent default, the risk makes it well worth the time and effort to make certain in every case that there are no unacceptable title exceptions.

Where title insurance is not commonly used, the same principles apply. Whatever form of title evidence is in use, the lender needs to make certain title is acceptable before closing. Clearing title exceptions after closing is difficult, at best, and often impossible.

Preparation of Documents

Once the mortgage insurance or guaranty commitment has been returned, the closing documents can be prepared. These include instructions to the closing agent, the note, the mortgage (or deed of trust), the deed conveying title from the seller to the buyer, the settlement statement (Form HUD-1), the HUD-FHA or VA commitment, the federal Truth in Lending disclosure statement (if it has not already been delivered), and any other legal documents required by the nature of the transaction.

Instructions to the Closing Agent

A letter with the instructions for closing begins with identification of the transaction and then lists the documents being forwarded as well as fees (such as discount points) to be collected. It further instructs the agent to close the loan and distribute the proceeds, and it usually imposes conditions that must be met before the transaction is considered complete, such as issuance of a title insurance policy with no exceptions.

The instructions can be detailed and specific to each case, or they can be simple and standard. Exhibit VIII-1 is an example of a detailed closing instruction.

The Note

The note is the borrower's promise to repay the debt. It states the amount of the loan, the interest rate, the place at which payments are to be made, the maturity date on which it is expected to be paid in full, the due date of the first and subsequent payments, the frequency of payments, and the change dates on adjustable rate mortgages.

The names of the borrowers on the note must be the same as the names on the mortgage and on the deed, unless there are cosigners who are not owners of the property. In that case, there might be a name or names on the note that do not appear on any other document. Even then all names appearing on the mortgage must also appear in the same form on the note and on the deed.

The due date of payments is usually the first of the month. (It must be the first of the month in HUD-FHA and VA transactions.) Typically, the first payment is scheduled to be due on the first day of the second month after closing. That is, if the closing takes place in January, the first payment is due March 1.

With HUD-FHA and VA loans, the first payment to principal and interest must be due no more than 60 days after the

EXHIBIT VIII-1: CONVENTIONAL LOAN CLOSING/ TITLE INSTRUCTIONS

[LENDER'S NAME AND ADDRESS]

PHONE # ____________

TO: ______________________ ATTN: ______________ GF # ____________

LOAN NO. __________ TYPE: ______________________ AMOUNT: ____________

BORROWER(S): ____

PROPERTY ADDRESS: ______________________________ SALES PRICE: ____________

INT. RATE: ______ TERM: ______ MOS. P&I PAYMENT: ________ DATE OF 1ST PMT.: ____________

SUBJECT LOAN IS MADE WITH CONDITION THAT IT SHALL BE RECORDED AND CREATE A 1ST LIEN AGAINST THE ABOVE PROPERTY.

Enclosed are papers pertinent to the closing of the above referenced loan. Please follow these instructions as set out. Should you not receive any document checked below, do not close this loan before contacting our office. If an error in the preparation of the documents is found, no change is to be made unless authorized by our office in advance.

___ Funds Request Form
___ Original Note
  ___ Addendum to Note
___ Original Deed of Trust/Mortgage (the "Security Instrument")
  ___ Original Condo/PUD Rider
  ___ Original 1-4 Family Rider
  ___ Adjustable Rate Rider
  ___ Balloon Rider
  ___ Other Rider:
___ Warranty Deed
___ Regulation Z Disclosure
___ FNMA 1009 Affidavit
___ Itemization of Amount Financed
___ Notice of Right to Cancel
___ Affidavit of Occupancy
___ Toxic & Hazardous Substance Warranty
___ Texas Business & Commerce Code Discl.
___ Acknow. of Receipt of Survey & Hold Harmless
___ Settlement Statement & Addendum to HUD-1 (to be completed)
___ Initial Escrow Account Statement
___ Address Information Form

___ Borrower's Accept. of Property & Authorization of Disbursement
___ Compliance Agreement
___ Flood Insurance Authorization
___ Notice of Insurance Requirements & Reserve Account Agreement
___ Name Affidavit(s)
___ Payment Letter & Consumer Information Sheet
___ Tax Information Sheet
___ W-9 Request for Taxpayer ID No. and Certification
___ ARM Disclosure
___ Conversion Option Compliance Agrmnt.
___ Notice to Convert Adjustable Rate Mortgage
___ Loan Application - to be signed by Borrower(s)
___ Sales Contract ___ - changes to be initialed
___ Copy of Payoff Statement
___ Premium Payment Authorization
___ Waiver of Escrow Impounds
___
___
___

PLEASE COLLECT THE FOLLOWING FUNDS AT CLOSING:

		FEES PAID OUTSIDE CLOSING	
______% ORIGINATION FEE	______	______	
______% LOAN DISCOUNT	______	______	
______% BUYDOWN SUBSIDY	______	______	Please issue separate check payable to:
______% PMI	______	______	______________
APPRAISAL	______	______	
FINAL INSPECTION	______	______	
CREDIT REPORT	______	______	Please issue separate check payable to:
DOCUMENT PREPARATION	______	______	YOUNGBLOOD, CLAYCOMBE & KING
	______	______	
	______	______	
	______	______	
	______	______	
	______	______	
	______	______	Please issue separate check payable to:
HAZARD INSURANCE	______	______	______________

NOTE: AMOUNTS SHOWN MARKED " -S " TO BE PAID BY SELLER.

PREPAID INTEREST should be collected from date of funding to ____ at ____ per day.

If disbursement of loan proceeds is _____, collect _____ days.

Please collect the following for **ESCROW/IMPOUNDS:**

______ mos. Taxes @ __________ per. month
______ mos. Taxes @ __________ per. month
______ mos. Hazard Insurance @ __________ per. month
______ mos. Flood Ins. (if applicable) @ __________ per. month
______ mos. Mortgage Insurance @ __________ per. month

EXHIBIT VIII-1—*continued*

UPON DISBURSEMENT OF FUNDS, THE FOLLOWING DOCUMENTS MUST BE FURNISHED TO [LENDER]:

___ Note - Original & 1 Copy
    ___ Addendum to Note
___ Deed of Trust/Mortgage - 2 Certified Copies of Executed, Notarized Document(s). Record original & return [Lender]
    ___ Rider(s)
___ Warranty Deed - 1 Certified Copy
___ FNMA 1009 Affidavit - Orig. signed by borrower(s)
___ Reg. Z Disclosure - Orig. to borrower(s), copy to [Lender]
___ Itemization of Amount Financed
___ Notice of Right to Cancel - Duplicate originals, fully executed original to [Lender].
___ Affidavit of Occupancy - Orig. signed by borrower(s)
___ Toxic & Hazardous Substance Warranty
___ Texas Business & Commerce Code Discl. - Orig. signed by borrower(s). Copy to each borrower/guarantor
___ Acknow. of Receipt of Survey & Hold Harmless
___ Settlement Statement & Addendum - 2 Originally executed copies or certified copies.
___ Initial Escrow Account Statement - Original to Borrowers Signed copy to [Lender].
___ Address Information Form
___ Borrower's Accept. of Property & Author. Disbursement
___ Compliance Agreement
___ Flood Insurance Authorization
___ Notice of Insurance Requirements & Reserve Account Agreement
___ Name Affidavit(s)

___ Payment Letter & Consumer Information Sheet
___ Tax Information Sheet
___ W-9 Request for Taxpayer ID No. and Certification
___ ARM Disclosure
___ Conversion Option Compliance Agrmnt.
___ Notice to Convert Adjustable Rate Mortgage
___ Loan Application - Original signed by Borrower(s)
___ Copy of Payoff Statement
___ Premium Payment Authorization
___ Waiver of Escrow Impounds - Orig. signed by Borrower(s)
___ Hazard Insurance Policy - Original **with first year's paid receipt** in an amount equal to or greater than or replacement cost coverage showing Loss Payee as: **[Lender]**
___ Flood Insurance
___ Survey (if applicable)
___
___
___

SPECIAL ITEMS NEEDED:

___ SEE ATTACHED ADDENDUM "1" FOR ADDITIONAL INSTRUCTIONS & REQUIREMENTS

<u>ANY CHANGES, WHITE-OUTS OR STRIKE-OUTS MUST BE INITIALED AT CLOSING.</u>

CHECKS TO BE RETURNED WITH PACKAGE (NO personal checks accepted)

___ Prepaid Interest and Escrow Deposit payable to **[Lender]**.
___ Mortgage Insurance Premium payable to ____________.
___ Hazard Insurance Premium payable to ____________.
___ Other: ____

___ **PACKAGE SHOULD BE RETURNED BY FEDERAL EXPRESS** ____________________

PLEASE MAKE SURE YOUR CLOSING IS IN COMPLIANCE WITH ALL REQUIREMENTS PRIOR TO DISBURSEMENT OF ANY FUNDS. CLOSING PACKAGE MUST BE EXPRESSED TO [LENDER] THE SAME DAY AS FUNDS ARE DISBURSED.

FUNDS WILL BE WIRED TOTALING $________________, INCLUSIVE OF THE LOAN AMOUNT OF _____ PLUS (OR MINUS) THE FOLLOWING:

____________________ ____________________
____________________ ____________________
____________________ ____________________
____________________ ____________________
____________________ ____________________

____
- CLOSER
PHONE:

EXHIBIT VIII-1—*continued*

ADDENDUM "1"

ADDITIONAL INSTRUCTIONS:

1. **Credits on the Settlement Statement** from Seller to Buyer (e.g., incomplete repairs, appliance allowance, etc.) are NOT to be shown without our prior approval. Notify Lender's office of any Closing Fees charged to the Borrower that in any way affect the Reg. Z Truth-in-Lending Disclosure by 1/8 of 1% of the APR or $10.00 of the Amount Financed in order to obtain a corrected disclosure.
2. The Title Policy must insure the Deed of Trust as a first lien with a coverage of no less than ____. **Mortgagee Clause** in favor of _________, **its successors and/or assigns.**
3. **Schedule A** must recite full recording data pertinent to the Mortgage/Deed of Trust and applicable Rider(s)/Schedule(s).
4. Only the following **Schedule B** Exceptions are allowed:
   a. The Exception to Restrictive Covenants shall state **"None of Record (except specified items)."**
   b. The Survey/Survey Endorsement Exception must be deleted from your policy to the extent allowed by law, showing only **"Shortages in Area."**
   c. Exceptions to Easements must be shown on Survey and must be specific as to size, purpose, location and recording data.
   d. Except as approved by Lender, no other items may be reflected in **Schedule B** to the policy other than the standard printed items and those permitted by a., b., c. and d. above.
5. No items on **Schedule C** of Title Commitment can be carried forward to the final Title Policy without Lender's approval.
6. You may record the necessary documents provided that you can issue an **ALTA or TLTA Policy of Title Insurance**, an **Environment Protection Endorsement** and an **ALTA Endorsement 100** (if applicable) insuring lender, subject only to **our Security Instrument. Please date title policy the same date as recording the Security Instrument** and use a standard tax clause on all policies, ie., taxes for the year _______, a lien, not yet due and payable.
7. **WE MUST HAVE THE RECORDED MORTGAGE OR COURTHOUSE CERTIFIED COPY OF THE RECORDED MORTGAGE AND THE FINAL TITLE POLICY WITHIN 45 DAYS AFTER CLOSING.**
8. ARM Endorsement (if applicable).
9. Balloon Mortage Endorsement (if applicable).
10. Survey Endorsement (if applicable).
11. Guarantee the authority of the agent to sell or mortgage the Property on behalf of the principal if the loan is closed with a Power of Attorney. The Power of Attorney must be recorded before the Deed or the Mortgage/Deed of Trust.

SPECIAL REQUIREMENTS

___ YOU MUST CALL FOR A FUNDING NUMBER PRIOR TO DISBURSEMENT **FUNDING #**__________________

___ PRIOR TO REQUEST FOR FUNDING, PLEASE FAX TO (214)__________ THE FOLLOWING DOCUMENTS:

1. Declaration Page of Hazard Insurance Policy   4. ____________________
2. Survey (if Applicable)   5. ____________________
3. ____________________   6. ____________________

___ CLEAR SEPTIC TANK CERTIFICATION.

___ CLEAR TERMITE/PEST INSPECTION SIGNED BY BORROWER.

___ FUNDING SUBJECT TO OUR RECEIPT OF A CLEAR FINAL INSPECTION - CONFIRM WITH US.

___ CLOSING AGENT TO COMPLETE 1ST PAYMENT LETTER WITH COUPON ATTACHED & RETURN COMPLETED COPY

___ WE WILL REQUIRE A PUD ENDORSEMENT TO THE TITLE POLICY.

___

___

___

___

___

___

___

___ **ABSOLUTELY NO CHANGES ALLOWED ON NOTE AND/OR MORTGAGE.**

___ FUNDING IS INVALID WITHOUT A FUNDING NUMBER. RETURN A COPY OF OUR CLOSING INSTRUCTIONS.

___ FINAL TITLE POLICY SHOULD REFLECT THE FOLLOWING CHANGES/CORRECTIONS:

lender signs the certificate on the commitment. (Be aware also that the dates on the note and on the mortgage must agree.)

Although the general content is the same, the language in the note is governed by state law, and different forms are used in different places. HUD-FHA and conventional loans use a multi-state note (Exhibits VIII-2 and VIII-3). These are used in the majority of states.

The Mortgage or Deed of Trust

Several different forms of mortgages and deeds of trust are in general use. Fannie Mae and Freddie Mac use a joint form, and HUD-FHA and VA each has its own. See Exhibits VIII-3, VIII-2, and VIII-4.

The mortgage or deed of trust includes the same basic information about the debt as the note, and it must agree with the note in every respect. If there were cosigners who are not owners of property, their names and signatures will appear on the note and not on the mortgage, but that should be the only difference.

For lenders who want to make changes by a separate rider to be recorded with the mortgage, HUD provides a rider. If you use such a rider, make sure the closing agent knows to record the rider with the basic mortgage.

The mortgage is a pledge of the property as security for the loan. It stands to reason, then, that it must clearly identify the property. That identification should be the legal description, and the description must match the one the title commitment, conditional commitment (in a HUD-FHA transaction), the VA certificate of reasonable value, the appraisal report (in a conventional transaction), and the deed.

While a reference to the place where the title is recorded is sometimes acceptable in ordering appraisals and a complete legal description might not appear on a commitment, the complete description must appear in the mortgage, and it must be accurate. An inaccurate legal description could make the mortgage unenforceable in the event of default.

EXHIBIT VIII-2: HUD-FHA MULTISTATE NOTE

Multistate

NOTE

FHA Case No.

[Date]

[Property Address]

1. PARTIES

"Borrower" means each person signing at the end of this Note, and the person's successors and assigns. "Lender" means

and its successors and assigns.

2. BORROWER'S PROMISE TO PAY; INTEREST

In return for a loan received from Lender, Borrower promises to pay the principal sum of

Dollars (U.S. $), plus interest, to the order of Lender. Interest will be charged on unpaid principal, from the date of disbursement of the loan proceeds by Lender, at the rate of
per cent (%) per year until the full amount of principal has been paid.

3. PROMISE TO PAY SECURED

Borrower's promise to pay is secured by a mortgage, deed of trust or similar security instrument that is dated the same date as this Note and called the "Security Instrument." That Security Instrument protects the Lender from losses which might result if Borrower defaults under this Note.

4. MANNER OF PAYMENT

(A) Time

Borrower shall make a payment of principal and interest to Lender on the first day of each month beginning on . Any principal and interest remaining on the first day of , will be due on that date, which is called the "Maturity Date."

(B) Place

Payment shall be made at

or at such other place as Lender may designate in writing by notice to Borrower.

(C) Amount

Each monthly payment of principal and interest will be in the amount of $. This amount will be part of a larger monthly payment required by the Security Instrument, that shall be applied to principal, interest and other items in the order described in the Security Instrument.

(D) Allonge to this Note for payment adjustments

If an allonge providing for payment adjustments is executed by Borrower together with this Note, the covenants of the allonge shall be incorporated into and shall amend and supplement the covenants of this Note as if the allonge were a part of this Note. [Check applicable box]

☐ Graduated Payment Allonge ☐ Growing Equity Allonge ☐ Other [specify]

5. BORROWER'S RIGHT TO PREPAY

Borrower has the right to pay the debt evidenced by this Note, in whole or in part, without charge or penalty, on the first day of any month.

6. BORROWER'S FAILURE TO PAY

(A) Late Charge for Overdue Payments

If Lender has not received the full monthly payment required by the Security Instrument, as described in Paragraph 4(C) of this Note by the end of fifteen calendar days after the payment is due, Lender may collect a late charge in the amount of per cent (%) of the overdue amount of each payment.

(B) Default

If Borrower defaults by failing to pay in full any monthly payment, then Lender may, except as limited by regulations of the Secretary in the case of payment defaults, require immediate payment in full of the principal balance remaining due and all accrued interest. Lender may choose not to exercise this option without waiving its rights in the event of any subsequent default. In many circumstances regulations issued by the Secretary will limit Lender's rights to require immediate payment in full in the case of payment defaults. This Note does not authorize acceleration when not permitted by HUD regulations. As used in this Note, "Secretary" means the Secretary of Housing and Urban Development or his or her designee.

(C) Payment of Costs and Expenses

If Lender has required immediate payment in full, as described above, Lender may require Borrower to pay costs and expenses including reasonable and customary attorneys' fees for enforcing this Note. Such fees and costs shall bear interest from the date of disbursement at the same rate as the principal of this Note.

7. WAIVERS

Borrower and any other person who has obligations under this Note waive the rights of presentment and notice of dishonor. "Presentment" means the right to require Lender to demand payment of amounts due. "Notice of dishonor" means the right to require Lender to give notice to other persons that amounts due have not been paid.

8. GIVING OF NOTICES

Unless applicable law requires a different method, any notice that must be given to Borrower under this Note will be given by delivering it or by mailing it by first class mail to Borrower at the property address above or at a different address if Borrower has given Lender a notice of Borrower's different address.

Any notice that must be given to Lender under this Note will be given by first class mail to Lender at the address stated in Paragraph 4(B) or at a different address if Borrower is given a notice of that different address.

9. OBLIGATIONS OF PERSONS UNDER THIS NOTE

If more than one person signs this Note, each person is fully and personally obligated to keep all of the promises made in this Note, including the promise to pay the full amount owed. Any person who is a guarantor, surety or endorser of this Note is also obligated to do these things. Any person who takes over these obligations, including the obligations of a guarantor, surety or endorser of this Note, is also obligated to keep all of the promises made in this Note. Lender may enforce its rights under this Note against each person individually or against all signatories together. Any one person signing this Note may be required to pay all of the amounts owed under this Note.

BY SIGNING BELOW, Borrower accepts and agrees to the terms and covenants contained in this Note.

______________________ (Seal) -Borrower	______________________ (Seal) -Borrower
______________________ (Seal) -Borrower	______________________ (Seal) -Borrower

Page 2 of 2

[Space Above This Line For Recording Data]

FHA Case No.

State of Illinois

MORTGAGE

THIS MORTGAGE ("Security Instrument") is made on . The Mortgagor is

("Borrower"). This Security Instrument is given to

which is organized and existing under the laws of , and whose address is ("Lender"). Borrower owes Lender the principal sum of

Dollars (U.S. $).

This debt is evidenced by Borrower's note dated the same date as this Security Instrument ("Note"), which provides for monthly payments, with the full debt, if not paid earlier, due and payable on

This Security Instrument secures to Lender: (a) the repayment of the debt evidenced by the Note, with interest, and all renewals, extensions and modifications; (b) the payment of all other sums, with interest, advanced under paragraph 6 to protect the security of this Security Instrument; and (c) the performance of Borrower's covenants and agreements under this Security Instrument and the Note. For this purpose, Borrower does hereby mortgage, grant and convey to Lender the following described property located in County, Illinois:

which has the address of [Street, City],

Illinois [Zip Code] ("Property Address");

FHA Illinois Mortgage - 2/91

-4R(IL) (9103)

Page 1 of 6

VMP MORTGAGE FORMS - (313)293-8100 - (800)521-7291

EXHIBIT VIII-2—*continued*

TOGETHER WITH all the improvements now or hereafter erected on the property, and all easements, rights, appurtenances, rents, royalties, mineral, oil and gas rights and profits, water rights and stock and all fixtures now or hereafter a part of the property. All replacements and additions shall also be covered by this Security Instrument. All of the foregoing is referred to in this Security Instrument as the "Property."

BORROWER COVENANTS that Borrower is lawfully seised of the estate hereby conveyed and has the right to mortgage, grant and convey the Property and that the Property is unencumbered, except for encumbrances of record. Borrower warrants and will defend generally the title to the Property against all claims and demands, subject to any encumbrances of record.

1. Payment of Principal, Interest and Late Charge. Borrower shall pay when due the principal of, and interest on, the debt evidenced by the Note and late charges due under the Note.

2. Monthly Payments of Taxes, Insurance and Other Charges. Borrower shall include in each monthly payment, together with the principal and interest as set forth in the Note and any late charges, an installment of any (a) taxes and special assessments levied or to be levied against the Property, (b) leasehold payments or ground rents on the Property, and (c) premiums for insurance required by paragraph 4.

Each monthly installment for items (a), (b), and (c) shall equal one-twelfth of the annual amounts, as reasonably estimated by Lender, plus an amount sufficient to maintain an additional balance of not more than one-sixth of the estimated amounts. The full annual amount for each item shall be accumulated by Lender within a period ending one month before an item would become delinquent. Lender shall hold the amounts collected in trust to pay items (a), (b), and (c) before they become delinquent.

If at any time the total of the payments held by Lender for items (a), (b), and (c), together with the future monthly payments for such items payable to Lender prior to the due dates of such items, exceeds by more than one-sixth the estimated amount of payments required to pay such items when due, and if payments on the Note are current, then Lender shall either refund the excess over one-sixth of the estimated payments or credit the excess over one-sixth of the estimated payments to subsequent payments by Borrower, at the option of Borrower. If the total of the payments made by Borrower for item (a), (b), or (c) is insufficient to pay the item when due, then Borrower shall pay to Lender any amount necessary to make up the deficiency on or before the date the item becomes due.

As used in this Security Instrument, "Secretary" means the Secretary of Housing and Urban Development or his or her designee. In any year in which the Lender must pay a mortgage insurance premium to the Secretary, each monthly payment shall also include either: (i) an installment of the annual mortgage insurance premium to be paid by Lender to the Secretary, or (ii) a monthly charge instead of a mortgage insurance premium if this Security Instrument is held by the Secretary. Each monthly installment of the mortgage insurance premium shall be in an amount sufficient to accumulate the full annual mortgage insurance premium with Lender one month prior to the date the full annual mortgage insurance premium is due to the Secretary, or if this Security Instrument is held by the Secretary, each monthly charge shall be in an amount equal to one-twelfth of one-half percent of the outstanding principal balance due on the Note.

If Borrower tenders to Lender the full payment of all sums secured by this Security Instrument, Borrower's account shall be credited with the balance remaining for all installments for items (a), (b), and (c) and any mortgage insurance premium installment that Lender has not become obligated to pay to the Secretary, and Lender shall promptly refund any excess funds to Borrower. Immediately prior to a foreclosure sale of the Property or its acquisition by Lender, Borrower's account shall be credited with any balance remaining for all installments for items (a), (b), and (c).

3. Application of Payments. All payments under paragraphs 1 and 2 shall be applied by Lender as follows:

First, to the mortgage insurance premium to be paid by Lender to the Secretary or to the monthly charge by the Secretary instead of the monthly mortgage insurance premium;
Second, to any taxes, special assessments, leasehold payments or ground rents, and fire, flood and other hazard insurance premiums, as required;
Third, to interest due under the Note;
Fourth, to amortization of the principal of the Note;
Fifth, to late charges due under the Note.

4. Fire, Flood and Other Hazard Insurance. Borrower shall insure all improvements on the Property, whether now in existence or subsequently erected, against any hazards, casualties, and contingencies, including fire, for which Lender requires insurance. This insurance shall be maintained in the amounts and for the periods that Lender requires. Borrower shall also insure all improvements on the Property, whether now in existence or subsequently erected, against loss by floods to the extent required by the Secretary. All insurance shall be carried with companies approved by Lender. The insurance policies and any renewals shall be held by Lender and shall include loss payable clauses in favor of, and in a form acceptable to, Lender.

In the event of loss, Borrower shall give Lender immediate notice by mail. Lender may make proof of loss if not made promptly by Borrower. Each insurance company concerned is hereby authorized and directed to make payment for such loss directly to Lender, instead of to Borrower and to Lender jointly. All or any part of the insurance proceeds may be applied by Lender, at its option, either (a) to the reduction of the indebtedness under the Note and this Security Instrument, first to any delinquent amounts applied in the order in paragraph 3, and then to prepayment of principal, or (b) to the restoration or repair of the damaged Property. Any application of the proceeds to the principal shall not extend or postpone the due date of the monthly payments which are referred to in paragraph 2, or change the amount of such payments. Any excess insurance proceeds over an amount required to pay all outstanding indebtedness under the Note and this Security Instrument shall be paid to the entity legally entitled thereto.

In the event of foreclosure of this Security Instrument or other transfer of title to the Property that extinguishes the indebtedness, all right, title and interest of Borrower in and to insurance policies in force shall pass to the purchaser.

5. Occupancy, Preservation, Maintenance and Protection of the Property; Borrower's Loan Application; Leaseholds. Borrower shall occupy, establish, and use the Property as Borrower's principal residence within sixty days after the execution of this Security Instrument and shall continue to occupy the Property as Borrower's principal residence for at least one year after the date of occupancy, unless the Secretary determines this requirement will cause undue hardship for Borrower, or unless extenuating circumstances exist which are beyond Borrower's control. Borrower shall notify Lenders of any extenuating circumstances. Borrower shall not commit waste or destroy, damage or substantially change the Property or allow the Property to deteriorate, reasonable wear and tear excepted. Lender may inspect the Property if the Property is vacant or abandoned or the loan is in default. Lender may take reasonable action to protect and preserve such vacant or abandoned Property. Borrower shall also be in default if Borrower, during the loan application process, gave materially false or inaccurate information or statements to Lender (or failed to provide Lender with any material information) in connection with the loan evidenced by the Note, including, but not limited to, representations concerning Borrower's occupancy of the Property as a principal residence. If this Security Instrument is on a leasehold, Borrower shall comply with the provisions of the lease. If Borrower acquires fee title to the Property, the leasehold and fee title shall not be merged unless Lender agrees to the merger in writing.

6. Charges to Borrower and Protection of Lender's Rights in the Property. Borrower shall pay all governmental or municipal charges, fines and impositions that are not included in paragraph 2. Borrower shall pay these obligations on time directly to the entity which is owed the payment. If failure to pay would adversely affect Lender's interest in the Property, upon Lender's request Borrower shall promptly furnish to Lender receipts evidencing these payments.

If Borrower fails to make these payments or the payments required by paragraph 2, or fails to perform any other covenants and agreements contained in this Security Instrument, or there is a legal proceeding that may significantly affect Lender's rights in the Property (such as a proceeding in bankruptcy, for condemnation or to enforce laws or regulations), then Lender may do and pay whatever is necessary to protect the value of the Property and Lender's rights in the Property, including payment of taxes, hazard insurance and other items mentioned in paragraph 2.

Any amounts disbursed by Lender under this paragraph shall become an additional debt of Borrower and be secured by this Security Instrument. These amounts shall bear interest from the date of disbursement, at the Note rate, and at the option of Lender, shall be immediately due and payable.

7. Condemnation. The proceeds of any award or claim for damages, direct or consequential, in connection with any condemnation or other taking of any part of the Property, or for conveyance in place of condemnation, are hereby assigned and shall be paid to Lender to the extent of the full amount of the indebtedness that remains unpaid under the Note and this Security Instrument. Lender shall apply such proceeds to the reduction of the indebtedness under the Note and this Security Instrument, first to any delinquent amounts applied in the order provided in paragraph 3, and then to prepayment of principal. Any application of the proceeds to the principal shall not extend or postpone the due date of the monthly payments, which are referred to in paragraph 2, or change the amount of such payments. Any excess proceeds over an amount required to pay all outstanding indebtedness under the Note and this Security Instrument shall be paid to the entity legally entitled thereto.

8. Fees. Lender may collect fees and charges authorized by the Secretary.

9. Grounds for Acceleration of Debt.

(a) Default. Lender may, except as limited by regulations issued by the Secretary in the case of payment defaults, require immediate payment in full of all sums secured by this Security Instrument if:

(i) Borrower defaults by failing to pay in full any monthly payment required by this Security Instrument prior to or on the due date of the next monthly payment, or

(ii) Borrower defaults by failing, for a period of thirty days, to perform any other obligations contained in this Security Instrument.

(b) Sale Without Credit Approval. Lender shall, if permitted by applicable law and with the prior approval of the Secretary, require immediate payment in full of all sums secured by this Security Instrument if:

(i) All or part of the Property, or a beneficial interest in a trust owning all or part of the Property, is sold or otherwise transferred (other than by devise or descent) by the Borrower, and

(ii) The Property is not occupied by the purchaser or grantee as his or her principal residence, or the purchaser or grantee does so occupy the Property but his or her credit has not been approved in accordance with the requirements of the Secretary.

(c) No Waiver. If circumstances occur that would permit Lender to require immediate payment in full, but Lender does not require such payments, Lender does not waive its rights with respect to subsequent events.

(d) Regulations of HUD Secretary. In many circumstances regulations issued by the Secretary will limit Lender's rights in the case of payment defaults to require immediate payment in full and foreclose if not paid. This Security Instrument does not authorize acceleration or foreclosure if not permitted by regulations of the Secretary.

(e) Mortgage Not Insured. Borrower agrees that should this Security Instrument and the Note secured thereby not be eligible for insurance under the National Housing Act within 60 days from the date hereof, Lender may, at its option and notwithstanding anything in paragraph 9, require immediate payment in full of all sums secured by this Security Instrument. A written statement of any authorized agent of the Secretary dated subsequent to 60 days from the date hereof, declining to insure this Security Instrument and the Note secured thereby, shall be deemed conclusive proof of such ineligibility. Notwithstanding the foregoing, this option may not be exercised by Lender when the unavailability of insurance is solely due to Lender's failure to remit a mortgage insurance premium to the Secretary.

10. Reinstatement. Borrower has a right to be reinstated if Lender has required immediate payment in full because of Borrower's failure to pay an amount due under the Note or this Security Instrument. This right applies even after foreclosure proceedings are instituted. To reinstate the Security Instrument, Borrower shall tender in a lump sum all amounts required to bring Borrower's account current including, to the extent they are obligations of Borrower under this Security Instrument, foreclosure costs and reasonable and customary attorneys' fees and expenses properly associated with the foreclosure proceeding. Upon reinstatement by Borrower, this Security Instrument and the obligations that it secures shall remain in effect as if Lender had not required immediate payment in full. However, Lender is not required to permit reinstatement if: (i) Lender has accepted reinstatement after the commencement of foreclosure proceedings within two years immediately preceding the commencement of a current foreclosure proceeding, (ii) reinstatement will preclude foreclosure on different grounds in the future, or (iii) reinstatement will adversely affect the priority of the lien created by this Security Instrument.

11. Borrower Not Released; Forbearance By Lender Not a Waiver. Extension of the time of payment or modification of amortization of the sums secured by this Security Instrument granted by Lender to any successor in interest of Borrower shall not operate to release the liability of the original Borrower or Borrower's successor in interest. Lender shall not be required to commence proceedings against any successor in interest or refuse to extend time for payment or otherwise modify amortization of the sums secured by this Security Instrument by reason of any demand made by the original Borrower or Borrower's successors in interest. Any forbearance by Lender in exercising any right or remedy shall not be a waiver of or preclude the exercise of any right or remedy.

VMP®-4R(IL) (9103) Page 4 of 6

12. Successors and Assigns Bound; Joint and Several Liability; Co-Signers. The covenants and agreements of this Security Instrument shall bind and benefit the successors and assigns of Lender and Borrower, subject to the provisions of paragraph 9.b. Borrower's covenants and agreements shall be joint and several. Any Borrower who co-signs this Security Instrument but does not execute the Note: (a) is co-signing this Security Instrument only to mortgage, grant and convey that Borrower's interest in the Property under the terms of this Security Instrument; (b) is not personally obligated to pay the sums secured by this Security Instrument; and (c) agrees that Lender and any other Borrower may agree to extend, modify, forbear or make any accommodations with regard to the terms of this Security Instrument or the Note without that Borrower's consent.

13. Notices. Any notice to Borrower provided for in this Security Instrument shall be given by delivering it or by mailing it by first class mail unless applicable law requires use of another method. The notice shall be directed to the Property Address or any other address Borrower designates by notice to Lender. Any notice to Lender shall be given by first class mail to Lender's address stated herein or any address Lender designates by notice to Borrower. Any notice provided for in this Security Instrument shall be deemed to have been given to Borrower or Lender when given as provided in this paragraph.

14. Governing Law; Severability. This Security Instrument shall be governed by federal law and the law of the jurisdiction in which the Property is located. In the event that any provision or clause of this Security Instrument or the Note conflicts with applicable law, such conflict shall not affect other provisions of this Security Instrument or the Note which can be given effect without the conflicting provision. To this end the provisions of this Security Instrument and the Note are declared to be severable.

15. Borrower's Copy. Borrower shall be given one conformed copy of this Security Instrument.

16. Assignment of Rents. Borrower unconditionally assigns and transfers to Lender all the rents and revenues of the Property. Borrower authorizes Lender or Lender's agents to collect the rents and revenues and hereby directs each tenant of the Property to pay the rents to Lender or Lender's agents. However, prior to Lender's notice to Borrower of Borrower's breach of any covenant or agreement in the Security Instrument, Borrower shall collect and receive all rents and revenues of the Property as trustee for the benefit of Lender and Borrower. This assignment of rents constitutes an absolute assignment and not an assignment for additional security only.

If Lender gives notice of breach to Borrower: (a) all rents received by Borrower shall be held by Borrower as trustee for benefit of Lender only, to be applied to the sums secured by the Security Instrument; (b) Lender shall be entitled to collect and receive all of the rents of the Property; and (c) each tenant of the Property shall pay all rents due and unpaid to Lender or Lender's agent on Lender's written demand to the tenant.

Borrower has not executed any prior assignment of the rents and has not and will not perform any act that would prevent Lender from exercising its rights under this paragraph 16.

Lender shall not be required to enter upon, take control of or maintain the Property before or after giving notice of breach to Borrower. However, Lender or a judicially appointed receiver may do so at any time there is a breach. Any application of rents shall not cure or waive any default or invalidate any other right or remedy of Lender. This assignment of rents of the Property shall terminate when the debt secured by the Security Instrument is paid in full.

NON-UNIFORM COVENANTS. Borrower and Lender further covenant and agree as follows:

17. Foreclosure Procedure. If Lender requires immediate payment in full under paragraph 9, Lender may foreclose this Security Instrument by judicial proceeding. Lender shall be entitled to collect all expenses incurred in pursuing the remedies provided in this paragraph 17, including, but not limited to, reasonable attorneys' fees and costs of title evidence.

18. Release. Upon payment of all sums secured by this Security Instrument, Lender shall release this Security Instrument without charge to Borrower. Borrower shall pay any recordation costs.

19. Waiver of Homestead. Borrower waives all right of homestead exemption in the Property.

VMP® -4R(IL) (9103) Page 5 of 6

EXHIBIT VIII-2—*continued*

20. Riders to this Security Instrument. If one or more riders are executed by Borrower and recorded together with this Security Instrument, the covenants of each such rider shall be incorporated into and shall amend and supplement the covenants and agreements of this Security Instrument as if the rider(s) were a part of this Security Instrument.
[Check applicable box(es)]

☐ Condominium Rider ☐ Graduated Payment Rider ☐ Other [Specify]
☐ Planned Unit Development Rider ☐ Growing Equity Rider

BY SIGNING BELOW, Borrower accepts and agrees to the terms contained in this Security Instrument and in any rider(s) executed by Borrower and recorded with it.
Witnesses:

_______________________________ (Seal)
-Borrower

____

_______________________________ (Seal)
-Borrower

____

_______________________________ (Seal)
-Borrower

_______________________________ (Seal)
-Borrower

STATE OF ILLINOIS, **County ss:**

I, , a Notary Public in and for said county and state do hereby certify that

, personally known to me to be the same person(s) whose name(s) subscribed to the foregoing instrument, appeared before me this day in person, and acknowledged that he signed and delivered the said instrument as free and voluntary act, for the uses and purposes therein set forth.

Given under my hand and official seal, this day of , .

My Commission Expires:

____
Notary Public

This Instrument was prepared by:

VMP-4R(IL) Page 6 of 6

[Space Above This Line For Recording Data]

State of Texas

DEED OF TRUST

FHA Case No.

THIS DEED OF TRUST ("Security Instrument") is made on . The Grantor is

("Borrower"). The trustee is

("Trustee"). The beneficiary is ,

which is organized and existing under the laws of and whose address is ("Lender"). Borrower owes Lender the principal sum of

Dollars (U.S. $).

This debt is evidenced by Borrower's note dated the same date as this Security Instrument ("Note"), which provides for monthly payments, with the full debt, if not paid earlier, due and payable on .
This Security Instrument secures to Lender: (a) the repayment of the debt evidenced by the Note, with interest, and all renewals, extensions and modifications; (b) the payment of all other sums, with interest, advanced under paragraph 6 to protect the security of this Security Instrument; and (c) the performance of Borrower's covenants and agreements under this Security Instrument and the Note. For this purpose, Borrower irrevocably grants and conveys to Trustee, in trust, with power of sale, the following described property located in County, Texas:

which has the address of [Street, City],
Texas [Zip Code] ("Property Address");

FHA Texas Deed of Trust - 2/91

EXHIBIT VIII-2—*continued*

TOGETHER WITH all the improvements now or hereafter erected on the property, and all easements, rights, appurtenances, rents, royalties, mineral, oil and gas rights and profits, water rights and stock and all fixtures now or hereafter a part of the property. All replacements and additions shall also be covered by this Security Instrument. All of the foregoing is referred to in this Security Instrument as the "Property."

BORROWER COVENANTS that Borrower is lawfully seised of the estate hereby conveyed and has the right to grant and convey the Property and that the Property is unencumbered, except for encumbrances of record. Borrower warrants and will defend generally the title to the Property against all claims and demands, subject to any encumbrances of record.

1. Payment of Principal, Interest and Late Charge. Borrower shall pay when due the principal of, and interest on, the debt evidenced by the Note and late charges due under the Note.

2. Monthly Payments of Taxes, Insurance and Other Charges. Borrower shall include in each monthly payment, together with the principal and interest as set forth in the Note and any late charges, an installment of any (a) taxes and special assessments levied or to be levied against the Property, (b) leasehold payments or ground rents on the Property, and (c) premiums for insurance required by paragraph 4.

Each monthly installment for items (a), (b), and (c) shall equal one-twelfth of the annual amounts, as reasonably estimated by Lender, plus an amount sufficient to maintain an additional balance of not more than one-sixth of the estimated amounts. The full annual amount for each item shall be accumulated by Lender within a period ending one month before an item would become delinquent. Lender shall hold the amounts collected in trust to pay items (a), (b), and (c) before they become delinquent.

If at any time the total of the payments held by Lender for items (a), (b), and (c), together with the future monthly payments for such items payable to Lender prior to the due dates of sucn items, exceeds by more than one-sixth the estimated amount of payments required to pay such items when due, and if payments on the Note are current, then Lender shall either refund the excess over one-sixth of the estimated payments or credit the excess over one-sixth of the estimated payments to subsequent payments by Borrower, at the option of Borrower. If the total of the payments made by Borrower for item (a), (b), or (c) is insufficient to pay the item when due, then Borrower shall pay to Lender any amount necessary to make up the deficiency on or before the date the item becomes due.

As used in this Security Instrument, "Secretary" means the Secretary of Housing and Urban Development or his or her designee. In any year in which the Lender must pay a mortgage insurance premium to the Secretary, each monthly payment shall also include either: (i) an installment of the annual mortgage insurance premium to be paid by Lender to the Secretary, or (ii) a monthly charge instead of a mortgage insurance premium if this Security Instrument is held by the Secretary. Each monthly installment of the mortgage insurance premium shall be in an amount sufficient to accumulate the full annual mortgage insurance premium with Lender one month prior to the date the full annual mortgage insurance premium is due to the Secretary, or if this Security Instrument is held by the Secretary, each monthly charge shall be in an amount equal to one-twelfth of one-half percent of the outstanding principal balance due on the Note.

If Borrower tenders to Lender the full payment of all sums secured by this Security Instrument, Borrower's account shall be credited with the balance remaining for all installments for items (a), (b), and (c) and any mortgage insurance premium installment that Lender has not become obligated to pay to the Secretary, and Lender shall promptly refund any excess funds to Borrower. Immediately prior to a foreclosure sale of the Property or its acquisition by Lender, Borrower's account shall be credited with any balance remaining for all installments for items (a), (b), and (c).

3. Application of Payments. All payments under paragraphs 1 and 2 shall be applied by Lender as follows:

First, to the mortgage insurance premium to be paid by Lender to the Secretary or to the monthly charge by the Secretary instead of the monthly mortgage insurance premium;

Second, to any taxes, special assessments, leasehold payments or ground rents, and fire, flood and other hazard insurance premiums, as required;

Third, to interest due under the Note;

Fourth, to amortization of the principal of the Note;

Fifth, to late charges due under the Note.

VMP® -4R(TX) Page 2 of 6

4. Fire, Flood and Other Hazard Insurance. Borrower shall insure all improvements on the Property, whether now in existence or subsequently erected, against any hazards, casualties, and contingencies, including fire, for which Lender requires insurance. This insurance shall be maintained in the amounts and for the periods that Lender requires. Borrower shall also insure all improvements on the Property, whether now in existence or subsequently erected, against loss by floods to the extent required by the Secretary. All insurance shall be carried with companies approved by Lender. The insurance policies and any renewals shall be held by Lender and shall include loss payable clauses in favor of, and in a form acceptable to, Lender.

In the event of loss, Borrower shall give Lender immediate notice by mail. Lender may make proof of loss if not made promptly by Borrower. Each insurance company concerned is hereby authorized and directed to make payment for such loss directly to Lender, instead of to Borrower and to Lender jointly. All or any part of the insurance proceeds may be applied by Lender, at its option, either (a) to the reduction of the indebtedness under the Note and this Security Instrument, first to any delinquent amounts applied in the order in paragraph 3, and then to prepayment of principal, or (b) to the restoration or repair of the damaged Property. Any application of the proceeds to the principal shall not extend or postpone the due date of the monthly payments which are referred to in paragraph 2, or change the amount of such payments. Any excess insurance proceeds over an amount required to pay all outstanding indebtedness under the Note and this Security Instrument shall be paid to the entity legally entitled thereto.

In the event of foreclosure of this Security Instrument or other transfer of title to the Property that extinguishes the indebtedness, all right, title and interest of Borrower in and to insurance policies in force shall pass to the purchaser.

5. Occupancy, Preservation, Maintenance and Protection of the Property; Borrower's Loan Application; Leaseholds. Borrower shall occupy, establish, and use the Property as Borrower's principal residence within sixty days after the execution of this Security Instrument and shall continue to occupy the Property as Borrower's principal residence for at least one year after the date of occupancy, unless the Secretary determines this requirement will cause undue hardship for Borrower, or unless extenuating circumstances exist which are beyond Borrower's control. Borrower shall notify Lenders of any extenuating circumstances. Borrower shall not commit waste or destroy, damage or substantially change the Property or allow the Property to deteriorate, reasonable wear and tear excepted. Lender may inspect the Property if the Property is vacant or abandoned or the loan is in default. Lender may take reasonable action to protect and preserve such vacant or abandoned Property. Borrower shall also be in default if Borrower, during the loan application process, gave materially false or inaccurate information or statements to Lender (or failed to provide Lender with any material information) in connection with the loan evidenced by the Note, including, but not limited to, representations concerning Borrower's occupancy of the Property as a principal residence. If this Security Instrument is on a leasehold, Borrower shall comply with the provisions of the lease. If Borrower acquires fee title to the Property, the leasehold and fee title shall not be merged unless Lender agrees to the merger in writing.

6. Charges to Borrower and Protection of Lender's Rights in the Property. Borrower shall pay all governmental or municipal charges, fines and impositions that are not included in paragraph 2. Borrower shall pay these obligations on time directly to the entity which is owed the payment. If failure to pay would adversely affect Lender's interest in the Property, upon Lender's request Borrower shall promptly furnish to Lender receipts evidencing these payments.

If Borrower fails to make these payments or the payments required by paragraph 2, or fails to perform any other covenants and agreements contained in this Security Instrument, or there is a legal proceeding that may significantly affect Lender's rights in the Property (such as a proceeding in bankruptcy, for condemnation or to enforce laws or regulations), then Lender may do and pay whatever is necessary to protect the value of the Property and Lender's rights in the Property, including payment of taxes, hazard insurance and other items mentioned in paragraph 2.

Any amounts disbursed by Lender under this paragraph shall become an additional debt of Borrower and be secured by this Security Instrument. These amounts shall bear interest from the date of disbursement, at the Note rate, and at the option of Lender, shall be immediately due and payable.

7. Condemnation. The proceeds of any award or claim for damages, direct or consequential, in connection with any condemnation or other taking of any part of the Property, or for conveyance in place of condemnation, are hereby assigned and shall be paid to Lender to the extent of the full amount of the indebtedness that remains unpaid under the Note and this Security Instrument. Lender shall apply such proceeds to the reduction of the indebtedness under the Note and this Security Instrument, first to any delinquent amounts applied in the order provided in paragraph 3, and then to prepayment of principal. Any application of the proceeds to the principal shall not extend or postpone the due date of the monthly payments, which are

VMP®-4R(TX) Page 3 of 6

referred to in paragraph 2, or change the amount of such payments. Any excess proceeds over an amount required to pay all outstanding indebtedness under the Note and this Security Instrument shall be paid to the entity legally entitled thereto.

8. Fees. Lender may collect fees and charges authorized by the Secretary.

9. Grounds for Acceleration of Debt.

(a) Default. Lender may, except as limited by regulations issued by the Secretary in the case of payment defaults, require immediate payment in full of all sums secured by this Security Instrument if:

(i) Borrower defaults by failing to pay in full any monthly payment required by this Security Instrument prior to or on the due date of the next monthly payment, or

(ii) Borrower defaults by failing, for a period of thirty days, to perform any other obligations contained in this Security Instrument.

(b) Sale Without Credit Approval. Lender shall, if permitted by applicable law and with the prior approval of the Secretary, require immediate payment in full of all sums secured by this Security Instrument if:

(i) All or part of the Property, or a beneficial interest in a trust owning all or part of the Property, is sold or otherwise transferred (other than by devise or descent) by the Borrower, and

(ii) The Property is not occupied by the purchaser or grantee as his or her principal residence, or the purchaser or grantee does so occupy the Property but his or her credit has not been approved in accordance with the requirements of the Secretary.

(c) No Waiver. If circumstances occur that would permit Lender to require immediate payment in full, but Lender does not require such payments, Lender does not waive its rights with respect to subsequent events.

(d) Regulations of HUD Secretary. In many circumstances regulations issued by the Secretary will limit Lender's rights in the case of payment defaults to require immediate payment in full and foreclose if not paid. This Security Instrument does not authorize acceleration or foreclosure if not permitted by regulations of the Secretary.

(e) Mortgage Not Insured. Borrower agrees that should this Security Instrument and the Note secured thereby not be eligible for insurance under the National Housing Act within 60 days from the date hereof, Lender may, at its option and notwithstanding anything in paragraph 9, require immediate payment in full of all sums secured by this Security Instrument. A written statement of any authorized agent of the Secretary dated subsequent to 60 days from the date hereof, declining to insure this Security Instrument and the Note secured thereby, shall be deemed conclusive proof of such ineligibility. Notwithstanding the foregoing, this option may not be exercised by Lender when the unavailability of insurance is solely due to Lender's failure to remit a mortgage insurance premium to the Secretary.

10. Reinstatement. Borrower has a right to be reinstated if Lender has required immediate payment in full because of Borrower's failure to pay an amount due under the Note or this Security Instrument. This right applies even after foreclosure proceedings are instituted. To reinstate the Security Instrument, Borrower shall tender in a lump sum all amounts required to bring Borrower's account current including, to the extent they are obligations of Borrower under this Security Instrument, foreclosure costs and reasonable and customary attorneys' fees and expenses properly associated with the foreclosure proceeding. Upon reinstatement by Borrower, this Security Instrument and the obligations that it secures shall remain in effect as if Lender had not required immediate payment in full. However, Lender is not required to permit reinstatement if: (i) Lender has accepted reinstatement after the commencement of foreclosure proceedings within two years immediately preceding the commencement of a current foreclosure proceeding, (ii) reinstatement will preclude foreclosure on different grounds in the future, or (iii) reinstatement will adversely affect the priority of the lien created by this Security Instrument.

11. Borrower Not Released; Forbearance By Lender Not a Waiver. Extension of the time of payment or modification of amortization of the sums secured by this Security Instrument granted by Lender to any successor in interest of Borrower shall not operate to release the liability of the original Borrower or Borrower's successor in interest. Lender shall not be required to commence proceedings against any successor in interest or refuse to extend time for payment or otherwise modify amortization of the sums secured by this Security Instrument by reason of any demand made by the original Borrower or Borrower's successors in interest. Any forbearance by Lender in exercising any right or remedy shall not be a waiver of or preclude the exercise of any right or remedy.

VMP-4R(TX) Page 4 of 6

12. Successors and Assigns Bound; Joint and Several Liability; Co-Signers. The covenants and agreements of this Security Instrument shall bind and benefit the successors and assigns of Lender and Borrower, subject to the provisions of paragraph 9.b. Borrower's covenants and agreements shall be joint and several. Any Borrower who co-signs this Security Instrument but does not execute the Note: (a) is co-signing this Security Instrument only to mortgage, grant and convey that Borrower's interest in the Property under the terms of this Security Instrument; (b) is not personally obligated to pay the sums secured by this Security Instrument; and (c) agrees that Lender and any other Borrower may agree to extend, modify, forbear or make any accommodations with regard to the terms of this Security Instrument or the Note without that Borrower's consent.

13. Notices. Any notice to Borrower provided for in this Security Instrument shall be given by delivering it or by mailing it by first class mail unless applicable law requires use of another method. The notice shall be directed to the Property Address or any other address Borrower designates by notice to Lender. Any notice to Lender shall be given by first class mail to Lender's address stated herein or any address Lender designates by notice to Borrower. Any notice provided for in this Security Instrument shall be deemed to have been given to Borrower or Lender when given as provided in this paragraph.

14. Governing Law; Severability. This Security Instrument shall be governed by federal law and the law of the jurisdiction in which the Property is located. In the event that any provision or clause of this Security Instrument or the Note conflicts with applicable law, such conflict shall not affect other provisions of this Security Instrument or the Note which can be given effect without the conflicting provision. To this end the provisions of this Security Instrument and the Note are declared to be severable.

15. Borrower's Copy. Borrower shall be given one conformed copy of this Security Instrument.

16. Assignment of Rents. Borrower unconditionally assigns and transfers to Lender all the rents and revenues of the Property. Borrower authorizes Lender or Lender's agents to collect the rents and revenues and hereby directs each tenant of the Property to pay the rents to Lender or Lender's agents. However, prior to Lender's notice to Borrower of Borrower's breach of any covenant or agreement in the Security Instrument, Borrower shall collect and receive all rents and revenues of the Property as trustee for the benefit of Lender and Borrower. This assignment of rents constitutes an absolute assignment and not an assignment for additional security only.

If Lender gives notice of breach to Borrower: (a) all rents received by Borrower shall be held by Borrower as trustee for benefit of Lender only, to be applied to the sums secured by the Security Instrument; (b) Lender shall be entitled to collect and receive all of the rents of the Property; and (c) each tenant of the Property shall pay all rents due and unpaid to Lender or Lender's agent on Lender's written demand to the tenant.

Borrower has not executed any prior assignment of the rents and has not and will not perform any act that would prevent Lender from exercising its rights under this paragraph 16.

Lender shall not be required to enter upon, take control of or maintain the Property before or after giving notice of breach to Borrower. However, Lender or a judicially appointed receiver may do so at any time there is a breach. Any application of rents shall not cure or waive any default or invalidate any other right or remedy of Lender. This assignment of rents of the Property shall terminate when the debt secured by the Security Instrument is paid in full.

NON-UNIFORM COVENANTS. Borrower and Lender further covenant and agree as follows:

17. Foreclosure Procedure. If Lender requires immediate payment in full under paragraph 9, Lender may invoke the power of sale and any other remedies permitted by applicable law. Lender shall be entitled to collect all expenses incurred in pursuing the remedies provided in this paragraph 17, including, but not limited to, reasonable attorneys' fees and costs of title evidence.

If Lender invokes the power of sale, Lender or Trustee shall give notice of the time, place and terms of sale by posting and recording the notice at least 21 days prior to sale as provided by applicable law. Lender shall mail a copy of the notice of sale to Borrower in the manner prescribed by applicable law. Sale shall be made at public vendue between the hours of 10 a.m. and 4 p.m. on the first Tuesday in any month. Borrower authorizes Trustee to sell the Property to the highest bidder for cash in one or more parcels and in any order Trustee determines. Lender or its designee may purchase the Property at any sale.

Trustee shall deliver to the purchaser Trustee's deed conveying indefeasible title to the Property with covenants of general warranty. Borrower covenants and agrees to defend generally the purchaser's title to the Property against all claims and demands. The recitals in the Trustee's deed shall be prima facie evidence of the truth of the statements made therein. Trustee shall apply the proceeds of the sale in the following order: (a) to all expenses of the sale, including, but not limited to, reasonable Trustee's and attorneys' fees; (b) to all sums secured by this Security Instrument; and (c) any excess to the person or persons legally entitled to it.

If the Property is sold pursuant to this paragraph 17, Borrower or any person holding possession of the Property

-4R(TX) Page 5 of 6

EXHIBIT VIII-2—*continued*

through Borrower shall immediately surrender possession of the Property to the purchaser at that sale. If possession is not surrendered, Borrower or such person shall be a tenant at sufferance and may be removed by writ of possession.

18. Release. Upon payment of all sums secured by this Security Instrument, Lender shall release this Security Instrument without charge to Borrower. Borrower shall pay any recordation costs.

19. Substitute Trustee. Lender, at its option and with or without cause, may from time to time remove Trustee and appoint, by power of attorney or otherwise, a successor trustee to any Trustee appointed hereunder. Without conveyance of the Property, the successor trustee shall succeed to all the title, power and duties conferred upon Trustee herein and by applicable law.

20. Subrogation. Any of the proceeds of the Note used to take up outstanding liens against all or any part of the Property have been advanced by Lender at Borrower's request and upon Borrower's representation that such amounts are due and are secured by valid liens against the Property. Lender shall be subrogated to any and all rights, superior titles, liens and equities owned or claimed by any owner or holder of any outstanding liens and debts, regardless of whether said liens or debts acquired by Lender by assignment or are released by the holder thereof upon payment.

21. Partial Invalidity. In the event any portion of the sums intended to be secured by this Security Instrument cannot be lawfully secured hereby, payments in reduction of such sums shall be applied first to those portions not secured hereby.

22. Riders to this Security Instrument. If one or more riders are executed by Borrower and recorded together with this Security Instrument, the covenants of each such rider shall be incorporated into and shall amend and supplement the covenants and agreements of this Security Instrument as if the rider(s) were a part of this Security Instrument.
[Check applicable box(es)]

☐ Condominium Rider ☐ Graduated Payment Rider ☐ Other [Specify]
☐ Planned Unit Development Rider ☐ Growing Equity Rider

23. Purchase Money; Vendor's Lien; Renewal and Extension. [Complete as appropriate]

BY SIGNING BELOW, Borrower accepts and agrees to the terms contained in this Security Instrument and in any rider(s) executed by Borrower and recorded with it.
Witnesses:

____________________ (Seal)
-Borrower

____

____________________ (Seal)
-Borrower

____

____________________ (Seal)
-Borrower

____________________ (Seal)
-Borrower

STATE OF TEXAS, **County ss:**

BEFORE ME, the undersigned, a Notary Public in and for said County and State, on this day personally appeared

, known to me to be the person(s) whose name(s) subscribed to the foregoing instrument, and acknowledged to me that he executed the same for the purposes and consideration therein expressed.

GIVEN UNDER MY HAND AND SEAL OF OFFICE, this day of

____
Notary Public

VMP®-4R(TX) Page 6 of 6

EXHIBIT VIII-3: CONVENTIONAL MULTISTATE NOTE

NOTE

, 19 ,

[City] [State]

[Property Address]

1. BORROWER'S PROMISE TO PAY

In return for a loan that I have received, I promise to pay U.S. $ (this amount is called "principal"), plus interest, to the order of the Lender. The Lender is

I understand that the Lender may transfer this Note. The Lender or anyone who takes this Note by transfer and who is entitled to receive payments under this Note is called the "Note Holder."

2. INTEREST

Interest will be charged on unpaid principal until the full amount of principal has been paid. I will pay interest at a yearly rate of %.

The interest rate required by this Section 2 is the rate I will pay both before and after any default described in Section 6(B) of this Note.

3. PAYMENTS

(A) Time and Place of Payments

I will pay principal and interest by making payments every month.

I will make my monthly payments on the day of each month beginning on , 19 . I will make these payments every month until I have paid all of the principal and interest and any other charges described below that I may owe under this Note. My monthly payments will be applied to interest before principal. If, on , , I still owe amounts under this Note, I will pay those amounts in full on that date, which is called the "maturity date."

I will make my monthly payments at

or at a different place if required by the Note Holder.

(B) Amount of Monthly Payments

My monthly payment will be in the amount of U.S. $

4. BORROWER'S RIGHT TO PREPAY

I have the right to make payments of principal at any time before they are due. A payment of principal only is known as a "prepayment." When I make a prepayment, I will tell the Note Holder in writing that I am doing so.

I may make a full prepayment or partial prepayments without paying any prepayment charge. The Note Holder will use all of my prepayments to reduce the amount of principal that I owe under this Note. If I make a partial prepayment, there will be no changes in the due date or in the amount of my monthly payment unless the Note Holder agrees in writing to those changes.

5. LOAN CHARGES

If a law, which applies to this loan and which sets maximum loan charges, is finally interpreted so that the interest or other loan charges collected or to be collected in connection with this loan exceed the permitted limits, then: (i) any such loan charge shall be reduced by the amount necessary to reduce the charge to the permitted limit; and (ii) any sums already collected from me which exceeded permitted limits will be refunded to me. The Note Holder may choose to make this refund by reducing the principal I owe under this Note or by making a direct payment to me. If a refund reduces principal, the reduction will be treated as a partial prepayment.

6. BORROWER'S FAILURE TO PAY AS REQUIRED

(A) Late Charge for Overdue Payments

If the Note Holder has not received the full amount of any monthly payment by the end of calendar days after the date it is due, I will pay a late charge to the Note Holder. The amount of the charge will be % of my overdue payment of principal and interest I will pay this late charge promptly but only once on each late payment.

(B) Default

If I do not pay the full amount of each monthly payment on the date it is due, I will be in default.

(C) Notice of Default

If I am in default, the Note Holder may send me a written notice telling me that if I do not pay the overdue amount by a certain date, the Note Holder may require me to pay immediately the full amount of principal which has not been paid and all the interest that I owe on that amount. That date must be at least 30 days after the date on which the notice is delivered or mailed to me.

(D) No Waiver By Note Holder

Even if, at a time when I am in default, the Note Holder does not require me to pay immediately in full as described above, the Note Holder will still have the right to do so if I am in default at a later time.

(E) Payment of Note Holder's Costs and Expenses

If the Note Holder has required me to pay immediately in full as described above, the Note Holder will have the right to be paid back by me for all of its costs and expenses in enforcing this Note to the extent not prohibited by applicable law. Those expenses include, for example, reasonable attorneys' fees.

MULTISTATE FIXED RATE NOTE—Single Family—FNMA/FHLMC UNIFORM INSTRUMENT Form 3200 12/83 Amended 5/91

EXHIBIT VIII-3—*continued*

7. GIVING OF NOTICES

Unless applicable law requires a different method, any notice that must be given to me under this Note will be given by delivering it or by mailing it by first class mail to me at the Property Address above or at a different address if I give the Note Holder a notice of my different address.

Any notice that must be given to the Note Holder under this Note will be given by mailing it by first class mail to the Note Holder at the address stated in Section 3(A) above or at a different address if I am given a notice of that different address.

8. OBLIGATIONS OF PERSONS UNDER THIS NOTE

If more than one person signs this Note, each person is fully and personally obligated to keep all of the promises made in this Note, including the promise to pay the full amount owed. Any person who is a guarantor, surety or endorser of this Note is also obligated to do these things. Any person who takes over these obligations, including the obligations of a guarantor, surety or endorser of this Note, is also obligated to keep all of the promises made in this Note. The Note Holder may enforce its rights under this Note against each person individually or against all of us together. This means that any one of us may be required to pay all of the amounts owed under this Note.

9. WAIVERS

I and any other person who has obligations under this Note waive the rights of presentment and notice of dishonor. "Presentment" means the right to require the Note Holder to demand payment of amounts due. "Notice of dishonor" means the right to require the Note Holder to give notice to other persons that amounts due have not been paid.

10. UNIFORM SECURED NOTE

This Note is a uniform instrument with limited variations in some jurisdictions. In addition to the protections given to the Note Holder under this Note, a Mortgage, Deed of Trust or Security Deed (the "Security Instrument"), dated the same date as this Note, protects the Note Holder from possible losses which might result if I do not keep the promises which I make in this Note. That Security Instrument describes how and under what conditions I may be required to make immediate payment in full of all amounts I owe under this Note. Some of those conditions are described as follows:

> **Transfer of the Property or a Beneficial Interest in Borrower.** If all or any part of the Property or any interest in it is sold or transferred (or if a beneficial interest in Borrower is sold or transferred and Borrower is not a natural person), without Lender's prior written consent, Lender may, at its option, require immediate payment in full of all sums secured by this Security Instrument. However, this option shall not be exercised by Lender if exercise is prohibited by federal law as of the date of this Security Instrument.
>
> If Lender exercises this option, Lender shall give Borrower notice of acceleration. The notice shall provide a period of not less than 30 days from the date the notice is delivered or mailed within which Borrower must pay all sums secured by this Security Instrument. If Borrower fails to pay these sums prior to the expiration of this period, Lender may invoke any remedies permitted by this Security Instrument without further notice or demand on Borrower.

WITNESS THE HAND(S) AND SEAL(S) OF THE UNDERSIGNED.

______________________________ (Seal)
-Borrower
SSN:

______________________________ (Seal)
-Borrower
SSN:

______________________________ (Seal)
-Borrower
SSN:

______________________________ (Seal)
-Borrower
SSN:

(Sign Original Only)

[Space Above This Line For Recording Data]

MORTGAGE

THIS MORTGAGE ("Security Instrument") is given on . The mortgagor is

("Borrower"). This Security Instrument is given to

which is organized and existing under the laws of , and whose address is

("Lender"). Borrower owes Lender the principal sum of

Dollars (U.S. $).

This debt is evidenced by Borrower's note dated the same date as this Security Instrument ("Note"), which provides for monthly payments, with the full debt, if not paid earlier, due and payable on

This Security Instrument secures to Lender: (a) the repayment of the debt evidenced by the Note, with interest, and all renewals, extensions and modifications of the Note; (b) the payment of all other sums, with interest, advanced under paragraph 7 to protect the security of this Security Instrument; and (c) the performance of Borrower's covenants and agreements under this Security Instrument and the Note. For this purpose, Borrower does hereby mortgage, grant and convey to Lender the following described property located in County, Illinois:

which has the address of [Street, City],

Illinois [Zip Code] ("Property Address");

ILLINOIS-Single Family-**Fannie Mae/Freddie Mac UNIFORM INSTRUMENT** Page 1 of 6 **Form 3014 9/90 Amended 5/91**

VMP -6R(IL) (9105) VMP MORTGAGE FORMS · (313)293-8100 · (800)521-7291

TOGETHER WITH all the improvements now or hereafter erected on the property, and all easements, appurtenances, and fixtures now or hereafter a part of the property. All replacements and additions shall also be covered by this Security Instrument. All of the foregoing is referred to in this Security Instrument as the "Property."

BORROWER COVENANTS that Borrower is lawfully seised of the estate hereby conveyed and has the right to mortgage, grant and convey the Property and that the Property is unencumbered, except for encumbrances of record. Borrower warrants and will defend generally the title to the Property against all claims and demands, subject to any encumbrances of record.

THIS SECURITY INSTRUMENT combines uniform covenants for national use and non-uniform covenants with limited variations by jurisdiction to constitute a uniform security instrument covering real property.

UNIFORM COVENANTS. Borrower and Lender covenant and agree as follows:

1. Payment of Principal and Interest; Prepayment and Late Charges. Borrower shall promptly pay when due the principal of and interest on the debt evidenced by the Note and any prepayment and late charges due under the Note.

2. Funds for Taxes and Insurance. Subject to applicable law or to a written waiver by Lender, Borrower shall pay to Lender on the day monthly payments are due under the Note, until the Note is paid in full, a sum ("Funds") for: (a) yearly taxes and assessments which may attain priority over this Security Instrument as a lien on the Property; (b) yearly leasehold payments or ground rents on the Property, if any; (c) yearly hazard or property insurance premiums; (d) yearly flood insurance premiums, if any; (e) yearly mortgage insurance premiums, if any; and (f) any sums payable by Borrower to Lender, in accordance with the provisions of paragraph 8, in lieu of the payment of mortgage insurance premiums. These items are called "Escrow Items." Lender may, at any time, collect and hold Funds in an amount not to exceed the maximum amount a lender for a federally related mortgage loan may require for Borrower's escrow account under the federal Real Estate Settlement Procedures Act of 1974 as amended from time to time, 12 U.S.C. Section 2601 *et seq.* ("RESPA"), unless another law that applies to the Funds sets a lesser amount. If so, Lender may, at any time, collect and hold Funds in an amount not to exceed the lesser amount. Lender may estimate the amount of Funds due on the basis of current data and reasonable estimates of expenditures of future Escrow Items or otherwise in accordance with applicable law.

The Funds shall be held in an institution whose deposits are insured by a federal agency, instrumentality, or entity (including Lender, if Lender is such an institution) or in any Federal Home Loan Bank. Lender shall apply the Funds to pay the Escrow Items. Lender may not charge Borrower for holding and applying the Funds, annually analyzing the escrow account, or verifying the Escrow Items, unless Lender pays Borrower interest on the Funds and applicable law permits Lender to make such a charge. However, Lender may require Borrower to pay a one-time charge for an independent real estate tax reporting service used by Lender in connection with this loan, unless applicable law provides otherwise. Unless an agreement is made or applicable law requires interest to be paid, Lender shall not be required to pay Borrower any interest or earnings on the Funds. Borrower and Lender may agree in writing, however, that interest shall be paid on the Funds. Lender shall give to Borrower, without charge, an annual accounting of the Funds, showing credits and debits to the Funds and the purpose for which each debit to the Funds was made. The Funds are pledged as additional security for all sums secured by this Security Instrument.

If the Funds held by Lender exceed the amounts permitted to be held by applicable law, Lender shall account to Borrower for the excess Funds in accordance with the requirements of applicable law. If the amount of the Funds held by Lender at any time is not sufficient to pay the Escrow Items when due, Lender may so notify Borrower in writing, and, in such case Borrower shall pay to Lender the amount necessary to make up the deficiency. Borrower shall make up the deficiency in no more than twelve monthly payments, at Lender's sole discretion.

Upon payment in full of all sums secured by this Security Instrument, Lender shall promptly refund to Borrower any Funds held by Lender. If, under paragraph 21, Lender shall acquire or sell the Property, Lender, prior to the acquisition or sale of the Property, shall apply any Funds held by Lender at the time of acquisition or sale as a credit against the sums secured by this Security Instrument.

3. Application of Payments. Unless applicable law provides otherwise, all payments received by Lender under paragraphs 1 and 2 shall be applied: first, to any prepayment charges due under the Note; second, to amounts payable under paragraph 2; third, to interest due; fourth, to principal due; and last, to any late charges due under the Note.

4. Charges; Liens. Borrower shall pay all taxes, assessments, charges, fines and impositions attributable to the Property which may attain priority over this Security Instrument, and leasehold payments or ground rents, if any. Borrower shall pay these obligations in the manner provided in paragraph 2, or if not paid in that manner, Borrower shall pay them on time directly to the person owed payment. Borrower shall promptly furnish to Lender all notices of amounts to be paid under this paragraph. If Borrower makes these payments directly, Borrower shall promptly furnish to Lender receipts evidencing the payments.

Borrower shall promptly discharge any lien which has priority over this Security Instrument unless Borrower: (a) agrees in writing to the payment of the obligation secured by the lien in a manner acceptable to Lender; (b) contests in good faith the lien by, or defends against enforcement of the lien in, legal proceedings which in the Lender's opinion operate to prevent the enforcement of the lien; or (c) secures from the holder of the lien an agreement satisfactory to Lender subordinating the lien to this Security Instrument. If Lender determines that any part of the Property is subject to a lien which may attain priority over this Security Instrument, Lender may give Borrower a notice identifying the lien. Borrower shall satisfy the lien or take one or more of the actions set forth above within 10 days of the giving of notice.

Form 3014 9/90

Page 2 of 6

5. Hazard or Property Insurance. Borrower shall keep the improvements now existing or hereafter erected on the Property insured against loss by fire, hazards included within the term "extended coverage" and any other hazards, including floods or flooding, for which Lender requires insurance. This insurance shall be maintained in the amounts and for the periods that Lender requires. The insurance carrier providing the insurance shall be chosen by Borrower subject to Lender's approval which shall not be unreasonably withheld. If Borrower fails to maintain coverage described above, Lender may, at Lender's option, obtain coverage to protect Lender's rights in the Property in accordance with paragraph 7.

All insurance policies and renewals shall be acceptable to Lender and shall include a standard mortgage clause. Lender shall have the right to hold the policies and renewals. If Lender requires, Borrower shall promptly give to Lender all receipts of paid premiums and renewal notices. In the event of loss, Borrower shall give prompt notice to the insurance carrier and Lender. Lender may make proof of loss if not made promptly by Borrower.

Unless Lender and Borrower otherwise agree in writing, insurance proceeds shall be applied to restoration or repair of the Property damaged, if the restoration or repair is economically feasible and Lender's security is not lessened. If the restoration or repair is not economically feasible or Lender's security would be lessened, the insurance proceeds shall be applied to the sums secured by this Security Instrument, whether or not then due, with any excess paid to Borrower. If Borrower abandons the Property, or does not answer within 30 days a notice from Lender that the insurance carrier has offered to settle a claim, then Lender may collect the insurance proceeds. Lender may use the proceeds to repair or restore the Property or to pay sums secured by this Security Instrument, whether or not then due. The 30-day period will begin when the notice is given.

Unless Lender and Borrower otherwise agree in writing, any application of proceeds to principal shall not extend or postpone the due date of the monthly payments referred to in paragraphs 1 and 2 or change the amount of the payments. If under paragraph 21 the Property is acquired by Lender, Borrower's right to any insurance policies and proceeds resulting from damage to the Property prior to the acquisition shall pass to Lender to the extent of the sums secured by this Security Instrument immediately prior to the acquisition.

6. Occupancy, Preservation, Maintenance and Protection of the Property; Borrower's Loan Application; Leaseholds. Borrower shall occupy, establish, and use the Property as Borrower's principal residence within sixty days after the execution of this Security Instrument and shall continue to occupy the Property as Borrower's principal residence for at least one year after the date of occupancy, unless Lender otherwise agrees in writing, which consent shall not be unreasonably withheld, or unless extenuating circumstances exist which are beyond Borrower's control. Borrower shall not destroy, damage or impair the Property, allow the Property to deteriorate, or commit waste on the Property. Borrower shall be in default if any forfeiture action or proceeding, whether civil or criminal, is begun that in Lender's good faith judgment could result in forfeiture of the Property or otherwise materially impair the lien created by this Security Instrument or Lender's security interest. Borrower may cure such a default and reinstate, as provided in paragraph 18, by causing the action or proceeding to be dismissed with a ruling that, in Lender's good faith determination, precludes forfeiture of the Borrower's interest in the Property or other material impairment of the lien created by this Security Instrument or Lender's security interest. Borrower shall also be in default if Borrower, during the loan application process, gave materially false or inaccurate information or statements to Lender (or failed to provide Lender with any material information) in connection with the loan evidenced by the Note, including, but not limited to, representations concerning Borrower's occupancy of the Property as a principal residence. If this Security Instrument is on a leasehold, Borrower shall comply with all the provisions of the lease. If Borrower acquires fee title to the Property, the leasehold and the fee title shall not merge unless Lender agrees to the merger in writing.

7. Protection of Lender's Rights in the Property. If Borrower fails to perform the covenants and agreements contained in this Security Instrument, or there is a legal proceeding that may significantly affect Lender's rights in the Property (such as a proceeding in bankruptcy, probate, for condemnation or forfeiture or to enforce laws or regulations), then Lender may do and pay for whatever is necessary to protect the value of the Property and Lender's rights in the Property. Lender's actions may include paying any sums secured by a lien which has priority over this Security Instrument, appearing in court, paying reasonable attorneys' fees and entering on the Property to make repairs. Although Lender may take action under this paragraph 7, Lender does not have to do so.

Any amounts disbursed by Lender under this paragraph 7 shall become additional debt of Borrower secured by this Security Instrument. Unless Borrower and Lender agree to other terms of payment, these amounts shall bear interest from the date of disbursement at the Note rate and shall be payable, with interest, upon notice from Lender to Borrower requesting payment.

8. Mortgage Insurance. If Lender required mortgage insurance as a condition of making the loan secured by this Security Instrument, Borrower shall pay the premiums required to maintain the mortgage insurance in effect. If, for any reason, the mortgage insurance coverage required by Lender lapses or ceases to be in effect, Borrower shall pay the premiums required to obtain coverage substantially equivalent to the mortgage insurance previously in effect, at a cost substantially equivalent to the cost to Borrower of the mortgage insurance previously in effect, from an alternate mortgage insurer approved by Lender. If substantially equivalent mortgage insurance coverage is not available, Borrower shall pay to Lender each month a sum equal to one-twelfth of the yearly mortgage insurance premium being paid by Borrower when the insurance coverage lapsed or ceased to be in effect. Lender will accept, use and retain these payments as a loss reserve in lieu of mortgage insurance. Loss reserve

Form 3014 9/90

Page 3 of 6

payments may no longer be required, at the option of Lender, if mortgage insurance coverage (in the amount and for the period that Lender requires) provided by an insurer approved by Lender again becomes available and is obtained. Borrower shall pay the premiums required to maintain mortgage insurance in effect, or to provide a loss reserve, until the requirement for mortgage insurance ends in accordance with any written agreement between Borrower and Lender or applicable law.

9. Inspection. Lender or its agent may make reasonable entries upon and inspections of the Property. Lender shall give Borrower notice at the time of or prior to an inspection specifying reasonable cause for the inspection.

10. Condemnation. The proceeds of any award or claim for damages, direct or consequential, in connection with any condemnation or other taking of any part of the Property, or for conveyance in lieu of condemnation, are hereby assigned and shall be paid to Lender.

In the event of a total taking of the Property, the proceeds shall be applied to the sums secured by this Security Instrument, whether or not then due, with any excess paid to Borrower. In the event of a partial taking of the Property in which the fair market value of the Property immediately before the taking is equal to or greater than the amount of the sums secured by this Security Instrument immediately before the taking, unless Borrower and Lender otherwise agree in writing, the sums secured by this Security Instrument shall be reduced by the amount of the proceeds multiplied by the following fraction: (a) the total amount of the sums secured immediately before the taking, divided by (b) the fair market value of the Property immediately before the taking. Any balance shall be paid to Borrower. In the event of a partial taking of the Property in which the fair market value of the Property immediately before the taking is less than the amount of the sums secured immediately before the taking, unless Borrower and Lender otherwise agree in writing or unless applicable law otherwise provides, the proceeds shall be applied to the sums secured by this Security Instrument whether or not the sums are then due.

If the Property is abandoned by Borrower, or if, after notice by Lender to Borrower that the condemnor offers to make an award or settle a claim for damages, Borrower fails to respond to Lender within 30 days after the date the notice is given, Lender is authorized to collect and apply the proceeds, at its option, either to restoration or repair of the Property or to the sums secured by this Security Instrument, whether or not then due.

Unless Lender and Borrower otherwise agree in writing, any application of proceeds to principal shall not extend or postpone the due date of the monthly payments referred to in paragraphs 1 and 2 or change the amount of such payments.

11. Borrower Not Released; Forbearance By Lender Not a Waiver. Extension of the time for payment or modification of amortization of the sums secured by this Security Instrument granted by Lender to any successor in interest of Borrower shall not operate to release the liability of the original Borrower or Borrower's successors in interest. Lender shall not be required to commence proceedings against any successor in interest or refuse to extend time for payment or otherwise modify amortization of the sums secured by this Security Instrument by reason of any demand made by the original Borrower or Borrower's successors in interest. Any forbearance by Lender in exercising any right or remedy shall not be a waiver of or preclude the exercise of any right or remedy.

12. Successors and Assigns Bound; Joint and Several Liability; Co-signers. The covenants and agreements of this Security Instrument shall bind and benefit the successors and assigns of Lender and Borrower, subject to the provisions of paragraph 17. Borrower's covenants and agreements shall be joint and several. Any Borrower who co-signs this Security Instrument but does not execute the Note: (a) is co-signing this Security Instrument only to mortgage, grant and convey that Borrower's interest in the Property under the terms of this Security Instrument; (b) is not personally obligated to pay the sums secured by this Security Instrument; and (c) agrees that Lender and any other Borrower may agree to extend, modify, forbear or make any accommodations with regard to the terms of this Security Instrument or the Note without that Borrower's consent.

13. Loan Charges. If the loan secured by this Security Instrument is subject to a law which sets maximum loan charges, and that law is finally interpreted so that the interest or other loan charges collected or to be collected in connection with the loan exceed the permitted limits, then: (a) any such loan charge shall be reduced by the amount necessary to reduce the charge to the permitted limit; and (b) any sums already collected from Borrower which exceeded permitted limits will be refunded to Borrower. Lender may choose to make this refund by reducing the principal owed under the Note or by making a direct payment to Borrower. If a refund reduces principal, the reduction will be treated as a partial prepayment without any prepayment charge under the Note.

14. Notices. Any notice to Borrower provided for in this Security Instrument shall be given by delivering it or by mailing it by first class mail unless applicable law requires use of another method. The notice shall be directed to the Property Address or any other address Borrower designates by notice to Lender. Any notice to Lender shall be given by first class mail to Lender's address stated herein or any other address Lender designates by notice to Borrower. Any notice provided for in this Security Instrument shall be deemed to have been given to Borrower or Lender when given as provided in this paragraph.

15. Governing Law; Severability. This Security Instrument shall be governed by federal law and the law of the jurisdiction in which the Property is located. In the event that any provision or clause of this Security Instrument or the Note conflicts with applicable law, such conflict shall not affect other provisions of this Security Instrument or the Note which can be given effect without the conflicting provision. To this end the provisions of this Security Instrument and the Note are declared to be severable.

16. Borrower's Copy. Borrower shall be given one conformed copy of the Note and of this Security Instrument.

Form 3014 9/90

Page 4 of 6

17. Transfer of the Property or a Beneficial Interest in Borrower. If all or any part of the Property or any interest in it is sold or transferred (or if a beneficial interest in Borrower is sold or transferred and Borrower is not a natural person) without Lender's prior written consent, Lender may, at its option, require immediate payment in full of all sums secured by this Security Instrument. However, this option shall not be exercised by Lender if exercise is prohibited by federal law as of the date of this Security Instrument.

If Lender exercises this option, Lender shall give Borrower notice of acceleration. The notice shall provide a period of not less than 30 days from the date the notice is delivered or mailed within which Borrower must pay all sums secured by this Security Instrument. If Borrower fails to pay these sums prior to the expiration of this period, Lender may invoke any remedies permitted by this Security Instrument without further notice or demand on Borrower.

18. Borrower's Right to Reinstate. If Borrower meets certain conditions, Borrower shall have the right to have enforcement of this Security Instrument discontinued at any time prior to the earlier of: (a) 5 days (or such other period as applicable law may specify for reinstatement) before sale of the Property pursuant to any power of sale contained in this Security Instrument; or (b) entry of a judgment enforcing this Security Instrument. Those conditions are that Borrower: (a) pays Lender all sums which then would be due under this Security Instrument and the Note as if no acceleration had occurred; (b) cures any default of any other covenants or agreements; (c) pays all expenses incurred in enforcing this Security Instrument, including, but not limited to, reasonable attorneys' fees; and (d) takes such action as Lender may reasonably require to assure that the lien of this Security Instrument, Lender's rights in the Property and Borrower's obligation to pay the sums secured by this Security Instrument shall continue unchanged. Upon reinstatement by Borrower, this Security Instrument and the obligations secured hereby shall remain fully effective as if no acceleration had occurred. However, this right to reinstate shall not apply in the case of acceleration under paragraph 17.

19. Sale of Note; Change of Loan Servicer. The Note or a partial interest in the Note (together with this Security Instrument) may be sold one or more times without prior notice to Borrower. A sale may result in a change in the entity (known as the "Loan Servicer") that collects monthly payments due under the Note and this Security Instrument. There also may be one or more changes of the Loan Servicer unrelated to a sale of the Note. If there is a change of the Loan Servicer, Borrower will be given written notice of the change in accordance with paragraph 14 above and applicable law. The notice will state the name and address of the new Loan Servicer and the address to which payments should be made. The notice will also contain any other information required by applicable law.

20. Hazardous Substances. Borrower shall not cause or permit the presence, use, disposal, storage, or release of any Hazardous Substances on or in the Property. Borrower shall not do, nor allow anyone else to do, anything affecting the Property that is in violation of any Environmental Law. The preceding two sentences shall not apply to the presence, use, or storage on the Property of small quantities of Hazardous Substances that are generally recognized to be appropriate to normal residential uses and to maintenance of the Property.

Borrower shall promptly give Lender written notice of any investigation, claim, demand, lawsuit or other action by any governmental or regulatory agency or private party involving the Property and any Hazardous Substance or Environmental Law of which Borrower has actual knowledge. If Borrower learns, or is notified by any governmental or regulatory authority, that any removal or other remediation of any Hazardous Substance affecting the Property is necessary, Borrower shall promptly take all necessary remedial actions in accordance with Environmental Law.

As used in this paragraph 20, "Hazardous Substances" are those substances defined as toxic or hazardous substances by Environmental Law and the following substances: gasoline, kerosene, other flammable or toxic petroleum products, toxic pesticides and herbicides, volatile solvents, materials containing asbestos or formaldehyde, and radioactive materials. As used in this paragraph 20, "Environmental Law" means federal laws and laws of the jurisdiction where the Property is located that relate to health, safety or environmental protection.

NON-UNIFORM COVENANTS. Borrower and Lender further covenant and agree as follows:

21. Acceleration; Remedies. Lender shall give notice to Borrower prior to acceleration following Borrower's breach of any covenant or agreement in this Security Instrument (but not prior to acceleration under paragraph 17 unless applicable law provides otherwise). The notice shall specify: (a) the default; (b) the action required to cure the default; (c) a date, not less than 30 days from the date the notice is given to Borrower, by which the default must be cured; and (d) that failure to cure the default on or before the date specified in the notice may result in acceleration of the sums secured by this Security Instrument, foreclosure by judicial proceeding and sale of the Property. The notice shall further inform Borrower of the right to reinstate after acceleration and the right to assert in the foreclosure proceeding the non-existence of a default or any other defense of Borrower to acceleration and foreclosure. If the default is not cured on or before the date specified in the notice, Lender, at its option, may require immediate payment in full of all sums secured by this Security Instrument without further demand and may foreclose this Security Instrument by judicial proceeding. Lender shall be entitled to collect all expenses incurred in pursuing the remedies provided in this paragraph 21, including, but not limited to, reasonable attorneys' fees and costs of title evidence.

22. Release. Upon payment of all sums secured by this Security Instrument, Lender shall release this Security Instrument without charge to Borrower. Borrower shall pay any recordation costs.

23. Waiver of Homestead. Borrower waives all right of homestead exemption in the Property.

Form 3014 9/90

Page 5 of 6

EXHIBIT VIII-3—*continued*

24. Riders to this Security Instrument. If one or more riders are executed by Borrower and recorded together with this Security Instrument, the covenants and agreements of each such rider shall be incorporated into and shall amend and supplement the covenants and agreements of this Security Instrument as if the rider(s) were a part of this Security Instrument.
[Check applicable box(es)]

- ☐ Adjustable Rate Rider
- ☐ Graduated Payment Rider
- ☐ Balloon Rider
- ☐ V.A. Rider
- ☐ Condominium Rider
- ☐ Planned Unit Development Rider
- ☐ Rate Improvement Rider
- ☐ Other(s) [specify]
- ☐ 1-4 Family Rider
- ☐ Biweekly Payment Rider
- ☐ Second Home Rider

BY SIGNING BELOW, Borrower accepts and agrees to the terms and covenants contained in this Security Instrument and in any rider(s) executed by Borrower and recorded with it.
Witnesses:

____________________ (Seal)
-Borrower

____

____________________ (Seal)
-Borrower

____

____________________ (Seal)
-Borrower

____________________ (Seal)
-Borrower

STATE OF ILLINOIS, **County ss:**

I, , a Notary Public in and for said county and state do hereby certify that

, personally known to me to be the same person(s) whose name(s) subscribed to the foregoing instrument, appeared before me this day in person, and acknowledged that he signed and delivered the said instrument as free and voluntary act, for the uses and purposes therein set forth.

Given under my hand and official seal, this day of

My Commission Expires:

____
Notary Public

This Instrument was prepared by:

Page 6 of 6 **Form 3014 9/90**

[Space Above This Line For Recording Data]

DEED OF TRUST

THIS DEED OF TRUST ("Security Instrument") is made on . The grantor is

("Borrower"). The trustee is

, whose address is

("Trustee"). The beneficiary is

,

which is organized and existing under the laws of , and whose address is

("Lender"). Borrower owes Lender the principal sum of

Dollars (U.S. $).

This debt is evidenced by Borrower's note dated the same date as this Security Instrument ("Note"), which provides for monthly payments, with the full debt, if not paid earlier, due and payable on

This Security Instrument secures to Lender: (a) the repayment of the debt evidenced by the Note, with interest, and all renewals, extensions and modifications of the Note; (b) the payment of all other sums, with interest, advanced under paragraph 7 to protect the security of this Security Instrument; and (c) the performance of Borrower's covenants and agreements under this Security Instrument and the Note. For this purpose, Borrower irrevocably grants and conveys to Trustee, in trust, with power of sale, the following described property located in County, Texas:

which has the address of [Street, City],

Texas [Zip Code] ("Property Address");

TOGETHER WITH all the improvements now or hereafter erected on the property, and all easements, appurtenances, and fixtures now or hereafter a part of the property. All replacements and additions shall also be covered by this Security Instrument. All of the foregoing is referred to in this Security Instrument as the "Property."

BORROWER COVENANTS that Borrower is lawfully seised of the estate hereby conveyed and has the right to grant and convey the Property and that the Property is unencumbered, except for encumbrances of record. Borrower warrants and will defend generally the title to the Property against all claims and demands, subject to any encumbrances of record.

THIS SECURITY INSTRUMENT combines uniform covenants for national use and non-uniform covenants with limited variations by jurisdiction to constitute a uniform security instrument covering real property.

UNIFORM COVENANTS. Borrower and Lender covenant and agree as follows:

1. Payment of Principal and Interest; Prepayment and Late Charges. Borrower shall promptly pay when due the principal of and interest on the debt evidenced by the Note and any prepayment and late charges due under the Note.

2. Funds for Taxes and Insurance. Subject to applicable law or to a written waiver by Lender, Borrower shall pay to Lender on the day monthly payments are due under the Note, until the Note is paid in full, a sum ("Funds") for: (a) yearly taxes and assessments which may attain priority over this Security Instrument as a lien on the Property; (b) yearly leasehold payments or ground rents on the Property, if any; (c) yearly hazard or property insurance premiums; (d) yearly flood insurance premiums, if any; (e) yearly mortgage insurance premiums, if any; and (f) any sums payable by Borrower to Lender, in accordance with the provisions of paragraph 8, in lieu of the payment of mortgage insurance premiums. These items are called "Escrow Items." Lender may, at any time, collect and hold Funds in an amount not to exceed the maximum amount a lender for a federally related mortgage loan may require for Borrower's escrow account under the federal Real Estate Settlement Procedures Act of 1974 as amended from time to time, 12 U.S.C. Section 2601 *et seq.* ("RESPA"), unless another law that applies to the Funds sets a lesser amount. If so, Lender may, at any time, collect and hold Funds in an amount not to exceed the lesser amount. Lender may estimate the amount of Funds due on the basis of current data and reasonable estimates of expenditures of future Escrow Items or otherwise in accordance with applicable law.

The Funds shall be held in an institution whose deposits are insured by a federal agency, instrumentality, or entity (including Lender, if Lender is such an institution) or in any Federal Home Loan Bank. Lender shall apply the Funds to pay the Escrow Items. Lender may not charge Borrower for holding and applying the Funds, annually analyzing the escrow account, or verifying the Escrow Items, unless Lender pays Borrower interest on the Funds and applicable law permits Lender to make such a charge. However, Lender may require Borrower to pay a one-time charge for an independent real estate tax reporting service used by Lender in connection with this loan, unless applicable law provides otherwise. Unless an agreement is made or applicable law requires interest to be paid, Lender shall not be required to pay Borrower any interest or earnings on the Funds. Borrower and Lender may agree in writing, however, that interest shall be paid on the Funds. Lender shall give to Borrower, without charge, an annual accounting of the Funds, showing credits and debits to the Funds and the purpose for which each debit to the Funds was made. The Funds are pledged as additional security for all sums secured by this Security Instrument.

If the Funds held by Lender exceed the amounts permitted to be held by applicable law, Lender shall account to Borrower for the excess Funds in accordance with the requirements of applicable law. If the amount of the Funds held by Lender at any time is not sufficient to pay the Escrow Items when due, Lender may so notify Borrower in writing, and, in such case Borrower shall pay to Lender the amount necessary to make up the deficiency. Borrower shall make up the deficiency in no more than twelve monthly payments, at Lender's sole discretion.

Upon payment in full of all sums secured by this Security Instrument, Lender shall promptly refund to Borrower any Funds held by Lender. If, under paragraph 21, Lender shall acquire or sell the Property, Lender, prior to the acquisition or sale of the Property, shall apply any Funds held by Lender at the time of acquisition or sale as a credit against the sums secured by this Security Instrument.

3. Application of Payments. Unless applicable law provides otherwise, all payments received by Lender under paragraphs 1 and 2 shall be applied: first, to any prepayment charges due under the Note; second, to amounts payable under paragraph 2; third, to interest due; fourth, to principal due; and last, to any late charges due under the Note.

4. Charges; Liens. Borrower shall pay all taxes, assessments, charges, fines and impositions attributable to the Property which may attain priority over this Security Instrument, and leasehold payments or ground rents, if any. Borrower shall pay these obligations in the manner provided in paragraph 2, or if not paid in that manner, Borrower shall pay them on time directly to the person owed payment. Borrower shall promptly furnish to Lender all notices of amounts to be paid under this paragraph. If Borrower makes these payments directly, Borrower shall promptly furnish to Lender receipts evidencing the payments.

Borrower shall promptly discharge any lien which has priority over this Security Instrument unless Borrower: (a) agrees in writing to the payment of the obligation secured by the lien in a manner acceptable to Lender; (b) contests in good faith the lien by, or defends against enforcement of the lien in, legal proceedings which in the Lender's opinion operate to prevent the enforcement of the lien; or (c) secures from the holder of the lien an agreement satisfactory to Lender subordinating the lien to this Security Instrument. If Lender determines that any part of the Property is subject to a lien which may attain priority over this Security Instrument, Lender may give Borrower a notice identifying the lien. Borrower shall satisfy the lien or take one or more of the actions set forth above within 10 days of the giving of notice.

Form 3044 9/90

Page 2 of 6

5. Hazard or Property Insurance. Borrower shall keep the improvements now existing or hereafter erected on the Property insured against loss by fire, hazards included within the term "extended coverage" and any other hazards, including floods or flooding, for which Lender requires insurance. This insurance shall be maintained in the amounts and for the periods that Lender requires. The insurance carrier providing the insurance shall be chosen by Borrower subject to Lender's approval which shall not be unreasonably withheld. If Borrower fails to maintain coverage described above, Lender may, at Lender's option, obtain coverage to protect Lender's rights in the Property in accordance with paragraph 7.

All insurance policies and renewals shall be acceptable to Lender and shall include a standard mortgage clause. Lender shall have the right to hold the policies and renewals. If Lender requires, Borrower shall promptly give to Lender all receipts of paid premiums and renewal notices. In the event of loss, Borrower shall give prompt notice to the insurance carrier and Lender. Lender may make proof of loss if not made promptly by Borrower.

Unless Lender and Borrower otherwise agree in writing, insurance proceeds shall be applied to restoration or repair of the Property damaged, if the restoration or repair is economically feasible and Lender's security is not lessened. If the restoration or repair is not economically feasible or Lender's security would be lessened, the insurance proceeds shall be applied to the sums secured by this Security Instrument, whether or not then due, with any excess paid to Borrower. If Borrower abandons the Property, or does not answer within 30 days a notice from Lender that the insurance carrier has offered to settle a claim, then Lender may collect the insurance proceeds. Lender may use the proceeds to repair or restore the Property or to pay sums secured by this Security Instrument, whether or not then due. The 30-day period will begin when the notice is given.

Unless Lender and Borrower otherwise agree in writing, any application of proceeds to principal shall not extend or postpone the due date of the monthly payments referred to in paragraphs 1 and 2 or change the amount of the payments. If under paragraph 21 the Property is acquired by Lender, Borrower's right to any insurance policies and proceeds resulting from damage to the Property prior to the acquisition shall pass to Lender to the extent of the sums secured by this Security Instrument immediately prior to the acquisition.

6. Occupancy, Preservation, Maintenance and Protection of the Property; Borrower's Loan Application; Leaseholds. Borrower shall occupy, establish, and use the Property as Borrower's principal residence within sixty days after the execution of this Security Instrument and shall continue to occupy the Property as Borrower's principal residence for at least one year after the date of occupancy, unless Lender otherwise agrees in writing, which consent shall not be unreasonably withheld, or unless extenuating circumstances exist which are beyond Borrower's control. Borrower shall not destroy, damage or impair the Property, allow the Property to deteriorate, or commit waste on the Property. Borrower shall be in default if any forfeiture action or proceeding, whether civil or criminal, is begun that in Lender's good faith judgment could result in forfeiture of the Property or otherwise materially impair the lien created by this Security Instrument or Lender's security interest. Borrower may cure such a default and reinstate, as provided in paragraph 18, by causing the action or proceeding to be dismissed with a ruling that, in Lender's good faith determination, precludes forfeiture of the Borrower's interest in the Property or other material impairment of the lien created by this Security Instrument or Lender's security interest. Borrower shall also be in default if Borrower, during the loan application process, gave materially false or inaccurate information or statements to Lender (or failed to provide Lender with any material information) in connection with the loan evidenced by the Note, including, but not limited to, representations concerning Borrower's occupancy of the Property as a principal residence. If this Security Instrument is on a leasehold, Borrower shall comply with all the provisions of the lease. If Borrower acquires fee title to the Property, the leasehold and the fee title shall not merge unless Lender agrees to the merger in writing.

7. Protection of Lender's Rights in the Property. If Borrower fails to perform the covenants and agreements contained in this Security Instrument, or there is a legal proceeding that may significantly affect Lender's rights in the Property (such as a proceeding in bankruptcy, probate, for condemnation or forfeiture or to enforce laws or regulations), then Lender may do and pay for whatever is necessary to protect the value of the Property and Lender's rights in the Property. Lender's actions may include paying any sums secured by a lien which has priority over this Security Instrument, appearing in court, paying reasonable attorneys' fees and entering on the Property to make repairs. Although Lender may take action under this paragraph 7, Lender does not have to do so.

Any amounts disbursed by Lender under this paragraph 7 shall become additional debt of Borrower secured by this Security Instrument. Unless Borrower and Lender agree to other terms of payment, these amounts shall bear interest from the date of disbursement at the Note rate and shall be payable, with interest, upon notice from Lender to Borrower requesting payment.

8. Mortgage Insurance. If Lender required mortgage insurance as a condition of making the loan secured by this Security Instrument, Borrower shall pay the premiums required to maintain the mortgage insurance in effect. If, for any reason, the mortgage insurance coverage required by Lender lapses or ceases to be in effect, Borrower shall pay the premiums required to obtain coverage substantially equivalent to the mortgage insurance previously in effect, at a cost substantially equivalent to the cost to Borrower of the mortgage insurance previously in effect, from an alternate mortgage insurer approved by Lender. If substantially equivalent mortgage insurance coverage is not available, Borrower shall pay to Lender each month a sum equal to one-twelfth of the yearly mortgage insurance premium being paid by Borrower when the insurance coverage lapsed or ceased to be in effect. Lender will accept, use and retain these payments as a loss reserve in lieu of mortgage insurance. Loss reserve

Form 3044 9/90

Page 3 of 6

payments may no longer be required, at the option of Lender, if mortgage insurance coverage (in the amount and for the period that Lender requires) provided by an insurer approved by Lender again becomes available and is obtained. Borrower shall pay the premiums required to maintain mortgage insurance in effect, or to provide a loss reserve, until the requirement for mortgage insurance ends in accordance with any written agreement between Borrower and Lender or applicable law.

9. Inspection. Lender or its agent may make reasonable entries upon and inspections of the Property. Lender shall give Borrower notice at the time of or prior to an inspection specifying reasonable cause for the inspection.

10. Condemnation. The proceeds of any award or claim for damages, direct or consequential, in connection with any condemnation or other taking of any part of the Property, or for conveyance in lieu of condemnation, are hereby assigned and shall be paid to Lender.

In the event of a total taking of the Property, the proceeds shall be applied to the sums secured by this Security Instrument, whether or not then due, with any excess paid to Borrower. In the event of a partial taking of the Property in which the fair market value of the Property immediately before the taking is equal to or greater than the amount of the sums secured by this Security Instrument immediately before the taking, unless Borrower and Lender otherwise agree in writing, the sums secured by this Security Instrument shall be reduced by the amount of the proceeds multiplied by the following fraction: (a) the total amount of the sums secured immediately before the taking, divided by (b) the fair market value of the Property immediately before the taking. Any balance shall be paid to Borrower. In the event of a partial taking of the Property in which the fair market value of the Property immediately before the taking is less than the amount of the sums secured immediately before the taking, unless Borrower and Lender otherwise agree in writing or unless applicable law otherwise provides, the proceeds shall be applied to the sums secured by this Security Instrument whether or not the sums are then due.

If the Property is abandoned by Borrower, or if, after notice by Lender to Borrower that the condemnor offers to make an award or settle a claim for damages, Borrower fails to respond to Lender within 30 days after the date the notice is given, Lender is authorized to collect and apply the proceeds, at its option, either to restoration or repair of the Property or to the sums secured by this Security Instrument, whether or not then due.

Unless Lender and Borrower otherwise agree in writing, any application of proceeds to principal shall not extend or postpone the due date of the monthly payments referred to in paragraphs 1 and 2 or change the amount of such payments.

11. Borrower Not Released; Forbearance By Lender Not a Waiver. Extension of the time for payment or modification of amortization of the sums secured by this Security Instrument granted by Lender to any successor in interest of Borrower shall not operate to release the liability of the original Borrower or Borrower's successors in interest. Lender shall not be required to commence proceedings against any successor in interest or refuse to extend time for payment or otherwise modify amortization of the sums secured by this Security Instrument by reason of any demand made by the original Borrower or Borrower's successors in interest. Any forbearance by Lender in exercising any right or remedy shall not be a waiver of or preclude the exercise of any right or remedy.

12. Successors and Assigns Bound; Joint and Several Liability; Co-signers. The covenants and agreements of this Security Instrument shall bind and benefit the successors and assigns of Lender and Borrower, subject to the provisions of paragraph 17. Borrower's covenants and agreements shall be joint and several. Any Borrower who co-signs this Security Instrument but does not execute the Note: (a) is co-signing this Security Instrument only to mortgage, grant and convey that Borrower's interest in the Property under the terms of this Security Instrument; (b) is not personally obligated to pay the sums secured by this Security Instrument; and (c) agrees that Lender and any other Borrower may agree to extend, modify, forbear or make any accommodations with regard to the terms of this Security Instrument or the Note without that Borrower's consent.

13. Loan Charges. If the loan secured by this Security Instrument is subject to a law which sets maximum loan charges, and that law is finally interpreted so that the interest or other loan charges collected or to be collected in connection with the loan exceed the permitted limits, then: (a) any such loan charge shall be reduced by the amount necessary to reduce the charge to the permitted limit; and (b) any sums already collected from Borrower which exceeded permitted limits will be refunded to Borrower. Lender may choose to make this refund by reducing the principal owed under the Note or by making a direct payment to Borrower. If a refund reduces principal, the reduction will be treated as a partial prepayment without any prepayment charge under the Note.

14. Notices. Any notice to Borrower provided for in this Security Instrument shall be given by delivering it or by mailing it by first class mail unless applicable law requires use of another method. The notice shall be directed to the Property Address or any other address Borrower designates by notice to Lender. Any notice to Lender shall be given by first class mail to Lender's address stated herein or any other address Lender designates by notice to Borrower. Any notice provided for in this Security Instrument shall be deemed to have been given to Borrower or Lender when given as provided in this paragraph.

15. Governing Law; Severability. This Security Instrument shall be governed by federal law and the law of the jurisdiction in which the Property is located. In the event that any provision or clause of this Security Instrument or the Note conflicts with applicable law, such conflict shall not affect other provisions of this Security Instrument or the Note which can be given effect without the conflicting provision. To this end the provisions of this Security Instrument and the Note are declared to be severable.

16. Borrower's Copy. Borrower shall be given one conformed copy of the Note and of this Security Instrument.

Form 3044 9/90

Page 4 of 6

17. Transfer of the Property or a Beneficial Interest in Borrower. If all or any part of the Property or any interest in it is sold or transferred (or if a beneficial interest in Borrower is sold or transferred and Borrower is not a natural person) without Lender's prior written consent, Lender may, at its option, require immediate payment in full of all sums secured by this Security Instrument. However, this option shall not be exercised by Lender if exercise is prohibited by federal law as of the date of this Security Instrument.

If Lender exercises this option, Lender shall give Borrower notice of acceleration. The notice shall provide a period of not less than 30 days from the date the notice is delivered or mailed within which Borrower must pay all sums secured by this Security Instrument. If Borrower fails to pay these sums prior to the expiration of this period, Lender may invoke any remedies permitted by this Security Instrument without further notice or demand on Borrower.

18. Borrower's Right to Reinstate. If Borrower meets certain conditions, Borrower shall have the right to have enforcement of this Security Instrument discontinued at any time prior to the earlier of: (a) 5 days (or such other period as applicable law may specify for reinstatement) before sale of the Property pursuant to any power of sale contained in this Security Instrument; or (b) entry of a judgment enforcing this Security Instrument. Those conditions are that Borrower: (a) pays Lender all sums which then would be due under this Security Instrument and the Note as if no acceleration had occurred; (b) cures any default of any other covenants or agreements; (c) pays all expenses incurred in enforcing this Security Instrument, including, but not limited to, reasonable attorneys' fees; and (d) takes such action as Lender may reasonably require to assure that the lien of this Security Instrument, Lender's rights in the Property and Borrower's obligation to pay the sums secured by this Security Instrument shall continue unchanged. Upon reinstatement by Borrower, this Security Instrument and the obligations secured hereby shall remain fully effective as if no acceleration had occurred. However, this right to reinstate shall not apply in the case of acceleration under paragraph 17.

19. Sale of Note; Change of Loan Servicer. The Note or a partial interest in the Note (together with this Security Instrument) may be sold one or more times without prior notice to Borrower. A sale may result in a change in the entity (known as the "Loan Servicer") that collects monthly payments due under the Note and this Security Instrument. There also may be one or more changes of the Loan Servicer unrelated to a sale of the Note. If there is a change of the Loan Servicer, Borrower will be given written notice of the change in accordance with paragraph 14 above and applicable law. The notice will state the name and address of the new Loan Servicer and the address to which payments should be made. The notice will also contain any other information required by applicable law.

20. Hazardous Substances. Borrower shall not cause or permit the presence, use, disposal, storage, or release of any Hazardous Substances on or in the Property. Borrower shall not do, nor allow anyone else to do, anything affecting the Property that is in violation of any Environmental Law. The preceding two sentences shall not apply to the presence, use, or storage on the Property of small quantities of Hazardous Substances that are generally recognized to be appropriate to normal residential uses and to maintenance of the Property.

Borrower shall promptly give Lender written notice of any investigation, claim, demand, lawsuit or other action by any governmental or regulatory agency or private party involving the Property and any Hazardous Substance or Environmental Law of which Borrower has actual knowledge. If Borrower learns, or is notified by any governmental or regulatory authority, that any removal or other remediation of any Hazardous Substance affecting the Property is necessary, Borrower shall promptly take all necessary remedial actions in accordance with Environmental Law.

As used in this paragraph 20, "Hazardous Substances" are those substances defined as toxic or hazardous substances by Environmental Law and the following substances: gasoline, kerosene, other flammable or toxic petroleum products, toxic pesticides and herbicides, volatile solvents, materials containing asbestos or formaldehyde, and radioactive materials. As used in this paragraph 20, "Environmental Law" means federal laws and laws of the jurisdiction where the Property is located that relate to health, safety or environmental protection.

NON-UNIFORM COVENANTS. Borrower and Lender further covenant and agree as follows:

21. Acceleration; Remedies. Lender shall give notice to Borrower prior to acceleration following Borrower's breach of any covenant or agreement in this Security Instrument (but not prior to acceleration under paragraph 17 unless applicable law provides otherwise). The notice shall specify: (a) the default; (b) the action required to cure the default; (c) a date, not less than 30 days from the date the notice is given to Borrower, by which the default must be cured; and (d) that failure to cure the default on or before the date specified in the notice will result in acceleration of the sums secured by this Security Instrument and sale of the Property. The notice shall further inform Borrower of the right to reinstate after acceleration and the right to bring a court action to assert the non-existence of a default or any other defense of Borrower to acceleration and sale. If the default is not cured on or before the date specified in the notice, Lender, at its option, may require immediate payment in full of all sums secured by this Security Instrument without further demand and may invoke the power of sale and any other remedies permitted by applicable law. Lender shall be entitled to collect all expenses incurred in pursuing the remedies provided in this paragraph 21, including, but not limited to, reasonable attorneys' fees and costs of title evidence.

If Lender invokes the power of sale, Lender or Trustee shall give notice of the time, place and terms of sale by posting and recording the notice at least 21 days prior to sale as provided by applicable law. Lender shall mail a copy of the notice of sale to Borrower in the manner prescribed by applicable law. Sale shall be made at public vendue between the hours of 10 a.m. and 4 p.m. on the first Tuesday of the month. Borrower authorizes Trustee to sell the Property to the highest bidder for cash in one or more parcels and in any order Trustee determines. Lender or its designee may purchase the Property at any sale.

Trustee shall deliver to the purchaser Trustee's deed conveying indefeasible title to the Property with covenants of general warranty. Borrower covenants and agrees to defend generally the purchaser's title to the Property against all claims and demands. The recitals in the Trustee's deed shall be prima facie evidence of the truth of the statements made therein. Trustee shall apply the proceeds of the sale in the following order: (a) to all expenses of the sale, including, but not limited to, reasonable Trustee's and attorneys' fees; (b) to all sums secured by this Security Instrument; and (c) any excess to the person or persons legally entitled to it.

If the Property is sold pursuant to this paragraph 21, Borrower or any person holding possession of the Property through Borrower shall immediately surrender possession of the Property to the purchaser at that sale. If possession is not surrendered, Borrower or such person shall be a tenant at sufferance and may be removed by writ of possession.

Form 3044 9/90

EXHIBIT VIII-3—*continued*

22. Release. Upon payment of all sums secured by this Security Instrument, Lender shall release this Security Instrument without charge to Borrower. Borrower shall pay any recordation costs.

23. Substitute Trustee. Lender, at its option and with or without cause, may from time to time remove Trustee and appoint, by power of attorney or otherwise, a successor trustee to any Trustee appointed hereunder. Without conveyance of the Property, the successor trustee shall succeed to all the title, power and duties conferred upon Trustee herein and by applicable law.

24. Subrogation. Any of the proceeds of the Note used to take up outstanding liens against all or any part of the Property have been advanced by Lender at Borrower's request and upon Borrower's representation that such amounts are due and are secured by valid liens against the Property. Lender shall be subrogated to any and all rights, superior titles, liens and equities owned or claimed by any owner or holder of any outstanding liens and debts, regardless of whether said liens or debts are acquired by Lender by assignment or are released by the holder thereof upon payment.

25. Partial Invalidity. In the event any portion of the sums intended to be secured by this Security Instrument cannot be lawfully secured hereby, payments in reduction of such sums shall be applied first to those portions not secured hereby.

26. Waiver of Notice of Intention to Accelerate. Borrower waives the right to notice of intention to require immediate payment in full of all sums secured by this Security Instrument except as provided in paragraph 21.

27. Riders to this Security Instrument. If one or more riders are executed by Borrower and recorded together with this Security Instrument, the covenants and agreements of each such rider shall be incorporated into and shall amend and supplement the covenants and agreements of this Security Instrument as if the rider(s) were a part of this Security Instrument.
[Check applicable box(es)]

☐ Adjustable Rate Rider	☐ Condominium Rider	☐ 1-4 Family Rider
☐ Graduated Payment Rider	☐ Planned Unit Development Rider	☐ Biweekly Payment Rider
☐ Balloon Rider	☐ Rate Improvement Rider	☐ Second Home Rider
☐ V.A. Rider	☐ Other(s) [specify]	

28. Purchase Money; Vendor's Lien; Renewal and Extension. [Complete as appropriate]

BY SIGNING BELOW, Borrower accepts and agrees to the terms and covenants contained in this Security Instrument and in any rider(s) executed by Borrower and recorded with it.

Witnesses:

_______________________________ (Seal)
-Borrower
Social Security Number

____

_______________________________ (Seal)
-Borrower
Social Security Number

____

_______________________________ (Seal)
-Borrower
Social Security Number

_______________________________ (Seal)
-Borrower
Social Security Number

STATE OF TEXAS, **County ss:**

BEFORE ME, the undersigned, a Notary Public in and for said County and State, on this day personally appeared

, known to me to be the person(s) whose name(s) subscribed to the foregoing instrument, and acknowledged to me that he executed the same for the purposes and consideration therein expressed.

GIVEN UNDER MY HAND AND SEAL OF OFFICE, this day of

____
Notary Public

Form 3044 9/90

EXHIBIT VIII-4: VA MORTGAGE AND MORTGAGE NOTE

VA Form 26—6310a (Home Loan)
Rev. October 1974. Use Optional.
Section 1810, Title 38, U.S.C.
Acceptable to Federal National
Mortgage Association
(Amended May, 1989)

ILLINOIS

MORTGAGE NOTE

NOTICE: THIS LOAN IS NOT ASSUMABLE WITHOUT THE APPROVAL OF THE DEPARTMENT OF VETERANS AFFAIRS OR ITS AUTHORIZED AGENT.

$ Illinois.
19

FOR VALUE RECEIVED, the undersigned, promise(s) to pay to the order of

the principal sum of

Dollars ($), with interest from date at the rate of
per centum (%) per annum on the unpaid balance until paid; the said principal and interest to be payable in monthly installments as follows:

Dollars ($) beginning on the first day of , 19 , and continuing on the first day of each month thereafter until this note is fully paid, except that, if not sooner paid, the final payment of principal and interest shall be due and payable on the first day of

Both principal and interest shall be payable at the office of
in
or at such other place as the holder may from time to time designate in writing delivered or mailed to the debtor.

Privilege is reserved to prepay at any time, without premium or fee, the entire indebtedness or any part thereof not less than the amount of one installment, or one hundred dollars ($100.00), whichever is less. Prepayment in full shall be credited on the date received. Partial prepayment, other than on an installment due date, need not be credited until the next following installment due date or thirty days after such prepayment, whichever is earlier.

If there be any deficiency in the payment of any such installment of principal and interest for a period of thirty (30) days after the due date thereof, the holder of this note may, at its option, and without notice, declare all the unpaid principal and accrued interest of said note immediately due and payable. Failure to exercise this option shall not constitute a waiver of the right to exercise the same in the event of any subsequent default.

This note is secured by mortgage of even date executed by the undersigned on certain property described therein and represents money actually used for the acquisition of said property or the improvements thereon.

Presentment for payment, protest, notice of protest, demand and notice of nonpayment are hereby waived. Each and all of the parties now or hereafter personally liable for the payment of any of the debt hereby evidenced agree, by executing or endorsing this note or by entering into or executing any agreement to pay any of said debt, that the legal owner or holder hereof shall have the right, without notice and at any time or times, to deal in any way with such party or any other person with respect to said debt or to grant to any such party or any other person any extensions of time for payment of any of said debt or any release of liability or any other indulgences or forebearances whatever, without releasing or in any way affecting the personal liability of any other party hereunder.

(Signature)	*(Signature)*
(Address)	*(Address)*
(Signature)	*(Signature)*
(Address)	*(Address)*

THIS IS TO CERTIFY that this is the note described in and secured by mortgage of even date herewith, in the same principal amount as herein stated and secured on real estate situated in the
of , county of , and State of Illinois.

Dated , 19

Notary Public.

VMP-2(IL) (8904) VMP MORTGAGE FORMS • (313)293-8100 • (800)521-7291

VA Form 26—6310 (Home Loan)
Rev. August 1981. Use Optional.
Section 1810, Title 38, U.S.C.
Acceptable to
Federal National Mortgage Association
(Amended May, 1989)

ILLINOIS

MORTGAGE

NOTICE: THIS LOAN IS NOT ASSUMABLE WITHOUT THE APPROVAL OF THE DEPARTMENT OF VETERANS AFFAIRS OR ITS AUTHORIZED AGENT. The attached RIDER is made a part of this instrument.

THIS INDENTURE, made this day of 19 , between

, Mortgagor, and

a corporation organized and existing under the laws of
Mortgagee.

WITNESSETH: That whereas the Mortgagor is justly indebted to the Mortgagee, as is evidenced by a certain promissory note executed and delivered by the Mortgagor, in favor of the Mortgagee, and bearing even date herewith, in the principal sum of

Dollars ($) payable with interest at the rate of
per centum (%) per annum on the unpaid balance until paid, and made payable to the order of the Mortgagee at its office in ,

, or at such other place as the holder may designate in writing, and delivered or mailed to the Mortgagor; the said principal and interest being payable in monthly installments of

Dollars ($) beginning on the first day of , 19 , and continuing on the first day of each month thereafter until the note is fully paid, except that the final payment of principal and interest, if not sooner paid, shall be due and payable on the first day of

NOW, THEREFORE, the said Mortgagor, for the better securing of the payment of said principal sum of money and interest and the performance of the covenants and agreements herein contained, does by these presents MORTGAGE and WARRANT unto the Mortgagee, its successors or assigns, the following described real estate situate, lying, and being in the county of and the State of Illinois, to wit:

TOGETHER with all and singular the tenements, hereditaments and appurtenances thereunto belonging, and the rents, issues, and profits thereof; and all fixtures now or hereafter attached to or used in connection with the premises herein described and in addition thereto the following described household appliances, which are, and shall be deemed to be, fixtures and a part of the realty, and are a portion of the security for the indebtedness herein mentioned;

VMP-3(IL) (8904) VMP MORTGAGE FORMS • (313)293-8100 • (800)521-7291

TO HAVE AND TO HOLD the above-described premises, with the appurtenances and fixtures, unto the said Mortgagee, its successors and assigns, forever, for the purposes and uses herein set forth, free from all rights and benefits under and by virtue of the Homestead Exemption Laws of the State of Illinois, which said rights and benefits the said Mortgagor does hereby expressly release and waive.

AND SAID MORTGAGOR covenants and agrees:

To keep said premises in good repair, and not to do, or permit to be done, upon said premises, anything that may impair the value thereof, or of the security intended to be effected by virtue of this instrument; not to suffer any lien of mechanics men or material men to attach to said premises; to pay to the Mortgagee, as hereinafter provided, until said note is fully paid, (1) a sum sufficient to pay all taxes and assessments on said premises, or any tax or assessment that may be levied by authority of the State of Illinois, or of the county, town, village, or city in which the said land is situate, upon the Mortgagor on account of the ownership thereof; (2) a sum sufficient to keep all buildings that may at any time be on said premises, during the continuance of said indebtedness, insured for the benefit of the Mortgagee in such type or types of hazard insurance, and in such amounts, as may be required by the Mortgagee.

In case of the refusal or neglect of the Mortgagor to make such payments, or to satisfy any prior lien or incumbrance other than that for taxes or assessments on said premises, or to keep said premises in good repair, the Mortgagee may pay such taxes, assessments, and insurance premiums, when due, and may make such repairs to the property herein mortgaged as may reasonably be deemed necessary for the proper preservation thereof, and any moneys so paid or expended shall become so much additional indebtedness, secured by this mortgage, shall bear interest at the rate provided for in the principal indebtedness, shall be payable thirty (30) days after demand and shall be paid out of proceeds of the sale of the mortgaged premises, if not otherwise paid by the Mortgagor.

Upon the request of the Mortgagee the Mortgagor shall execute and deliver a supplemental note or notes for the sum or sums advanced by the Mortgagee for the alteration, modernization, improvement, maintenance, or repair of said premises, for taxes or assessments against the same and for any other purpose authorized hereunder. Said note or notes shall be secured hereby on a parity with and as fully as if the advance evidenced thereby were included in the note first described above. Said supplemental note or notes shall bear interest at the rate provided for in the principal indebtedness and shall be payable in approximately equal monthly payments for such period as may be agreed upon by the creditor and debtor. Failing to agree on the maturity, the whole of the sum or sums so advanced shall be due and payable thirty (30) days after demand by the creditor. In no event shall the maturity extend beyond the ultimate maturity of the note first described above.

It is expressly provided, however (all other provisions of this mortgage to the contrary notwithstanding), that the Mortgagee shall not be required nor shall it have the right to pay, discharge, or remove any tax, assessment, or tax lien upon or against the premises described herein or any part thereof or the improvements situated thereon, so long as the Mortgagor shall, in good faith, contest the same or the validity thereof by appropriate legal proceedings brought in a court of competent jurisdiction, which shall operate to prevent the collection of the tax, assessment, or lien so contested and the sale or forfeiture of the said premises or any part thereof to satisfy the same.

AND the said Mortgagor further covenants and agrees as follows:

Privilege is reserved to prepay at any time, without premium or fee, the entire indebtedness or any part thereof not less than the amount of one installment, or one hundred dollars ($100.00), whichever is less. Prepayment in full shall be credited on the date received. Partial prepayment, other than on an installment due date, need not be credited until the next following installment due date or thirty days after such prepayment, whichever is earlier.

Together with, and in addition to, the monthly payments of principal and interest payable under the terms of the note secured hereby, the Mortgagor will pay to the Mortgagee as Trustee under the terms of this trust as hereinafter stated, on the first day of each month until the said note is fully paid, the following sums:

(a) A sum equal to the ground rents, if any, next due, plus the premiums that will next become due and payable on policies of fire and other hazard insurance covering the mortgaged property, plus taxes and assessments next due on the mortgaged property (all as estimated by the Mortgagee, and of which the Mortgagor is notified) less all sums already paid therefor divided by the number of months to elapse before one month prior to the date when such ground rents, premiums, taxes and assessments will become delinquent, such sums to be held by Mortgagee in trust to pay said ground rents, premiums, taxes and assessments.

(*b*) The aggregate of the amounts payable pursuant to subparagraph *(a)* and those payable on the note secured hereby, shall be paid in a single payment each month, to be applied to the following items in the order stated:

I. ground rents, if any, taxes, assessments, fire, and other hazard insurance premiums;

II. interest on the note secured hereby; and

III. amortization of the principal of the said note.

Any deficiency in the amount of any such aggregate monthly payment shall, unless made good prior to the due date of the next payment, constitute an event of default under this Mortgage. At Mortgagee's option, Mortgagor will pay a "late charge" not exceeding four per centum (4%) of any installment when paid more than fifteen (15) days after the due date thereof to cover the extra expense involved in handling delinquent payments, but such "late charge" shall not be payable out of the proceeds of any sale made to satisfy the indebtedness secured hereby, unless such proceeds are sufficient to discharge the entire indebtedness and all proper costs and expenses secured hereby.

If the total of the payments made by the Mortgagor under subparagraph (a) of the preceding paragraph shall exceed the amount of payments actually made by the Mortgagee as Trustee for ground rents, taxes, and assessments, or insurance premiums, as the case may be, such excess shall be credited on subsequent payments to be made by the Mortgagor for such items or, at the Mortgagee's option as Trustee, shall be refunded to the Mortgagor. If, however, such monthly payments shall not be sufficient to pay such items when the same shall become due and payable, the Mortgagor shall pay to the Mortgagee as Trustee any amount necessary to make up the deficiency. Such payments shall be made within thirty (30) days after written notice from the Mortgagee stating the amount of the deficiency, which notice may be given by mail. If at any time the Mortgagor shall tender to the Mortgagee, in accordance with the provisions of the note secured hereby, full payment of the entire indebtedness represented thereby, the Mortgagee as Trustee shall, in computing the amount of such indebtedness, credit to the account of the Mortgagor any credit balance remaining under the provisions of subparagraph (a) of the preceding paragraph. If there shall be a default under any of the provisions of this mortgage, resulting in a public sale of the premises covered hereby, or if the Mortgagee acquires the property otherwise after default, the Mortgagee as Trustee shall apply, at the time of the commencement of such proceedings or at the time the property is otherwise acquired, the amount then remaining to credit of Mortgagor under said subparagraph (a) as a credit on the interest accrued and unpaid and the balance to the principal then remaining unpaid under said note.

AS ADDITIONAL SECURITY for the payment of the indebtedness aforesaid the Mortgagor does hereby assign to the Mortgagee all the rents, issues, and profits now due or which may hereafter become due for the use of the premises hereinabove described. The Mortgagor shall be entitled to collect and retain all of said rents, issues and profits until default hereunder, EXCEPT rents, bonuses and royalties resulting from oil, gas or other mineral leases or conveyances thereof now or hereafter in effect. The lessee, assignee or sublessee of such oil, gas or mineral lease is directed to pay any profits, bonuses, rents, revenues or royalties to the owner of the indebtedness secured hereby.

MORTGAGOR WILL CONTINUOUSLY maintain hazard insurance, of such type or types and amounts as Mortgagee may from time to time require, on the improvements now or hereafter on said premises, and except when payment for all such premiums has theretofore been made, he/she will pay promptly when due any premiums therefor. All insurance shall be carried in companies approved by the Mortgagee and the policies and renewals thereof shall be held by the Mortgagee and have attached thereto loss payable clauses in favor of and in form acceptable to the Mortgagee. In event of loss Mortgagor will give immediate notice by mail to the Mortgagee, who may make proof of loss if not made promptly by Mortgagor, and each insurance company concerned is hereby authorized and directed to make payment for such loss directly to the Mortgagee instead of to the Mortgagor and the Mortgagee jointly, and the insurance proceeds, or any part thereof, may be applied by the Mortgagee at its option either to the reduction of the indebtedness hereby secured or to the restoration or repair of the property damaged. In event of foreclosure of this mortgage, or other transfer of title to the mortgaged property in extinguishment of the indebtedness secured hereby, all right, title and interest of the Mortgagor in and to any insurance policies then in force shall pass to the purchaser or grantee.

IN THE EVENT of default in making any monthly payment provided for herein and in the note secured hereby, or in case of a breach of any other covenant or agreement herein stipulated, then the whole of said principal sum remaining unpaid together with accrued interest thereon, shall, at the election of the Mortgagee, without notice, become immediately due and payable.

IN THE EVENT that the whole of said debt is declared to be due, the Mortgagee shall have the right immediately to foreclose this mortgage, and upon the filing of any bill for that purpose, the court in which such bill is filed may at any time thereafter, either before or after sale, and without notice to the said Mortgagor, or any party claiming under said Mortgagor, and without regard to the solvency or insolvency at the time of such application for a receiver, of the person or persons liable for the payment of the indebtedness secured hereby, and without regard to the value of said premises or whether the same shall then be occupied by the owner of the equity of redemption, as a homestead, appoint a receiver for the benefit of the Mortgagee, with power to collect the rents, issues, and profits of the said premises during the pendency of such foreclosure suit and, in case of sale and a deficiency, during the full statutory period of redemption, and such rents, issues, and profits when collected may be applied toward the payment of the indebtedness, costs, taxes, insurance, and other items necessary for the protection and preservation of the property.

IN CASE OF FORECLOSURE of this mortgage by said Mortgagee in any court of law or equity, a reasonable sum shall be allowed for the solicitor's fees of the complainant and for stenographers' fees of the complainant in such proceeding, and also for all outlays for documentary evidence and the cost of a complete abstract of title for the purpose of such foreclosure; and in case of any other suit, or legal proceeding, wherein the Mortgagee shall be made a party thereto by reason of this mortgage, its costs and expenses, and the reasonable fees and charges of the attorneys or solicitors of the Mortgagee, so made parties, for services in such suit or proceed-

EXHIBIT VIII-4—*continued*

ings, shall be a further lien and charge upon the said premises under this mortgage, and all such expenses shall become so much additional indebtedness secured hereby and be allowed in any decree foreclosing this mortgage.

THERE SHALL BE INCLUDED in any decree foreclosing this mortgage and be paid out of the proceeds of any sale made in pursuance of any such decree: (1) All the costs of such suit or suits, advertising, sale, and conveyance, including reasonable attorneys', solicitors', and stenographers' fees, outlays for documentary evidence and cost of said abstract and examination of title; (2) all the moneys advanced by the Mortgagee, if any, for any purpose authorized in the mortgage, with interest on such advances at the rate provided for in the principal indebtedness, from the time such advances are made; (3) all the accrued interest remaining unpaid on the indebtedness hereby secured; (4) all the said principal money remaining unpaid; (5) all sums paid by the Department of Veterans Affairs on account of the guaranty or insurance of the indebtedness secured hereby. The overplus of the proceeds of sale, if any, shall then be paid to the Mortgagor.

If Mortgagor shall pay said note at the time and in the manner aforesaid and shall abide by, comply with and duly perform all the covenants and agreements herein, then this conveyance shall be null and void and Mortgagee will, within thirty days after written demand therefor by Mortgagor, execute a release or satisfaction of this mortgage, and Mortgagor hereby waives the benefits of all statutes or laws which require the earlier execution or delivery of such release or satisfaction by Mortgagee.

The lien of this instrument shall remain in full force and effect during any postponement or extension of the time of payment of the indebtedness or any part thereof hereby secured; and no extension of the time of payment of the debt hereby secured given by the Mortgagee to any successor in interest of the Mortgagor shall operate to release, in any manner, the original liability of the Mortgagor.

If the indebtedness secured hereby be guaranteed or insured under Title 38, United States Code, such Title and Regulations issued thereunder and in effect on the date hereof shall govern the rights, duties and liabilities of the parties hereto, and any provisions of this or other instruments executed in connection with said indebtedness which are inconsistent with said Title or Regulations are hereby amended to conform thereto.

THE COVENANTS HEREIN CONTAINED shall bind, and the benefits and advantages shall inure, to the respective heirs, executors, administrators, successors, and assigns of the parties hereto. Wherever used, the singular number shall include the plural, the plural the singular, and the term "Mortgagee" shall include any payee of the indebtedness hereby secured or any transferee thereof whether by operation of law or otherwise.

WITNESS the hand and seal of the Mortgagor, the day and year first written.

______________________________ [SEAL] ______________________________ [SEAL]

______________________________ [SEAL] ______________________________ [SEAL]

STATE OF ILLINOIS *ss:*

COUNTY OF

I, , a notary public, in and for the county and State aforesaid, Do Hereby Certify That and , his/her spouse, personally known to me to be the same person whose name subscribed to the foregoing instrument appeared before me this day in person and acknowledged that signed, sealed, and delivered the said instrument as free and voluntary act for the uses and purposes therein set forth, including the release and waiver of the right of homestead.

My Commission Expires:

This instrument was prepared by: GIVEN under my hand and Notarial Seal this

______________________________ day of , 19

______________________________ ______________________________

Notary Public.

STATE OF ILLINOIS

Mortgage

TO

Doc. No.

Filed for Record in the Recorder's Office of

County, Illinois,

on the day of

A.D. 19 , at o'clock m.,

and duly recorded in Book

of page

Clerk.

All owners of the property as identified on the deed must sign the mortgage. It is common in some areas to require that all persons who signed the note also sign the mortgage, even if they are not owners of the property. This is what some attorneys call "surplusage," since one cannot pledge as security for a debt something that is not owned by that person.

However, the addition of these surplus signatures to the mortgage does not affect its enforceability against the property. What is important is that all owners of the property join in the pledge of it as security, since the mortgage will generally not be enforceable against the property interest of someone who has not signed it.

The Deed

The deed conveys title from the sellers to the buyers, and, while it is not technically a part of the loan closing, it is very important to it. The borrowers cannot pledge as security a piece of property they do not own; thus, title to the property is generally transferred at the same time as the loan closing.

Here, three things are very important: (1) The sellers identified in the deed as grantors are the same as the owners of record of the property; (2) The buyers identified in the deed as grantees are the same as the borrowers identified in the mortgage; and (3) The property identified in the deed is the same as the property identified in the mortgage. Again, the complete legal description is used, and it must be identical in both documents.

The Settlement Statement

Regardless of the type of loan, the record of what went on at closing is kept on Form HUD-1 (See Exhibit VI-4), a standard settlement sheet developed to comply with the Real Estate Settlement Procedures Act. RESPA does not specifically require the form to be used in connection with all loans, but it does require that it be used with all federally related loans.

The definition of "federally related" is broad enough to make its practical application virtually universal. For example, a conventional loan made by a mortgage banking firm that is partly owned by a bank holding company (which is regulated by the Federal Reserve Board) is a federally related loan.

The HUD-1 summarizes every payment made by each party in the transaction, even though payments may have been made at a time prior to closing. When the form is completed, those amounts are entered on the appropriate lines, with the notation "POC" (paid outside closing) on the same line. They are not included in any of the totals.

There may be two or three different HUD-1s in a transaction. The copy given to the borrower need not show costs paid by the seller, and the copy given to the seller need not show costs paid by the borrower. However, the lender may want a copy showing all costs.

Take care in completing the HUD-1; errors can create problems later. If an error is made, do not erase it or white it out. Line through the mistake, enter the correct figure, and initial the change.

The sales contract or purchase agreement must outline the distribution of closing costs between the buyer and the seller. In some areas, the buyer normally pays all closing costs; in others, the seller normally pays all of them; and in still others, the costs are normally divided between the buyer and seller—sometimes evenly, sometimes not. It is important that all those involved in the origination process, from the loan officer through the closing agent, know what local practice dictates and review the sales contract or purchase agreement in each situation.

Generally, any cost paid by the seller that would normally be paid by the buyer is considered a "seller contribution" and may reduce or at least affect the maximum mortgage available in a transaction. In some situations, even costs normally paid by sellers fall into this category.

Discounts, contributions to buydown escrows, closing costs normally paid by the buyer, the value of sales incentives (premiums and trips, for example), and the like are all a part of the "seller contribution," and they are deducted from the contract sales price in determining the maximum insurable mortgage, to the extent they exceed 6 percent of whatever the maximum mortgage would be if only closing costs paid by the seller were deducted.

Other agencies and investors are not as restrictive as HUD-FHA, but each has its own rules. The VA has a 4 percent limitation.

Fees for services associated with bringing the loan into being are also closing costs, even though they may be paid outside the actual settlement transaction. As with other costs, who pays is a matter of local custom and practice. This category includes payments for termite inspections and treatment, powers of attorney, credit reports, appraisals, and so on.

These charges are itemized on the HUD-1 settlement statement, but they are not included in the totals unless they are actually paid with the settlement proceeds. If these services are paid when rendered, they are identified on the HUD-1 with the notation "POC" in the proper column.

The closing agent, the buyer, and the seller must all sign certifications related to the accuracy of the HUD-1. In the case of the buyer and the seller, these certifications also establish that none of the buyer's cash requirement was borrowed. A sample certification form appears as Exhibit VIII-5.

The Commitment

While it should always accompany the other documents, nothing need be done with or to the commitment at closing unless it is a HUD-FHA commitment. In HUD-FHA cases, the firm commitment contains several certifications on the reverse side, which must be signed by the borrower (Exhibit VIII-6). One of the blocks in item (d) must be checked. If the third block is checked, the appropriate amount from the sales contract must be entered in the blank space in the middle of the paragraph. On Direct Endorsement cases, these certifications are contained in page 4 of the HUD/VA addendum.

The rest of the certifications are self-explanatory, but they should be discussed with the borrowers as part of the closing

EXHIBIT VIII-5: ADDENDUM TO HUD-1 SETTLEMENT STATEMENT

ADDENDUM TO HUD-1 SETTLEMENT STATEMENT

NOTICE TO ALL PARTIES: If information is obtained which indicates that the source of the borrower's financial contribution is other than from the borrower or other than stated by the lender in its closing instructions, the settlement agent is to obtain written instructions from the lender before proceeding with settlement.

CERTIFICATION OF BUYER IN AN FHA-INSURED LOAN TRANSACTION

I certify that I have no knowledge of any loans that have been or will be made to me (us) or loans that have been or will be assumed by me (us) for purposes of financing this transaction, other than those described in the sales contract dated (including addenda). I certify that I (we) have not been paid or reimbursed for any of the cash downpayment. I certify that I (we) have not and will not receive any payment or reimbursement for any of my (our) closing costs which have not been previously disclosed in the sales contract (including addenda) and/or my application for mortgage insurance submitted to my (our) mortgage lender.

Borrower Date | Borrower Date

Borrower Date | Borrower Date

CERTIFICATION OF SELLER IN AN FHA-INSURED LOAN TRANSACTION

I certify that I have no knowledge of any loans that have been or will be made to the borrower(s), or loans that have been or will be assumed by the borrower(s), for purposes of financing this transaction, other than those described in the sales contract dated (including addenda). I certify that I have not and will not pay or reimburse the borrower(s) for any part of the cash downpayment. I certify that I have not and will not pay or reimburse the borrower(s) for any part of the borrower's closing costs which have not been previously disclosed in the sales contract (including any addenda).

Seller Date | Seller Date

Seller Date | Seller Date

CERTIFICATION OF SETTLEMENT AGENT IN AN FHA-INSURED LOAN TRANSACTION

To the best of my knowledge, the HUD-1 Settlement Statement which I have prepared is a true and accurate account of the funds which were (i) received, or (ii) paid outside closing, and the funds received have been or will be disbursed by the undersigned as part of the settlement of this transaction. I further certify that I have obtained the above certifications which were executed by the borrower(s) and seller(s) as indicated.

Settlement Agent Date

(The certifications contained herein may be obtained from the respective parties at different times or may be obtained on separate addenda)

WARNING: It is a crime to knowingly make false statements to the United States on this or any other similar form. Penalties upon conviction can include a fine and imprisonment. For details, see: Title 18 U.S. Code Sections 1001 and 1010.

VMP-445 (9103) VMP MORTGAGE FORMS • (313)293-8100 • (800)521-7291 3/91

EXHIBIT VIII-6: HUD/FHA FIRM COMMITMENT

Firm Commitment

U.S. Department of Housing
and Urban Development
Office of Housing
Federal Housing Commissioner

This is to certify, in compliance with the Right to Financial Privacy Act of 1978, that, in connection with any subsequent request for access to financial records for the purpose of considering or administering assistance to this applicant, the Department of Housing and Urban Development is in compliance with the applicable provisions of said Act.

Instructions to Lender — Forward to the HUD Service Office: (1) this commitment signed by the lender and borrower; (2) a copy of the note, bond or other credit instrument; (3) a copy of the mortgage or other security instrument; and (4) a copy of the settlement statement, (form HUD-1) signed by the lender which itemizes all charges and fees collected by the lender from the borrower and seller.

Date ____________________ 19 ___

Lender's Certificate — The undersigned certifies that to the best of its knowledge:

(a) None of the statements made in its application for insurance nor in the Borrower's Certificate are untrue or incorrect.

(b) The conditions listed below or appearing in any outstanding commitment issued under the case number shown below have been fulfilled.

(c) Complete disbursement of the loan has been made to the Borrower, or to his/her creditors for his/her account and with his/her consent.

(d) The security instrument has been recorded and is a good and valid first lien on the property described.

(e) No charge has been made to or paid by the Borrower except as permitted under HUD Regulations.

(f) The copies of the credit and security instruments which are submitted herewith are true and exact copies as executed and filed for record.

(g) It has not paid any kickbacks, fees or consideration of any type, directly or indirectly, on or after May 1, 1972, to any party in connection with this transaction except as permitted under Section 203.27 of the HUD Regulations and administrative instructions issued pursuant thereto.

____
(Signature and Title of Lender Official)

☐ Accepted Firm Commitment for mortgage insurance under the National Housing Act Section

☐ Notice of return/rejection (see below)

Action Date

By

Lender I.D.

FHA Case No.

Lender Name and Address

Property Address:

Borrower Name

Co-Borrower Name

Other Borrower Name

A note and mortgage described above or as modified below will be insured under the National Housing Act provided one of the borrowers will be an owner-occupant and all conditions appearing in any outstanding commitment used under the above case number and those set forth below are fulfilled.

						Commitment	
As Applied For	Mortgage Amount Without MIP $	Interest Rate %	No. of Mos	Monthly Payment Principal & Interest $	Discount $	Issued	Expires
	Total MIP $	Financed Yes ☐ No ☐	Total Mortgage Amount $				
As Modified and/or Accepted	Mortgage Amount Without MIP $	Interest Rate %	No. of Mos	Monthly Payment Principal & Interest $	Discount $	Est. Value of Property $	
	Total MIP $	Financed Yes ☐ No ☐	Total Mortgage Amount $			Est. Closing Cost $	
Commitment Conditions	☐ HUD-92544 Builders warranty required ☐ Owner-occupancy NOT required ☐ The property is to be insured under Section 221(d)(2); a code compliance inspection is required ☐ See the following additional conditions on reverse					Total (for Mortgage Insurance Purposes) $	

____
(Authorized Agent for the Federal Housing Commissioner) (Date) (Field Office)

Replaces HUD-92900.4T which is obsolete

Page 1 of 2 Pages

HUD-92900.4 (10-86)

Mortgage Credit

Application Return
If this is a Return, the reasons for return are indicated by code on the front of this form:

R-01. **Submit Form HUD-92900.**
R-02. Submit Credit Report.
R-03. Reserved.
R-04. Submit Copy of Sales Contract.
R-05. Submit Verification of Deposit.
R-06. Submit Verification of Employment
R-07 through R-12. Reserved
R-13. Submit Disclosure Statement.
R-15. Complete Block 5a or 5b (Form HUD-92900).

Application Rejection
If this is a Rejection, the applicable reasons are indicated by code on the front of this form:

M-01. Stability of income not established.
M-02. Insufficient income to support mortgage.
M-03. Insurable loan limited.
M-04. Gift letter unacceptable.
M-05. Exhibits indicate borrower resorting to unacceptable secondary financing.
M-06. Borrower has insufficient assets to close.
M-07. Verify source of funds to close.
M-08. Reserved.
M-09. Borrower's credit rating unacceptable.

Firm Commitment Specific Conditions
The applicable conditions are indicated by code on the front of this form.

C-01. Submit with the closing documents a statement signed by the seller acknowledging receipt of payment in cash from the buyer in the full amount stated in the contract for the purchase of the property and declaring that the owners of said property are in no way indebted to the seller and to the best of his/her knowledge and beliefs said owners do not have any outstanding unpaid obligation contracted in connection with the purchase or construction of said property other than the mortgage to be insured and, further, that there has not been nor will there be any refund of any portion of the equity payment.
C-02. Submit with the closing documents a corrected, signed GPM certification for the loan.
C-03. Submit evidence at the time of insurance showing all obligations that are paid in full.
C-04. Submit evidence of compliance with all specific conditions contained on the VA/CRV.

Fair Credit Reporting Act
In compliance with P.L. 91-508 (Fair Credit Reporting Act), this is to advise that the borrower has been rejected because of an unacceptable credit standing. The determination was made in whole or in part on the basis of information supplied in a consumer credit report from the credit bureau named on the front of this form.

Equal Credit Opportunity Notice
The Federal Equal Credit Opportunity Act prohibits creditors from discriminating against credit applicants on the basis of race, color, religion, national origin, sex, marital status, age (provided that the applicant has the capacity to enter into a binding contract); because all or part of the applicant's income derives from any public assistance program; or because the applicant has in good faith exercised any right under the Consumer Credit Protection Act. The government agency that administers compliance with this law concerning the Department of Housing and Urban Development is the Federal Trade Commission, Equal Credit Opportunity, Washington, D.C. 20580.

Borrower's Certificate
The undersigned certifies that:

(a) I will not have outstanding any other unpaid obligations contracted in connection with the mortgage transaction or the purchase of said property except obligations which are secured by property or collateral owned by me independently of the said mortgaged property or obligations approved by the Commissioner.

(b) One of the undersigned intends to occupy the subject property (NOTE: Delete this item if owner occupancy not required by commitment.)

(c) All charges and fees collected from me as shown in the settlement statement have been paid from my own funds, and no other charges have been or will be paid by me in respect to this transaction.

(d) Check applicable box:
- ☐ Amendatory clause not required in this transaction.
- ☐ The HUD/FHA Statement of Appraised Value or the VA Certificate of Reasonable Value was given to me prior to my signing the purchase contract for the property.
- ☐ The HUD/FHA Statement of Appraised Value or the VA Certificate of Reasonable Value was not given to me prior to my signing the contract to purchase, but the contract to purchase contained the following language: "It is expressly agreed that, notwithstanding any other provisions of this contract, the purchaser shall not be obligated to complete the purchase of the property described herein or to incur any penalty by forfeiture of earnest money deposits or otherwise unless the seller has delivered to the purchaser a written statement issued by the Federal Housing Commissioner setting forth the appraised value of the property (excluding closing costs) or not less than $ ________ which statement the seller hereby agrees to deliver to the purchaser promptly after such appraised value statement is available to the seller. The purchaser shall, however, have the privilege and option of proceeding with the consummation of the contract without regard to the amount of the appraised valuation made by the Federal Housing Commissioner. The appraised valuation is arrived at to determine the maximum mortgage the Department of Housing and Urban Development will insure. HUD does not warrant the value or the condition of the property. The purchaser should satisfy himself/herself that the price and condition of the property are acceptable." (IF THE AMENDATORY PROCEDURE WAS NECESSARY, THE DOLLAR AMOUNT USED IN THE AMENDATORY CLAUSE IS INSERTED IN THE ABOVE BLANK SPACE.)

(e) Neither I, nor anyone authorized to act for me, will refuse to sell or rent, after the making of a bona fide offer, or refuse to negotiate for the sale or rental of, or otherwise make unavailable or deny the dwelling or property covered by this loan to any person because of race, color, religion, sex, marital status or national origin. I recognize that any restrictive covenant on this property relating to race, color, religion, sex marital status or national origin is illegal and void and any such covenant is hereby specifically disclaimed. I understand that civil action for preventative relief may be brought by the Attorney General of the United States in any appropriate U.S. District Court against any person responsible for a violation of this certification.

Signature(s): ____________________

____

____

Date: ____________________ 19 ____

HUD-92900.4 (10-86)

Page 2 of 2 Pages

process before they are signed. The front of the firm commitment contains certifications made by and signed by the lender.

Truth in Lending Disclosure

Within three days of the taking of the loan application (preliminary TIL) and at or before settlement (final TIL), the borrower must receive a statement disclosing the actual cost of financing and several key terms of the transaction. This process is part of Federal Reserve Board regulations, and there must be a record of delivery. There is no prescribed form for this disclosure, but the regulations itemize the specific pieces of information it must include. Most forms in use around the country are fairly standard.

While the final disclosure statement can be provided to the borrowers at any time, it is probably best to make its delivery a part of the closing process. This not only avoids having to revise the statement in the event of any last-minute changes in the terms of the loan, but it also makes it possible to secure the signatures of the borrowers on the statement itself, which is the best way of establishing that it was actually delivered.

Disbursement

Disbursement can be handled in either of two ways, as a management decision based on local custom. First, the lender may wire funds to the closing agent. Because these funds are guaranteed and immediate, closing agents may prefer this process. The closing agent then issues its own checks to the ultimate recipients of the loan proceeds.

With the second method, the lender gives the closing agent a single check, drawn in favor of the closing agent, for the full amount of the loan proceeds. Again, the closing agent issues its own checks to the ultimate recipients of the loan proceeds.

Care is essential: Remember that the funds have not been disbursed simply because you wrote a check. The funds must actually be delivered to the closing agent. This is seldom a problem in conventional transactions, but it could be a problem in HUD-FHA or VA cases. Both agencies—but particularly HUD-FHA—look at dates of disbursement in their periodic reviews of lenders, and they often require lenders to refund interest to borrowers whose funds were not actually in the hands of the closing agent at closing.

Finally, when a case is submitted to HUD-FHA or VA for insurance or guaranty, it is accompanied by the settlement agent's and lender's certification that the funds have been disbursed. Both agencies look unfavorably on false certifications, even when they are unintentional.

Also, even though the rules say the funds are disbursed when the closing agent has them, significant delays on the part of the closing agent in getting them to their ultimate recipients should cause concern for the lender.

Recording

The final step in the closing process is recording. Title to the property is transferred when the deed is signed by the sellers and delivered. The debt becomes enforceable as soon as the note and mortgage are signed—enforceable as far as the people who signed them are concerned, that is. Recordation is not necessary for that.

A court will enforce a buyer's claim against a seller if the seller sold the property to the buyer, signed and delivered a deed, and subsequently tried to take back the property, even if the deed was not recorded. It will not, however, support the buyer against someone else who claims to own the property and who also has a deed, whether that deed was recorded or not. Those deeds were both valid between the people who signed the deeds and the people to whom the deeds were delivered, but not with the respect to anyone else.

The same is true of the note and mortgage. The idea is that an agreement can be binding to a specific individual only if that person knew there was an agreement.

It is impossible to give personal notice to everyone in the world that a property has been sold to another person, but one can give what is termed "constructive notice." Recording the documents that serve as evidence of the agreement acts as public notice that the agreement exists.

The assumption is that anyone who is interested in the property has the opportunity to visit the courthouse and search the public record to find out who really owns it, or what restrictions there are on that ownership—a mortgage, for example. This makes recordation of the documents an important step.

It also is critical to record the documents as soon as possible after the closing. In theory, the seller could fraudulently sign and deliver another deed to another person. If that deed is recorded before the deed to the first buyer (the borrower), there is serious question as to who actually owns the property and whether the mortgage is enforceable or not.

If the mortgage company itself can prepare the legal documents, it should seriously consider doing so. When documents are prepared by the settlement agent, the lender does not usually have an opportunity to review them until after the closing, making it difficult to correct any errors.

Documents prepared by the lender can be reviewed for accuracy before closing. In some jurisdictions, however, the preparation of these documents, even if it involves only filling in blank spaces on a preprinted form, is considered the practice of law, and the function must be performed by an attorney.

Conclusion

Regardless of who prepares the documents, the ultimate responsibility for their accuracy and the enforceability of the lien rests with the lender. It is essential, therefore, that they be reviewed meticulously for accuracy after closing. This is sometimes the responsibility of the branch office that originated the loan.

Many companies, however, have centralized the process and assigned it to post-closing review specialists. This can have both advantages and disadvantages. On the positive side, centralized control ensures that specialists will perform the review. But if errors are discovered, they will usually have to be corrected in the originating branch, and time can be lost and confusion created in the process of communicating between the centralized post-closing unit and the branches.

The lender must rely on closing agents to correct any errors they were clearly warned against in closing instructions. If, on the other hand, an error relates to something that was not included in the closing instructions, the closing agent may properly be able to disclaim responsibility.

Glossary

Handbook of Mortgage Processing

abstract of title: A written history of ownership of a parcel of land, summarizing the material parts of any occurrence affecting title of said land.

acceptance: An offeree's consent to enter into a contract and be bound by the terms of the offer.

accident and health premium: A portion of the amount paid by a borrower for mortgage insurance that ensures the continuance of mortgage payments in the event of a mortgagor's disability or illness.

accommodation party: A person who lends his name to guarantee a loan for another by signing a note, bill, or other negotiable instrument. The endorser becomes the guarantor of the loan and is therefore responsible for its repayment.

acquisition costs: In a HUD/FHA transaction, the sum of the price paid for the property and any costs of closing, repairs, or financing (except discounts in other that a refinance transaction) properly paid by the borrower. Does not include prepaid discounts in a purchase transaction, mortgage insurance premiums, etc.

addendum: An agreement or list that is added to a contract, agreement, or other document such as a letter of intent. FHA and VA require that an addendum be added to or incorporated in a sales contract, if it is written prior to the appraisal.

add-on interest: The full amount of interest calculated on the original principal for the term of the loan. This interest is added to the original principal, thereby becoming a part of the face amount of the promissory note.

adjustable rate mortgage (ARM): A mortgage loan or deed of trust that allows the lender to adjust the interest rate in accordance with a specified index periodically and as agreed to at the inception of the loan. Also called a variable rate mortgage (VRM).

adjusted basis: The original cost of a property, plus the value of any capital expenditures for improvements to the property, minus any depreciation taken.

advance: In real estate, a partial disbursement of funds under a note. Most often used in connection with construction lending.

advance commitment (conditional): A written promise to make an investment at some time in the future if specified conditions are met.

affidavit: A sworn statement in writing, usually requiring notarization.

after-tax equity reversion: The sale of property less transaction costs, outstanding debts, and disposition of taxes.

agreement for deed: A contract for the sale of property in which transfer of title to the buyer is contingent on the fulfillment of certain conditions.

agreement for sale: A written document in which the purchaser agrees to buy certain real estate or personal property and the seller agrees to sell under stated conditions. Also called a sales contract, binder, or earnest money contract.

alienation: The transfer of title to real property from one owner to another.

alienation clause: A type of acceleration clause that demands payment of the entire balance upon sale or other transfer of title. Also called a due-on-sale clause.

all-inclusive trust deed (AITD): A refinancing technique involving the creation of a new deed of trust that includes the balance due on the existing note plus new funds advanced; also known as a wrap-around mortgage.

allowance for vacancy and income loss: In accounting, an estimated amount reflecting probable vacancy, non-payment of rent by tenants, and any other income loss. These funds are set aside to cover either expected or unanticipated income losses.

alternative mortgage instrument: A mortgage that differs from the typical mortgage instrument either in the amount of principal, the interest rate, the periodic or monthly payments, or terms for repayment.

amenity: A feature that enhances property value. Examples are off-street reserved parking within a condominium community, or the proximity of public transportation, tennis courts, or a swimming pool.

amortization: Repayment of a mortgage debt with equal periodic payments of both principal and interest, calculated to retire the obligation at the end of a fixed period of time.

amortization schedule: A table showing the amounts of principal and interest due at regular intervals and the unpaid mortgage balance after each payment is made.

annual percentage rate (APR): A term defined in section 106 of the federal Truth-in-Lending Act (PL 90-321; 15 USC 1606), which expresses on an annualized basis the charges imposed on the borrower to obtain a loan (defined in the Act as -finance charges-), including interest, discount, and other costs.

applicant: A prospective borrower who has completed an application. An application is series of steps, usually including the completion of documents, that a lender requires of those seeking a loan.

application: A form used to record pertinent information about a prospective borrower and the proposed security. Application for Property Appraisal and Commitment (HUD Form 92800): The basic application to HUD/FHA requesting appraisal of the property and determination of its eligibility for insurance. VA Form 26-1805 is the corresponding VA form. The VA form may be used in HUD/FHA applications, but the HUD/FHA form may not be used in VA applications.

apportionment: A pro-rated division and distribution of prepaid or accrued taxes, prepaid insurance premiums, prepaid rents, and other income and expenses. When a property is sold, apportionment is used to distribute or collect funds due from the buyer and seller for income and expenses.

appraisal: An opinion or estimate of value. Also refers to the process by which a value estimate is obtained.

appraised value: An opinion of value reached by an appraiser based upon knowledge, experience, and a study of pertinent data.

appraiser: One qualified by education, training, and experience to estimate the value of real estate and personal property.

ARM: See adjustable rate mortgage (ARM).

arm's length transaction: A transaction in which the parties involved are entirely independent of each other, deal with each other as strangers, and have no reason for collusion.

assessed valuation: The value that a taxing authority places upon real property that becomes the base for computing local property taxes.

asset: A property or right owned, tangible or intangible, that has monetary value and is capable of providing future benefits to its owner.

assignee: The person to whom ownership, rights, or interest in property is transferred.

assignment of mortgage: A document that evidences the transfer of a mortgage from one party to another.

assignor: One who transfers to another ownership or interest in property.

assumption agreement: A written agreement by one party to pay an obligation originally incurred by another.

assumption fee: The amount paid a lender for the paperwork and processing of records necessary to approve and document a new debtor.

assumption of mortgage: A buyer's acceptance of primary liability for payment of an existing note secured by a mortgage or deed of trust. The seller remains secondarily liable, unless specifically released by the lender.

audit: The official examination and verification of bookkeeping accounts to prove the accuracy of figures and the adequacy of accounting controls. An audit may be done by public accountants hired for this purpose or by a company's own employees. The latter is called an internal audit.

automatic lender program: A VA program that enables eligible single-family lenders to conduct the processing and closing of VA single-family loan applications without VA's prior review. The VA, however, is responsible for producing the appraisal report for all VA loans including those performed via the automatic lender program unless lender is participating in LAPP.

back-to-back escrow: An escrow set up to facilitate the simultaneous purchase of one property and the sale of another property by the same party.

balance sheet: A report of the financial position of a business at a specific point in time, showing its assets, liabilities, and owner's equity.

balloon mortgage: A mortgage with periodic installments of principal and interest that do not fully amortize the loan. The balance of the mortgage is due in a lump sum at a specified date, usually at the end of the term.

balloon payment: A scheduled payment on a mortgage that is larger than other, periodic payments, usually the unamortized final payment.

bankrupt: An individual, firm, or corporation who, through a court proceeding, is relieved from the payment of all debts. Bankruptcy may be declared under one of several chapters of the federal bankruptcy code: Chapter 7, which covers liquidation of individual or business assets; Chapter 11, which covers reorganization of bankrupt businesses; Chapter 12, which covers certain farm bankruptcies; and Chapter 13, which covers workouts of debts by individuals.

basis point: One one-hundredth of one percent. Used primarily to describe changes in yield or price on debt instruments, including mortgages and mortgage-backed securities.

before-tax income: Gross income minus all expenses, except income taxes.

binder: Temporary hazard or title insurance granted prior to the issuance of a permanent policy. In real estate, a preliminary agreement between a buyer and seller that includes the price and terms of the contract.

borrower: One who receives funds in the form of a loan with the obligation of repaying the loan in full with interest.

building code: Regulations based on safety and health standards that govern design, construction, and materials used in construction.

buy-down escrow agreement: An unnumbered, local, lender-reproduced form used to formalize the terms of an escrow established to finance the reduced initial payments made available to the buyer by a buydown agreement. Before insurance of such a mortgage by HUD, the agreement must have been executed by the contributor, the buyer, the lender, and the escrow agent.

capital: The net worth of a business represented by the amount by which its assets exceed liabilities. Money invested to create income.

capitalization: The process of converting into present value a series of anticipated future installments of net income by discounting them into a present worth using a specific desired rate of earnings.

cash flow: The spendable cash (income) from an income-producing property after deducting from gross income all operating expenses and debt service.

certificate of claim: A contingent promise to reimburse an insured mortgagee for certain costs incurred during foreclosure of an insured mortgage, provided the proceeds from the sale of the property are sufficient to cover the lender's claim.

Certificate of Commitment for VA Loan Guaranty (VA Form 26-1866a): The form by which VA notifies the lender that an application has been found acceptable and will be guaranteed if conditions imposed by VA have been met and the loan is closed within six months. Performs the same function as the HUD/FHA firm commitment.

certificate of deposit (CD): Certificates issued by financial institutions with a stated return or interest rate, and with a set maturity. The bank pays the holder in due course at maturity.

Certificate of Eligibility (VA Form 26-8320): Evidence that the veteran is eligible for VA loan guarantee benefits. The form identifies the veteran and details the status of his or her eligibility.

certificate of reasonable value (CRV): A document issued by the Veterans Administration that establishes a maximum value and loan amount for a VA guaranteed mortgage.

certificate of title: A confirmation written by a title attorney or company stating that the title to a parcel of real property is legally vested in the present owner.

change order: A document evidencing a change in the original plan of construction by a building owner or general contractor.

chattel: Personal property.

clear title: Unencumbered title to real property, free of liens or defects. Also -free and clear.-

closing: In real estate, the delivery of a deed, financial adjustments, the signing of notes, and the disbursement of funds necessary to consummate a sale or loan transaction.

closing costs: Money paid by any party to the transaction to effect the closing of a mortgage loan. Does not include prepaid expenses, apportionments, and the like, but does normally include an origination fee (almost always paid by the borrower), title insurance, survey, attorney's fees, etc.

closing statement: A financial disclosure giving an account of all funds received and expected at closing, including escrow deposits for taxes, hazard insurance and mortgage insurance. A FHA, VA, and most conventionally financed loans use a uniform settlement statement called the -HUD-1.-

cloud on title: Any outstanding claim or encumbrance which, if valid, would affect or impair title. It can be removed by a quit- claim deed, release, or court action.

CMB: Certified Mortgage Banker. A professional designation awarded by the Mortgage Bankers Association of America (MBA) to those in the industry who have demonstrated superior knowledge and skills in the field of real estate finance. Candidates must be employed by MBA member firms and meet various educational, experience, and examination requirements.

coinsurance: A type of insurance where the insured agrees to carry a specified proportion of the policy amount to the actual value of the property insured at the time of loss. Thus, a portion of the property value is self insured. In federal multifamily housing programs, it refers to a sharing of the risk of mortgage default between a mortgage firm and the federal government.

collateral: Property pledged as security for a debt, for example, mortgaged real estate.

commitment: An agreement, often in writing, between a lender and a borrower, to loan money at a future date, subject to specified conditions. In secondary marketing, an agreement, in writing, between a lender and an investor to buy and sell mortgages under specific terms.

commitment fee: Any fee paid by a potential borrower to a potential lender for the lender's promise to loan money at a specified date in the future. The lender may or may not expect to fund the commitment. In secondary marketing, a fee paid by the loan seller to the investor in return for the investor's promise to purchase a loan or package of loans at a future date.

common area: An area owned by the owners or tenants of a complex or subdivision, for the common use of residents.

community property: In some states, a form of ownership under which property acquired during a marriage is presumed to be owned jointly unless acquired as separate property of either spouse.

co-mortgagor: A second borrower who signs a mortgage loan with a mortgagor. The co-mortgagor's income, assets, and debts are combined with the mortgagor's for underwriting and ratio analysis purposes. The co-mortgagor's name must appear on the FHA Certificate of Commitment and the mortgage or deed of trust. For full guarantee under the VA's program, the co-mortgagor must be either a spouse or another eligible veteran.

comparables: Properties used for comparative purposes in the appraisal process that have similar characteristics to the subject property.

compensating balance: A non-interest paying bank deposit maintained by the borrower that induces the bank to make credit available to the borrower on more favorable terms than would otherwise be available. computerized home underwriting management system (CHUMS): HUD's automated system that tracks the application for mortgage insurance from the initial application (for the appraiser) through to loan closing and the MIC issuance. The system enables HUD to track activity and streamline the process.

conditional commitment: An agreement to lend money to a borrower that has yet to be identified, but is still subject to the approval of the lender. During HUD/FHA mortgage insurance processing, it indicates the satisfactory completion of technical processing involving the estimated cost of the project, the -as is- value of the site, a detailed estimate of operating expenses and taxes, supportable costs, the financial and credit capacity of sponsors, financial requirements, and mortgage amounts.

conditional commitment requirements (VC sheet): A form reproduced locally by HUD/FHA offices and varying in content depending on local conditions. It lists the most common conditions imposed on conditional commitment, giving each a number (VC-10, VC-4, etc.). Only the number of the condition is entered on the commitment itself, and the list is attached.

condominium: A form of property ownership whereby the purchaser receives title to a unit in a multiunit structure and a proportionate interest in common areas.

condominium declarations: The basic condominium documents that must be registered by the originating property owner prior to the conveyance of the first unit sold. The declaration thoroughly describes the entire condominium entity, including each unit and all common areas, and specifies essential elements of ownership that permanently govern its operation. Also known as a master deed.

consideration: Something of value offered and accepted in exchange for a promise, without which a contract is unenforceable.

co-signer: One who agrees to assume the debt obligation if the principal borrower should default on mortgage payments. A co-signer assumes only personal liability and has no ownership interest in the property.

contiguous: Adjoining.

contingency: A clause in a contract that requires the completion of a certain act or the occurrence of a certain event before the contract is binding.

contract of sale: A contract between a purchaser and seller of real property to convey title after certain conditions have been met and payments have been made.

conventional financing: In real estate, mortgage financing that is not insured or guaranteed by a government agency such as HUD/FHA, VA, or the Farmers Home Administration.

convey: The act of transferring title to real property from one party to another.

conveyance: The document, such as a deed, lease, or mortgage, used to effect a transfer.

cooperative: In real estate, a form of multiple ownership in which a corporation or business trust entity holds title to a property (usually an apartment complex) and grants occupancy rights to shareholder tenants through proprietary leases. Also called a co-op.

corporation: A business entity owned by a group of owners, called stockholders. A corporation is considered an artificial person under law.

correlation: The final step in the appraisal process whereby the appraiser considers three estimates of value derived from cost, income, and market data approaches. The correlation process weighs the influence of each method in relation to the specific property type and final estimate of value.

correspondent: A specialized type of mortgage banker whose function is limited to the origination of mortgage loans that are sold to other mortgage bankers or investment bankers.

cost approach to value: A valuation approach in which the value of a property is determined by computing the replacement value of improvements, depreciation, and the value of the land.

coupon rate: The annual interest rate on a debt instrument. In mortgage banking, the term is used to describe the contract interest rate on the face of the note or bond.

credit rating: A rating given to a person or company that establishes creditworthiness based upon present financial condition, experience, and past credit history.

credit report: A report to a prospective lender on the credit standing of a prospective borrower, used to aid in the determination of creditworthiness.

custodial accounts: Bank accounts for the deposit of funds belonging to others.

debt service: A borrower's periodic mortgage payments comprised of principal plus interest on the unpaid mortgage balance.

deed of trust: A type of security instrument in which the borrower conveys title to real property to a third party (trustee) to be held in trust as security for the lender, with the condition that the trustee shall reconvey the title upon the payment of the debt, and, conversely, will sell the land and pay the debt in the event of a default by the borrower. See mortgage.

deposit: A sum of money given to (1) bind a sale of real estate, or (2) assure payment or an advance of funds in the processing of a loan. Also called earnest money.

deposit receipt: A form used to acknowledge the acceptance of the earnest money that binds an offer to purchase real property.

discount: In loan originations, a discount refers to an amount withheld from loan proceeds by a lender. In secondary market sales, a discount is the amount by which the sale price of a note is less than its face value. In both instances, the purpose of a discount is to adjust the yield upward, either in lieu of interest or in addition to interest. The rate or amount of discount depends on money market conditions, the credit of the borrower, and the rate or terms of the note.

discount point: Amount payable to the lending institution by the borrower or seller to increase the lender's effective yield. One point is equal to one percent of the loan.

draw: Periodic advances of funds according to the schedule of payments in a construction loan agreement. Also called advance, disbursement, payout, progress payment, or takedown.

due-on-sale: A clause in a mortgage stating that if the mortgagor sells, transfers, or in any way encumbers the property, then the mortgagee has the right to implement an acceleration clause, making the balance of the obligation due.

earnest money: A sum of money given to bind a sale of real estate, or assure payment or an advance of funds in the processing of a loan; a deposit.

ECOA: Equal Credit Opportunity Act. A federal law that requires lenders and other creditors to make credit equally available without discrimination based on race, color, religion, national origin, age, sex, marital status, or receipt of income from public assistance programs. Also called Regulation B.

effective gross income (personal): Normal annual income including overtime, before deductions, that is regular or guaranteed. It may be from more than one source. Salary is generally the principal source, but other income may be significant and stable and thus qualify. Effective gross income is used as the basis for borrower qualification by most conventional lenders and private mortgage insurers. Contrast with net income.

effective interest rate: The actual rate of return to the investor, considering commitment fees, loan points, or other fees. Also called yield.

endorsement: A signature on a negotiable instrument by which title to property mentioned therein is assigned and transferred. Also, a notation added to an instrument after execution to change or clarify its contents. In insurance, coverage may be restricted or enlarged by endorsing a policy. In FHA loans, a notation placed on the note by the FHA indicating that the loan is insured under the National Housing Act.

equity: Net ownership, the difference between fair market value and current indebtedness, sometimes called owner's interest.

escrow: An item of value, money or documents, deposited with a third party to be delivered upon the fulfillment of a condition. For example, the deposit by a borrower with the lender of funds to pay taxes and insurance premiums when they become due, or the deposit of funds or documents with an attorney or escrow agent to be disbursed upon the closing of a sale of real estate. In some parts of the country, escrows of taxes and insurance premiums are called impounds or reserves.

escrow account: The segregated trust account in which escrow funds are held.

escrow agent: The person or organization having a fiduciary responsibility to both the buyer and seller (or lender and borrower) to see that the terms of the purchase/sale (or loan) are carried out. Also called escrow company or escrow depository.

escrow company: An organization established to act as an escrow agent.

escrow contract: A three-party agreement between the buyer, seller, and the escrow agent, specifying the rights and duties of each.

escrow payment: That portion of a mortgagor's monthly payments held by a lender or servicer to pay taxes, hazard insurance, mortgage insurance, lease payments, and other items as they become due. Also called impounds or reserves in some states.

examination of title: The review of the chain of title as revealed by an abstract of title or public record.

exception: In legal descriptions, that portion of land to be deleted or excluded. The term is often used in a different sense to mean an objection to title or encumbrance on title.

execute: Recordation of the appropriate signatures on a document such as a mortgage note, to render it -in effect.-

existing construction: In HUD/FHA transactions, a house that was not approved by HUD/FHA or VA before the beginning of construction, but which has been completed more than one year.

existing, less than one year old: In HUD/FHA transactions, a house that was not approved by HUD/FHA or VA before the beginning of construction, and is less than one year old. Reduced mortgage amounts may be applied to these properties.

face value: Par value or the actual selling price of a security; the amount the issuer contracts to repay.

Farmers Home Administration (FmHA): A government agency within the Department of Agriculture that operates under the Consolidated Farm and Rural Development Act of 1921 and Title V of the Housing Act of 1949. This agency provides financing to farmers and other qualified borrowers who are unable to obtain loans elsewhere.

Federal Home Loan Mortgage Corporation (FHLMC): Created by Congress in Title III of the Emergency Home Finance Act of 1970 (12 USC 1451 et seq.). This stockholder-owned corporation, a portion of whose board of directors is appointed by the president of the United States, supports the secondary market in mortgages on residential property with mortgage purchase and securitization programs. Also called Freddie Mac.

Federal Housing Administration (FHA): A federal agency within the Department of Housing and Urban Development (HUD) that provides mortgage insurance for residential mortgages and sets standards for construction and underwriting. The FHA does not lend money, nor does it plan or construct housing.

Federal National Mortgage Association (FNMA): The nation's largest mortgage investor. Created in 1968 by an amendment to Title III of the National Housing Act (12 USC 1716 et seq.), this stockholder-owned corporation, a portion of whose board of directors is appointed by the president of the United States, supports the secondary market in mortgages on residential property with mortgage purchase and securitization programs. Also called Fannie Mae.

fee simple: The greatest possible interest a person can have in real estate, including the right to dispose of the property or pass it on to one's heirs.

FHA case number: The number used to identify a HUD/FHA mortgage in HUD's records. It is a 13-digit number, in three sections (XXX-XXXXXXX-XXX). The first three digits identify the HUD/FHA office in whose jurisdiction the property is located and the office responsible for processing the application (which may be different in some cases). The next seven digits are assigned by the HUD/FHA office, in the order applications are received. The final three digits identify the program under which the mortgage is insured.

FHA loan: A loan insured by the Federal Housing Administration open to all qualified home purchasers. While there are limits to the size of FHA loans, they are generous enough to handle moderately priced homes almost anywhere in the country.

FHA value: The value established by FHA as the basis for determining the maximum mortgage that may be insured on a specific property. It includes the appraised value of the property and 57 percent of the good faith estimate of closing costs.

final closing: The date upon which the permanent mortgage lender funds the mortgage loan.

firm commitment: (1) A lender's agreement to make a loan to a specific borrower on a specific property, sometimes on specific terms. (2) A HUD/FHA or PMI agreement to insure a loan on a specific property, for a specific borrower, at a maximum amount, interest rate, and term. In HUD/FHA transactions, the firm commitment is conditioned on compliance with requirements imposed by the conditional commitment with respect to the property, and other conditions imposed by the firm commitment itself, usually with respect to the borrower or to the transaction as a whole.

firm commitment condition: A condition imposed at the time of issue of the firm commitment and made a part of the commitment. Some are standard and are preprinted on the commitment form. Such conditions are made a part of the commitment if they are checked when the commitment is issued. Others are standardized with local HUD/FHA office jurisdictions.

first mortgage: A mortgage that gives the mortgagee a security right over all other mortgages of the mortgaged property.

first-time home buyer: In most government programs, a person applying for mortgage insurance or guaranty who has not owned real estate during the three years immediately preceding the date of the application. There are some exceptions; for example, a person who sold a home to move to a distant community might qualify as first-time home buyer in the new community.

gift affidavit: An unnumbered form, standardized locally by most HUD/FHA and VA offices. When an applicant intends to rely upon a gift to meet settlement requirements, all investors and insurers require evidence that the funds are truly a gift, from someone who could logically be expected to make the gift, and that repayment is neither required nor expected. Some also require verification that the donor actually has the funds on deposit.

GI loan: Nickname for a mortgage loan guaranteed by the VA.

Government National Mortgage Association (GNMA): Created in 1968 by an amendment to Title III of the National Housing Act (12 USC 1716 et seq.), this federal government corporation is a constituent part of the Department of Housing and Urban Development. Among other governmental functions, it guarantees securities backed by mortgages that are insured or guaranteed by other government agencies. Also called Ginnie Mae.

graduated payment mortgage (GPM): A type of flexible payment mortgage where the payments increase for a specified period of time and then level off. Usually results in negative amortization.

grantee: The person to whom an interest in real property is conveyed.

grantor: The person conveying an interest in real property.

ground lease: A lease of land only, usually on a long-term basis.

ground rent: Rent paid for land in accordance with the terms of a ground lease.

guaranteed loan: A loan guaranteed by a government agency or any other interested party.

hazard insurance: Insurance coverage that provides compensation to the insured in case of property loss or damage.

home or condominium owners association (HOA): A nonprofit corporation or association that manages the common areas and services of a planned unit development or condominium project. In a condominium project, it has no ownership interest in the common areas; in a planned unit development, it holds title to common areas.

homeowner's policy: A multiple peril insurance policy available to owners of private dwellings that covers the dwelling and its contents, as well as personal liability.

homestead estate: In some states, a statutory exemption that prohibits the attachment or sale of owner-occupied properties to pay the claims of creditors.

housing code: Standards to ensure that housing maintenance and improvements are adequate for occupancy.

HUD: The Department of Housing and Urban Development. A governmental entity responsible for the implementation and administration of housing and urban development programs. HUD was established by the Housing and Urban Development Act of 1965 to supersede the Housing and Home Finance Agency.

improved land: Land having utilities, roads, or other improvements.

improvements: Additions to raw land that normally increase its value, such as buildings, streets, and sewers.

income and expense statement: The actual or estimated schedule of income and expense items reflecting net gain or loss during a specified period.

income approach to value: The appraisal technique used to estimate real property value by capitalizing net income.

installment: The periodic payment that a borrower agrees to pay a mortgage lender.

institutional lender: A financial institution that lends to the public. Examples are mutual savings banks, life insurance companies, commercial banks, pension and trust funds, and savings and loan associations.

insured closing letter: A document issued by a title insurance company that protects a mortgagee against embezzlement or failure to follow specific closing instructions.

insured mortgage: A mortgage insured by FmHa, FHA or a private mortgage company.

interest: Consideration in the form of money paid for the use of money, usually expressed as an annual percentage. Also, a right, share, or title in property.

investor: Any person or institution that invests in mortgages or mortgage-backed securities.

joint and several note: Note signed by two or more persons, each of whom is liable for the full amount of the debt.

joint tenancy: Form of co-ownership giving each tenant equal interest and equal rights in the property, including the right of survivorship.

jointly-owned property: Property held in the name of more than one person.

jumbo loan: A loan that exceeds the statutory size limit eligible for purchase or securitization by federal agencies.

junior mortgage: A mortgage that is subordinate to the claims of a prior lien or mortgage.

land acquisition loan: A loan made for the purpose of purchasing land only, not improvements on or to the land. Also called an acquisition loan.

land contract: An agreement to transfer title to a property once conditions of the contract have been fulfilled.

landlord: Owner or lessor of real property.

LAPP: Lender Appraisal Processing Program. This program eliminates the VA's involvement in processing a loan and allows the lender to oversee the appraisal and underwriting process. Lenders must be preapproved by the VA to participate in this program.

late charge: An additional charge that a borrower is required to pay as a penalty for failure to pay a regular installment when due.

lease: A written document containing the conditions under which the possession and use of real and/or personal property are given by the owner to another for a stated period and consideration.

leasehold: An estate or interest in real property held by virtue of a lease.

leasehold mortgage: A loan to a lessee secured by a leasehold interest in a property.

legal description: A property description, recognized by law, that is sufficient to locate and identify the property without oral testimony.

lessee: One holding rights of possession and use of property under the terms of a lease. Also called tenant.

lessor: One who leases property to a lessee. Also called landlord.

lien: A legal hold or claim of a creditor on the property of another as security for a debt. Liens are always against property, usually real property.

lien waiver: A waiver of mechanic's lien rights; a document signed by a supplier or subcontractor stating that the firm has been compensated for its work, thereby giving up its right to file a claim against the property.

limited partnership: A form of business ownership that consists of one or more general partners who are fully liable, and one or more limited partners who are liable only for the amount of their investment.

listing: A written authorization for an agent to sell or lease real estate.

loan administration: A mortgage banking function which includes the receipt of payments, customer service, escrow administration, investor accounting, collections, and foreclosures. Also called servicing.

loan analysis (VA Form 26-6393): A form used by the VA as a worksheet to analyze the data submitted.

loan guaranty certificate: A VA document that states the portion of a loan that is guaranteed.

loan-to-value ratio: The ratio of mortgage amount to appraised value or sales price of real property. Used by lenders to determine maximum loan amounts as set by law.

loss payable clause: An insurance policy provision for payment of a claim to someone other than the insured, who holds an insurable interest in the insured property.

manufactured home: Factory-built or pre-fabricated housing, including mobile homes.

marketable title: A title that may not be completely clear, but has only minor objections that a well-informed and prudent buyer of real estate would accept.

market approach to value: In appraisal, a market value estimate of property based on actual prices paid in similar market transactions.

market value: The highest price that a buyer and the lowest price that a seller would accept, neither one being compelled to buy or sell.

master mortgage: A standard form mortgage recorded in the public record to help reduce recording fees, as mortgage documents thereafter refer to the record and the master mortgage.

maturity: The date on which an agreement expires; termination of a mortgage note.

MIC: See mortgage insurance certificate.

minimum property standards: Regulations or guidelines used as underwriting criteria that set forth acceptable property standards and specifications.

MIP: See mortgage insurance premium.

mobile home: A factory-assembled residence consisting of one or more modules, in which a chassis and wheels are an integral part of the structure, and can be readied for occupancy without removing the chassis or wheels.

modular house: A factory-assembled residence built in units or sections, transported to a permanent site, and erected on a foundation. Excludes mobile homes.

mortgage: A pledge of property, especially real property, as security for a debt. By extension, the document evidencing the pledge. In many states this document is a deed of trust. The document may contain the terms of repayment of the debt. By further extension, -mortgage- is used to describe both the mortgage proper and the separate promissory note evidencing the debt and providing the terms of the debt's repayment.

mortgage-backed security (MBS): An investment instrument backed by mortgage loans as security. Ownership is evidenced by an undivided interest in a pool of mortgages or trust deeds. Income from the underlying mortgages is used to pay interest and principal on the securities.

mortgage banker: An individual, firm or corporation that originates, sells or services loans secured by mortgages on real property.

mortgage broker: A firm or individual who, for a commission, matches borrowers and lenders. A mortgage broker does not retain servicing, does not use its own firms, and is not a principal.

Mortgage Credit Analysis Worksheet (HUD Form 92900-WS): A worksheet used by HUD/FHA or a direct endorsement underwriter to analyze the applicant's eligibility for an insured mortgage.

mortgage discount: The percentage difference between the principal amount of a mortgage and the selling price.

mortgage insurance (MI): Insurance that protects mortgage lenders against loss in the event of default by the borrower. This allows lenders to make loans with lower down payments. The federal government offers MI through HUD/FHA; private entities offer MI for conventional loans.

mortgage insurance certificate (MIC): Certificate issued by HUD/FHA as evidence that a mortgage has been insured, and that a contract of mortgage insurance exists between HUD/FHA and the lender incorporating the HUD/FHA regulations identified in the certificate.

mortgage insurance premium (MIP): The amount paid by a mortgagor for mortgage insurance either to FHA or a private mortgage insurance company.

mortgage note: A written promise to pay a sum of money at a stated interest rate during a specified term. A mortgage note is secured by a mortgage.

mortgagee: The lender in a mortgage transaction.

mortgagee clause: A clause that may be attached to an insurance policy stipulating that the lender will receive a portion of insurance proceeds sufficient to satisfy the unpaid amount of a loan in the event of a loss.

mortgagor: The borrower in a mortgage transaction who pledges property as a security for a debt.

Mutual Mortgage Insurance Fund (MMIF): The actuarially sound FHA insurance fund for the 203(b) unsubsidized single family mortgage program. It is -mutual- because mortgagors whose mortgages are insured by the fund receive rebates of premiums in excess of the amounts needed to pay costs and losses.

mutual savings bank: An institution owned by its depositors as evidenced by certificates of deposit rather than stock.

negative amortization: The unpaid interest that is added to the mortgage principal in a loan where the principal balance increases rather than decreases because the mortgage payments do not cover the full amount of interest due.

new construction: In HUD/FHA or VA transactions, construction approved by HUD/FHA or VA before the beginning of construction. -Approval- means using a conditional commitment or certificate of reasonable value. The -beginning of construction- means pouring footings. The foundation may be prepared for pouring, but if any concrete has been laid, construction has already begun. If this happens before the conditional commitment or CRV is issued, the property will not qualify as new construction. In HUD/FHA cases, this affects the maximum loan-to-value ratio of the insured mortgage. Until one year after construction is complete, HUD/FHA considers the house to be -existing, less than one year old.- After one year, it is said to be -existing.- On the HUD/FHA and VA Application for Appraisal (VA Form 26-1805 and HUD Form 92800-1), the block marked -proposed- is checked for new construction.

notary: A person authorized by the state to take acknowledgements and administer oaths.

on-site improvements: Any construction of buildings or other improvements within the boundaries of a property that increase its value.

origination fee: The lender's fee charged a borrower to prepare documents, make credit checks, inspect and sometimes appraise a property. Usually stated as a percentage of the face value of the loan.

originator: A person who solicits builders, brokers, and others to obtain applications for mortgage loans. Often called a loan officer.

par: A price of 100 percent of face value.

percolation test: A test performed on soil to determine its ability to absorb liquid, for either septic tank or construction purposes.

personal property: Any property that is not real property. Also called chattel.

physical approach to value: An appraisal method whereby property value is derived by estimating the replacement cost of improvements, less estimated depreciation, plus the estimated land value. Synonymous with cost approach.

PITI: Acronym for the items included in a monthly mortgage payment: principal, interest, taxes, and insurance.

planned unit development (PUD): A comprehensive development plan for a large land area. A PUD usually includes residences, roads, schools, recreational facilities, commercial, office and industrial areas. Also, a subdivision having lots or areas owned in common and reserved for the use of some or all of the owners of the separately owned lots.

plans and specifications: Architectural and engineering drawings and specifications for construction of a building or project. They include a description of materials to be used and the manner in which they are to be applied.

plat: A map representing a piece of land subdivided into lots with streets, boundaries, easements, and dimensions shown thereon.

point: An amount equal to one percent of the principal amount of a mortgage. Loan discount points are a one-time charge assessed at closing by the lender to increase the yield on the mortgage loan to a competitive position with other types of investments.

power of sale: A provision in a deed of trust that empowers a trustee, without any judicial procedure, to sell property in the event of default by the mortgagor and to apply the proceeds of the sale to satisfy the obligation, the costs of invoking the procedure, and the expenses of the sale.

preclosing: A meeting preceding formal closing in which documents are reviewed and signed and estimated prorations are made. Often used in the conversion of apartment units to condominium units.

preliminary title search: A title search by a title company prior to issuance of a title binder or commitment to insure.

premises: A defined portion of land and the improvements thereon as described in a deed, deed of trust, or mortgage.

premium: A security trading at a price in excess of par or 100 percent. In insurance, a payment for coverage.

prepayment penalty: A charge the mortgagor pays the mortgagee for the privilege to prepay the loan.

prepayment privilege: The right given a borrower in the mortgage to pay all or part of a mortgage debt without penalty prior to its maturity.

primary financing: A loan secured by a first mortgage or deed of trust on real property.

principal: The original balance of money lent, excluding interest. Also, the remaining balance of a loan, excluding interest.

priority: The order of precedence of liens against property or assets. Priority is usually established by filing or recordation of liens, but may be established by statute or agreement.

private mortgage insurance (PMI): Insurance written by a private company protecting the mortgage lender against financial loss occasioned by a borrower defaulting on the mortgage.

processing: The preparation of a mortgage loan application and supporting documents for underwriting.

promissory note: A written promise to pay a specific amount at a specified time.

pro rate: The allocation of proportionate shares of income, ownership, or of an obligation, which a buyer and seller share at the time of closing.

purchase agreement: A written agreement between a buyer and seller of real property, setting forth the price and terms of sale.

purchase-money mortgage: A mortgage a purchaser of real property gives a seller as all or part of the consideration in the sales transaction.

quiet title action: Legal action taken to eliminate any interest or claim to property by others; the procedure used to perfect title when a quitclaim deed is unobtainable.

quitclaim deed: A deed relinquishing all interest, title, or claim an owner has in a property. A quitclaim deed implies no warranty.

Real Estate Settlement Procedures Act (RESPA): A federal statute and regulation promulgated by HUD governing real estate lending practices and disclosures. Its main features pertain to the provision of a good faith estimate of loan settlement costs and the provision of the HUD settlement booklet within three days of making a loan application.

real property: Land and objects permanently attached to it, such as buildings and fences.

Realtor-: A person licensed to sell and/or lease real property, acting as an agent for others, and who is a member of a local real estate board affiliated with the National Association of Realtors- (NAR). -Realtor- is a registered trademark of the NAR.

recording: The filing of documents or details of a legal document to make them a matter of public record. Usually requires the witnessing and notarizing of the document or instrument to be recorded.

red lining: Arbitrary denial of real estate loan applications in certain geographical areas, without considering individual applicant qualifications.

refinancing: The repayment of a debt from the proceeds of a new loan using the same property as security.

Regulation B: See ECOA.

release of liability: An agreement by a lender to terminate personal obligation of a mortgagor in connection with payment of a debt.

Report of Home Loan Processed on Automatic Basis (VA Form 26-1820): A form used instead of the certificate of loan disbursement (VA Form 26-1826) when the mortgagee has processed and closed the loan under the VA Direct program, which permits certain qualified lenders to close loans without prior VA approval of the borrower. Request for Certificate of Veterans Status (VA Form 26-8261a): Form used if the applicant intends to apply for the special downpayment terms available to veterans on most HUD/FHA loans. It is submitted to VA with proof of the veteran's military service.

request for credit report: An unnumbered form, usually provided by credit bureaus, used to order credit reports from the specific bureau providing the form.

Request for Determination of Eligibility and Available Loan Guaranty Entitlement (VA Form 26-1880): The form used to request a certificate of eligibility. It is forwarded to the local VA office with proof of the veteran's military service. If the veteran does not already have a certificate of eligibility, this request should be submitted as one of the first actions in the application process.

Request for Determination of Reasonable Value for Real Estate (VA Form 26-1805): The basic application to VA, requesting appraisal of the property and determination of its eligibility for guaranty. This form may be used with HUD/FHA applications, but the HUD/FHA form (HUD Form 92800-1) may not be used with VA applications.

sales contract: A written agreement between buyer and seller stating terms and conditions of a sale or exchange of property.

savings and loan association: A mutual or stock association chartered and regulated by the Office of Thrift Supervision. Traditionally, deposits are invested in residential mortgage loans, although savings and loans now have broader lending powers.

savings bond list: An unnumbered, locally produced form used to list savings bonds when they are used as a source of funds for closing. Such a listing should include the bond numbers, the face amounts, and the current redemption value and should be certified by a mortgagee employee who has actually seen the bonds.

secondary mortgage market: The market in which lenders and investors buy and sell existing mortgages or mortgage-backed securities, thereby providing greater availability of funds for additional mortgage lending.

second mortgage: A mortgage that has rights subordinate to a first mortgage.

security instrument: A written document, such as a mortgage, deed of trust, or land contract, that is used to make property security (collateral) for the repayment of a debt.

seller-servicer: A term used by Fannie Mae and Freddie Mac for a mortgage banker or other entity that has met the requirements necessary to sell and service mortgages for Fannie Mae or Freddie Mac.

settlement costs: Money paid by borrowers and sellers to effect the closing of a mortgage loan, including payments for title insurance, survey, attorney fees, and such prepaid items as taxes and insurance escrow.

Settlement Statement (HUD Form 1): A statement showing the full details of the loan closing, including costs paid by both the buyer and the seller and a detailed breakdown of the manner in which the loan proceeds were distributed. RESPA requires that this standardized form be used in all loan closings involving purchase money first mortgages in which the federal government is involved in any way, even though the loan itself may not be insured or guaranteed by a government agency. For practical purposes, the form must be used with all purchase money first mortgage loan closings and may be used in other transactions, such as second mortgages, refinancing transactions, etc.

shipping: In the sale or securitization of mortgage loans, the preparation and delivery of documents for loans sold to investors.

spot loans: Single-family loans solicited on an individual basis, rather than through Realtor- referrals.

subdivision: Improved or unimproved land divided into a number of parcels for sale, lease, financing, or development.

subordination: The act of a party acknowledging, by written record, that a debt is inferior to the interest of another in the same property. Subordination may apply not only to mortgages, but to leases, real estate rights, and any other types of debt instruments.

survey: A measurement of land, prepared by a registered land surveyor, showing the location of the land with reference to known points, its dimensions, and the location and dimensions of any improvements.

surveyor's certificate: A formal statement signed, certified, and dated by a surveyor giving the pertinent facts about a particular property and any easements or encroachments affecting it.

tax deed: A deed on property purchased at public sale for nonpayment of taxes.

tax lien: A claim against property for unpaid taxes.

tax sale: The sale of property by a taxing authority or an officer of the court acting on a judgment to satisfy the payment of delinquent taxes.

tenancy: The use of real estate under any kind of right of title.

tenancy in common: A form of undivided ownership interest by two or more persons that provides for no right of survivorship. The interest need not be of equal percentage.

tenancy by entirety: A form of ownership in which husband and wife are co-owners with rights of survivorship.

tenant: One who is not the owner but occupies real property under consent of the owner and in subordination to the owner's title. The tenant is entitled to exclusive possession, use, and enjoyment of the property, usually for a time and amount specified in the lease.

term: The period of time between the commencement date and termination date of a note, mortgage, legal document, or other contract.

term mortgage: A mortgage in which, for a specified period of time, only interest is paid, after which the principal is due.

title: Written evidence of the right to or ownership in property. In the case of real estate, the documentary evidence of ownership is the title deed that specifies in whom the legal estate is vested and the history of ownership and transfers. Title may be acquired through purchase, inheritance, devise, gift, or through foreclosure of a mortgage.

title insurance policy: A contract by which the insurer agrees to pay the insured a specific amount for any loss caused by defects of title to real estate, wherein the insured has an interest as purchaser, mortgagee, or otherwise.

title search: An examination of public records, laws, and court decisions to ensure that no one except the seller has a valid claim to the property, and to disclose past and current facts regarding ownership of the subject property.

townhouse: A row house on a small lot that has exterior limits common to other similar units. Title to the unit and its lot is vested in the individual buyer with a fractional interest in common areas, if any.

transfer fees: Fees a buyer or seller pays a municipality to defray the cost of recording a transfer of ownership.

trust deed: The instrument given by a borrower (trustor) to a trustee vesting title to a property in the trustee to ensure the borrower's fulfillment of an obligation. A mortgage.

trustee: One who holds legal title to property for the benefit of another, or to secure performance of an obligation.

trustee in bankruptcy: An agent of the court authorized to liquidate and protect the assets of the bankrupt, and bring them to court for final distribution for the benefit of the bankrupt and creditors.

Truth-in-Lending law: The Truth-in-Lending Act (PL 90-321; 15 USC 1601 et seq.). Part of the Consumer Credit Protection Act, a federal law that requires lenders to provide full written disclosure of credit terms and conditions, the finance charge, the annual percentage rate, and other charges incurred in a loan contract.

underwriting: In mortgage banking, the analysis of the risk involved in making a mortgage loan to determine whether the risk is acceptable to the lender. Underwriting involves the evaluation of the property as outlined in the appraisal report, and of the borrower's ability and willingness to repay the loan.

unencumbered property: A property that is free and clear of debts or liens.

Uniform Residential Appraisal Report (FNMA Form 1004/FHLMC Form 65): Standard form used by appraisers to detail value for single-family properties.

Uniform Commercial Code (UCC): A comprehensive code of laws regulating important legal aspects of business and financial transactions. The code has been accepted by every state except Louisiana.

Uniform Residential Loan Application (URLA) (FNMA Form 1003/ FHLMC Form 65): The basic application for mortgages sold to Fannie Mae or Freddie Mac, insured by HUD/FHA or guaranteed by VA.

usury: The act of charging borrowers a rate of interest greater than that permitted by law.

usury ceiling: A maximum legal rate, established by state law, for interest, discounts, or other fees that may be charged for the use of money. The ceiling may vary depending on the nature or type of loan.

VA funding fee: A fee the VA charges to guarantee a mortgage loan.

valuation: The estimation of a property's price through appraisal.

vendee: The party to whom personal or real property is sold.

vendor: The seller of personal or real property.

vendor's lien: An unpaid seller's right to prior lien on property until the purchase price has been recovered.

verification of deposit (VOD): A form that requests and secures verifications of amounts on deposit at financial institutions. When a depository institution is also the applicant's creditor, the VOD verifies the obligation.

verification of earnest money deposit: An unnumbered, locally produced form used in some HUD/FHA and VA offices. Generally, the sales contract itself acknowledges the seller's receipt of a deposit in a specific amount. In some cases, however, the contract language does not make it clear that the deposit was actually paid in cash. Where the deposit was in the form of a note of check, or where the language of the contract does not clearly acknowledge receipt, additional verification is required. This form is used for that purpose.

verification of employment (VOE): A form that requests and secures documentation of a mortgage applicant's work history and occupation, to assist in the lender's credit investigation.

verification of source of funds for closing: An unnumbered, locally produced from, required by most HUD/FHA and VA offices when the source of funds for closing is unclear from the basic documentation accompanying the application.

Veterans Administration (VA): The Department of Veterans Affairs, a cabinet-level agency of the federal government. The Servicemen's Readjustment Act of 1944 authorized the agency to administer a variety of benefit programs designed to facilitate the adjustment of returning veterans to civilian life. Among the benefit programs is the VA Home Loan Guaranty program, which encourages mortgage lenders to offer long-term, low down payment financing to eligible veterans by partially guaranteeing the lender against loss.

waiver of lien: The written evidence from a contractor or supplier, surrendering the right of lien to enforce collection of debt against a property.

warehousing: The short-term borrowing of funds by a mortgage banker using permanent mortgage loans as collateral. This form of interim financing is used until the mortgages are sold to a permanent investor.

Wood Destroying Insect Information, Existing Construction (VA Form 26-8850/HUD Form 92053): A form used to report the findings of a pest control operator, in response to a condition imposed on conditional commitment or certificate of reasonable value, that an existing property be inspected for insect damage. The inspector reports the presence or absence of infestation or damage and indicates whether damage, if any, has been or will be repaired.

wraparound mortgage: A refinancing technique involving the creation of a second mortgage which includes the balance due on any existing mortgages, plus the amount of the new secondary or junior lien.

yield: The ratio of investment income to the total amount invested over a given period of time.

yield to maturity: The lender's percentage of annual return on actual funds loaned, assuming that the loan will be paid in full at maturity.